Beyond Spin

The Power of Strategic Corporate Journalism

Markos Kounalakis

Drew Banks

Kim Daus

Jossey-Bass Publishers
San Francisco

Jossey-Bass books and products are available through most bookstores. To contact Jossey-Bass directly, call (888) 378–2537, fax to (800) 605–2665, or visit our website at www.josseybass.com.

Substantial discounts on bulk quantities of Jossey-Bass books are available to corporations, professional associations, and other organizations. For details and discount information, contact the special sales department at Jossey-Bass.

 Manufactured in the United States of America on Lyons Falls Turin Book. This paper is acid-free and 100 percent totally chlorine-free.

Library of Congress Cataloging-in-Publication Data

Kounalakis, Markos.
  Beyond spin: the power of strategic corporate journalism / Markos Kounalakis, Drew Banks, Kim Daus. — 1st ed.
    p. cm.— (The Jossey-Bass business & management series)
  Includes bibliographical references and index.
  ISBN 0-7879-4550-1
  1. Communication in organizations. 2. Communication in management. 3. Journalism. I. Banks, Drew, 1961. II. Daus, Kim. III. Title. IV. Series.
  HD30.3.K68 1999
  658.4'53.—dc21   99-6555

FIRST EDITION
HB Printing   10 9 8 7 6 5 4 3 2 1

The Jossey-Bass
Business & Management Series

CONTENTS

FOREWORD

JAMES ADAMS
  FORMER CEO, UNITED PRESS INTERNATIONAL (UPI)
  CURRENT CEO, INFRASTRUCTURE DEFENSE (iDEFENSE)
  AUTHOR, *THE NEXT WORLD WAR*

In 1998, I was attempting to reposition UPI to a new vision—from an "information-over-the-wire" company to a "knowledge-via-the-Internet" operation. At that time, I met one of the authors of this book, who shared with me the concept of corporate journalism. Because of the shift UPI was undergoing, this new communication concept intrigued me.

The synthesis of journalism, publishing, business, and communication strategies represented in this authorship team is unique. Markos Kounalakis, Drew Banks, and Kim Daus have captured elements of the complex corporate environments in which we find ourselves, and combined the elements in a way that leads to new insight into how to communicate within organizations. Anyone inside the corporate walls struggling to manage or produce or make sense of the data whirling at them in the knowledge environment should read this book.

As *Beyond Spin* makes clear, at both strategic and tactical levels, how corporate communications is managed in this world will directly impact us all. Failure to meet the many challenges of the knowledge age will ensure the demise of some traditional media companies, and many traditional methods of communicating. Failure will also produce a fundamental challenge to democracy and to our cultural bastions that have sustained humankind down through the centuries. There is a lot at stake here, and this is the first book to set out both the challenges and the opportunities of this new world environment. Clearly, it is required reading for everyone who, like me, is wrestling with these challenges and trying to position a company to prosper in the next century.

If you think you've seen a lot of change during the past couple of decades, you'd better think again. The end of the twentieth century is being stirred by comparatively gentle breezes of change. They are the harbingers of a coming storm of social and technological restructuring that will be unprecedented in human history.

Technology is at the heart of this change. Not simply technology in the sense of the tools that we manipulate, or of the computers that perform for us the everyday functions that we can't quite manage to do ourselves. Technology is a much larger force that blends with society, integrating to the extent that people become increasingly subservient to the process.

Why does all this matter? The answer is simple: the foundations that have underpinned the evolution of mankind over the centuries are being rapidly eroded as we move from a terrestrial to a virtual environment. Almost every cornerstone of our lives—family, democracy, the rule of law, communication, and civilized discourse—is under attack. Yet this is only the beginning. In all our critical industries—finance, communications, transportation, utilities, emergency services—the growing tumult and chaos is merely the overture for the main performance that lies just ahead. The changes we will see during the next three to five years will dwarf those of the previous decade. And beyond five years, the rate of change and the consequent impact of change on society is anybody's guess.

This trend, this inevitable acceleration of technologically driven social change, poses a serious threat to the nation state. In many respects, governments are becoming superfluous entities in the real world of commerce and finance and communications. More and more, market forces and industrial alliances are moving in to assume the functions that governments, burdened with their incredible inertia, are unable to deal with.

Filling the vacuum, though, is no simple task. We as citizens of the world are in that precarious position of having one foot on the dock and the other in the boat. The dock, in this case, is the current world order, held in increasingly unstable balance by a crazy quilt of governments. The boat is the private sector solution to the problems that face our increasingly infrastructure-dependent world.

Why is private sector leadership so important? Government's strength is in its stability, but therein also lies its weakness. It is constrained by traditions and locked in bureaucratic inertia. For all its talk of responsiveness and reinvention, government remains years behind industry in the ability to recognize new problems and deal effectively with them. Progress, wherever it appears, is generally cosmetic rather than substantive.

If the rise of the market state is going to be the new paradigm in the new century, then we need to think about different ways of communicating with the people who are going to be engaged by the processes. In the recent past, this communication in both the corporate environment and the media has rested on three traditional pillars: information, education, and entertainment. Although the balance has switched in favor of entertainment in recent years, we need to continue relying on these three pillars. The question is, how should this be done?

We already know that the balance of information flow has moved away from delivering news, through providing information, and on to acquiring knowledge. The traditional media and other communication delivery systems have not yet fully understood this change, but there is no doubt that it has already taken place. Those who use the resources of the Web know what they want, demand it instantly, and do not want to be distracted by extraneous information. In other words, the old model of a media distributing general information from which the user might glean specific knowledge is over. We want to know more about what we know and we want to know very little, if anything, about what we don't know.

Another particular challenge produced by the technology of information has given new meaning to the phrase "free flow of information." In the twentieth century, the phrase was used as a hammer to attack totalitarian regimes that used information as a way of controlling people. This contrasted with democratic states that generally claimed to have a free press. But the Web has created an information and knowledge flow that is available to all, in real time, and at no cost. As speech recognition and simultaneous language translation becomes a reality, this model of free knowledge for all will become the accepted paradigm.

With real knowledge available to everyone in real time, the ability of any individual, organization, or government to control information flow is compromised. In a world where "spin" has evolved into an art form and propaganda is a pliant tool for corporation and government alike, this environment creates a whole new canvas on which to paint. But this is not just about blank canvas but rather about paint, brushes, content, and audience. How and why those choices are made is going to be fundamental to the future success of corporations.

Employees will demand a different level of interaction between themselves and their employers. There is likely to be intense competition for labor in a market where the knowledge worker is king and queen. Employers will continue to offer generous packages of salary, benefits, and options, but in the end this will not distinguish one company from another. Already there is very high mobility of labor in high-technology companies, which makes each worker more expensive and has a serious impact on the bottom line. The key to retention is not going to be money, but trust.

Generating a corporate culture that truly honors the contribution of every employee, embraces that worker and his or her family into the corporate family, and establishes a climate where every voice is recognized and heard will be exceptionally difficult. Many companies already claim to have a culture of trust while, in fact, the internal public relations is simply a convenient cover for the same old climate of fear. It takes more than mere words to instill trust and integrity in a corporation; it requires leadership by example from the very top down through the ranks. Beyond just good deeds and words, this too is something that will have a direct impact on the bottom line. Every competent CEO knows that a happy worker is more productive and makes a larger contribution to the bottom line.

What all this means is that internal communications within a corporation are going to have to reach a whole new level of excellence. Just what that looks like and how it might work in this new world is what *Beyond Spin* is about. There are no templates for this new world; we are building it from scratch, and many of us are making it up as we go along. In a revolution, those who survive and prosper tend to become revolutionaries themselves and then evolve to become the standard-bearers of the new order that arises out of the chaos. Those who read this book will become the standard-bearers for the new paradigm that will mean the difference between success and failure in the twenty-first-century corporation.

There will be no single point of entry for the spin control experts. There will be no practical way to control debate or even to directly influence its outcome. Freedom of the press will become freedom of the people to discuss, disagree, and define their own positions in ways that were unthinkable before the Web. In some respects, this is true democracy in action, where every voice has a chance to be heard.

PREFACE

A few years ago, there were two prevailing and competing political and economic systems in the world. One was open, the other closed. One was nimble, the other rigid. One was successful, the other doomed.

The factors that allowed one to survive and the other to disappear are similar to those by which one company evolves into a leader in today's global economy and another devolves into a future footnote.

At the heart of the USSR's communist regime was a government controlling its people. Control meant centrally mandated and implemented government programs. It also meant centrally crafted and orchestrated communications. Given this, it's not surprising that the communist party's official daily newspaper, *Pravda* (which translates as *truth* in English) has become synonymous with propaganda.

In *Beyond Spin*, we examine the concept of strategic corporate journalism: the blending of journalistic principles with organizational communications strategies. Journalistic practices of open, credible, accurate, and timely reporting have become central in democratized societies to create fluid information flow and a balance of power critical to the success of these societies. Similarly to a dictatorial political structure, most organizations today try to control their success through centralized vision and strategy development and centrally crafted and orchestrated communications. This dictatorial modality has its roots in the mechanistic management practices of the industrial age.

As we demonstrate, in the past three decades many macro sociotechnological factors have transformed the landscape within which organizations must operate. Knowledge has surpassed labor. Hierarchy has given way to flattened organizations where once-centralized control is now distributed. Mechanistic systems have evolved into organic models. For organic systems to survive, they need to communicate in dramatically new ways. This is where strategic corporate journalism plays a role. By systematically contextualizing these factors in the following chapters, we show how organizations can not only survive but also sharpen their competitive edge through institutional checks and intellectually innovative interaction catalyzed by corporate journalism.

Interestingly enough, our work with the term *corporate journalism* yielded three completely different perceptions from the people we interviewed. First were the "adverse impact skeptics," who equate the word *journalism* with the populist trend toward sensationalism in American journalism. These people interpret corporate journalism as manipulative writing, or corporatespeak. Then we uncovered the "what's the big deal" crowd, who confine journalism to newspapers and magazines and tend to view corporate journalism merely as the company magazine or the company newsletter. Finally, the "ah-ha" folks (who often came from a journalism or communications background) fully apprehend the journalistic practices and principles behind societal journalism and understand the implications of journalism in the corporate world. This final group simultaneously showed excitement about the possibilities yet recognized the complexities of merging the two worlds.

If, in reading this Preface, you find yourself skeptical or if "what's the big deal" resonates with you, then you might want to jump first to Chapter Four, where we explain the underlying practices and principles behind societal journalism. Our hope is that after this inside look you will see the potential impact within the corporation.

In *Beyond Spin*, we discuss the fundamentals of information fluidity within today's organizations. Most of the current organizational communication literature focuses on the role of dialogue or interactivity in achieving trust, message internalization, and adaptation to change. We touch on interactivity in Chapter Two and include it as an integral element in the "knowledge equation" that ends Chapter Four. Trust, internalization, and adaptation are laudable goals, but they are nearly impossible to attain without first creating aware-ness and understanding through open, timely, and accurate in-formation flow. Achieving this information flow, which we call strategic corporate journalism, should be the core of an organiza-tional communications strategy that opens the psychological door for interaction and dialogue.

Although in *Beyond Spin* we focus primarily on business ex-amples, the concepts that we introduce could apply to any orga-nization, be it a governing body, a community group, a religious institution, or even a family unit.

This book is for organizational leaders who are currently expe-riencing challenges managing the quantity and timing of the infor-mation flowing in and out of the organization; directing a confused, unproductive, demoralized, or transient workforce; getting ahead of the constantly advancing competitive curve; or succeeding in the global economy.

Once fear and threats to individuals were diminished or elim-inated, the USSR became an enlightening study of how the gov-erning institutions of a large-scale organization can no longer effectively control information dissemination and technologies from reaching a literate and increasingly critical populace. The system's rigidity prevented it from exploiting the intellectual capital it had so blatantly corrupted and diffused while state institutions also kept it immune from the checks and balances of noninstitutional pres-sure. The result was not a nation that exploded with creativity and competitive strength, but rather one that imploded and collapsed thanks to the weight of top-heavy structures that had no broad-based foundations or legitimacy.

In the Prelude, we illustrate a high-technology company in Sil-icon Valley during different periods of corporate success and chal-lenge. SGI (formerly Silicon Graphics), an early high-flier in the computer systems industry, experienced phenomenal growth rates, built an envied corporate culture of creativity and innovation, and enjoyed an environment that was characterized by a CEO who taught meditation and was lauded as an industry and social visionary. A few years later, the company that had known only continuous growth was suddenly faced with its first operating losses and the departure of its embattled CEO.

With this occurring during one of Silicon Valley's hottest-ever growth spurts, how did the company manage to keep itself together and stave off the imminent threats to personnel, products, and profitability? Its communications organization was central to maintaining a thread of community and was able to prolong some sense of stability where it existed, as well as contain a sense of panic and crisis when stability was scarce. The Prelude presents a practical look at an objective case of journalistic practices and principles being applied in a corporation's central communications function to help create forward momentum during an extremely tumultuous and uncertain period. During this time, the success of communications could promote the corporation's resurgence—or failed communications could undermine it.

In Chapter One, we look at today's global social and technological environment and how this environment is shaping information perceptions and communication expectations. Changes in the world of information technologies, educational levels, and general sophistication make obsolete many of the old models of communication and previous assumptions about how organizations are structured. In the opening chapter, we focus on five specific trends: the dominance of the knowledge workforce, democratization of the workplace, diversification of the organization (in terms of both a diverse workforce and a global economy), the challenges of the information age, and an overwhelming increase in the pace of change.

Throughout *Beyond Spin*, we build upon a number of assumptions about this new landscape within which today's organization must operate. The bases for these assumptions are presented in Chapter One. Skip the first chapter if you already operate under these assumptions. What is important in the first chapter is not the specific details of the five trends but their aggregate interrelated effect.

In Chapter Two, we move from the external world to the internal world of organizations and take a deterministic, deconstructionist view of organizational communications. We analyze the three basic elements of organizational communications—content, distribution, and style—breaking each one into the factors that determine effectiveness. We then reconstruct the organizational communications strategy, considering the effect of specific factors within an organizational landscape that comprises the external trends discussed in Chapter Two and the internal environment specific to the organization. This deconstructive and reconstructive perspective exposes the enormous complexity of organizational communications that has been so compounded in recent times.

In Chapter Three, we provide a historical overview of how Western journalistic principles and practices have evolved in a larger world context, and how they have worked as an institutional check, an educational medium, and a cornerstone of democratic societies. Over the years, journalism has developed the means for open, accurate, and timely delivery of news and information, such that people generally have more than enough information with which to make well-informed decisions, whether about their political institutions, their economic well-being, or any other facet of their lives that is affected by public and private institutions.

Developments in technology have pressured journalistic organs to keep pace with faster news cycles and the multiple news sources that are available, in order to compete for larger, more global, diverse, and discerning audiences. By the same token, private and public institutions have been under pressure to respond to closer scrutiny and the forced transparency of their activities and behaviors. Those institutions that have been able to respond quickly and change accordingly are the ones that continue to thrive and survive. The rest will take the back seat.

In Chapter Four, we discuss the basics of how a knowledge-based organization needs to set up its communications networks and newsrooms in order to sustain a fluid informational infrastructure supporting alignment, productivity, and creativity goals. In fact, this chapter begins to show the convergence between the public realm's development and reliance on journalism and the private sector's growing interest and dependence upon the very same principles and practices that are addressed in greater detail in Chapter Five.

In Chapter Four, we translate the journalistic principles and practices outlined in the previous chapter to their practical applicability for knowledge-based organizations. As a result of the factors outlined in Chapters Two and Three, leading global corporations and organizations—particularly those on the cutting edge of technological innovation—increasingly resemble democratic societies and institutions. The corporation is structured more as a collaborative society with a unique culture, value set, and purpose. Although motivated by financial remuneration, it is just as important that employees feel aligned to the organizational vision, valued as enablers of that vision, and instrumental in bringing about organizational results and success.

It is in this chapter that we conjoin the environmental trends of Chapter One, the organizational communication strategy process of Chapter Two, and the historical context of Chapter Three into our central thesis: strategic corporate journalism is the necessary core of a communications strategy within today's knowledge-based organizations.

In Chapter Five, we demonstrate how some organizations have incorporated elements of corporate journalism. We begin this chapter by highlighting specific elements essential to the effectiveness of corporate journalism and then move on to demonstrate how some organizations have bravely attempted journalistic principles and practices and how others reject them. We outline examples such as Arco's communications following the Alaska pipeline rupture, Hewlett-Packard's publishing of an article titled "I'm Losing My Job," and Tandem's groundbreaking introduction of an internal televised news show as examples of noteworthy early integrations of corporate journalism.

In Chapter Six, we detail a specific case study at SGI that shows how the company dealt with the bipolar challenges outlined in the Prelude by using—or failing to use—some of the journalistic principles and practices it committed to adopting as part of its strategic communications plan. This is a telling chapter that shows how an organization, bereft of its leadership and embattled by the marketplace, was still able to function and maintain its ability to survive through timely and open organizational communications. This case study paints a vivid picture of the external and internal forces at work; it presents a highly complex environment under siege for the first time following years of unencumbered growth, profitability, and adulation by hitherto uncritical external and internal audiences that were willing to believe the myths and magic of an organization that was seen as exceptional in every way.

The final chapter is an exploratory one, in which we examine the future of organizational communications. We investigate the sociotechnological trends discussed in Chapter One as well as legal, business, and societal trends dealing with boundaries, information fluidity, and knowledge disparity. We offer no conclusions other than the belief that all trends are leading us away from mechanistic systems toward organic ones that require boundaryless, instantaneous, perfectly contextualized communications.

In their book *A Simpler Way*, Margaret Wheatley and Myron Kellner-Rogers describe the advanced communication infrastructure within ecosystems: "In ecosystems, members seem to have access to the whole system. The quality of their communication is dazzling. . . . Nothing we have created in any human organization comes close" (1996, p. 39). In ecosystems, open, timely, and accurate information flow is part of the system's fabric; it naturally replicates what journalism in its purest form is designed to provide. Until the time when organizations develop a communication infrastructure analogous to an ecosystem, strategic corporate journalism will remain the critical core of the organizational communication strategy.

Beyond Spin

"Headless Body in Topless Boardroom!"

I t is one of those unforgettable headlines branded into journalistic lore. New York City and its hard-competing tabloid press are the perfect combination of grit and gristle, meat and potatoes. When a nudey joint in New York had an unexpected decapitation, the *New York Post* delivered the goods in a fast, punchy, and pithy way. The "Headless" headline has since appeared in a number of permutations, such as a 1998 cover of *Mother Jones* magazine featuring Rupert Murdoch and reading, "Spineless Man in Heartless World!" Here is a corporate contribution to the oeuvre: "Headless Body in Topless Boardroom!"

JULY 1995

The "News" was loud and clear. Strong backbeat and solid chords. Huey Lewis and his amped backup, the News, rocked the corporate

---

The observations made regarding SGI reflect the personal opinions of the authors.

rally into near frenzy on the rolling grass knolls that make up the SGI campus.* This was yet another private company affair where an internationally renowned rock group was considered only the warm-up act. SGI did things big.

Circling above the gathering was a propeller plane pulling a banner of congratulations: "The Best Employees on the Planet." It was a phrase echoed on the T-shirt every employee received on the first day of work. It read, "Silicon Graphics—The Best Computer Company on the Planet." Superlatives were second nature at a place that could seemingly do no wrong.

The sun was shining on all who could stand and feel its radiant heat. In the glare and the heat, and onto the stage to the bounce of the beat, strode two men in dark sunglasses. The crowd roared. Sure, Huey Lewis and the News were a big deal, but these two were the real big deal. The CEO, Ed McCracken, and President Tom Jermoluk (affectionately known as T.J.)—the Iowa farmboy and the Hawaiian party animal—an odd couple made of the mettle that constitutes the mythology of Silicon Valley, came on with their air guitars looking like stars.

On the way to campus that morning, employees listening to commute-time radio heard Jermoluk thanking them for blowing away financial predictions—and for doing it, once again, in the midst of a flat economy. Life was good.

Performance art is perfected by the hucksters and the high fliers in Silicon Valley. It can whip up enthusiasm, charm doubters, seduce investors, and inspire people to do things they never thought possible. Apple Computer's Steve Jobs, a master stagecraft performer, set the bar high for those ascending the high-tech throne. T.J. was a close second. Harnessing his energy and blond, boyish enthusiasm was one of SGI's secret weapons in the marketplace.

On this day, he bantered with McCracken, and they both beamed as they announced the 1994 fiscal year financial results. It

---

* In April 1999 Silicon Graphics, Inc., formally changed its name to SGI.

was not only the show and the showmanship that would tantalize the audience that July day. McCracken and Jermoluk had presents to give away: an $800 Tag Heuer watch for all 6,300 employees around the globe, and additional stock options. The crowd sprang to its feet, incredulous at the news, and applauded hard. Life was very good.

It looked good from the outside, too. In mid-1994, *Business-Week*'s cover story dubbed SGI the "Gee Whiz" company. SGI, then a relatively small, unknown computer systems developer and man-ufacturer, was growing at an unheard-of annual rate of nearly 50 percent. It was breaking into high-profile markets such as enter-tainment, and getting publicity from work with Hollywood film stu-dios that used SGI's equipment to create digital special effects. It was the company that made *Jurassic Park* possible—helped make dinosaurs come alive in the twentieth century—and was partner-ing with the likes of Steven Spielberg.

In that field, at that moment, SGI employees were certain that the company would far outsucceed not only the press's predictions but those of the financial community too. Employees left the field with their T-shirt and sunshade giveaways, racing back to their desks to watch the stock price creep steadily up toward 50. The employ-ees made bets about when the stock would split for the third time in five years. Life was damn good.

OCTOBER 1997

The news was loud and clear. Results were rocky and employees were still reeling from the unexpected and continuous downturn that the company was inexplicably experiencing in what were boom times for just about everyone else. Employees tentatively filed into the auditorium of building 43 in Mountain View, California, for the quarterly All Hands meeting. The dark room matched the employ-ees' somber mood. As a tired McCracken took the stage, a sti-fling silence hung in the air. Just a few short months prior to that moment, *BusinessWeek's* cover read in large print, tabloid style: "The Sad Saga of Silicon Graphics." The article exposed, among other things, the personal travails of many current and former SGI executives, including the charismatic Jermoluk, who had since left SGI to run a start-up called @Home . . . and it was popularly believed that he did not leave of his own accord. In that room, after two years of poor financial results and a stock price that plummeted from 46 to 7, employees were angry and looking to McCracken for answers.

Although bits of information about the financial results had leaked and rumors about the company were rampant, no one was prepared for the news that hit them. SGI reported its first loss in eleven years, McCracken—the twelve-year CEO of the sixteen-year-old company—was stepping down, and a layoff of 10 percent of the workforce was announced. The three-pronged announcement stunned employees. The once-and-future high-flying company was now in a seeming nosedive.

As "the best employees on the planet" exited the auditorium, local media reporters wrangled them for information. A plane flew overhead trailing an advertisement for job opportunities at Lucent, one of Silicon Valley's newest darlings; the sight led human resource managers to wish that the air space above campus be declared a no-fly zone. Headhunters and recruiters pounded employee voice mail and e-mail boxes. Employees' cars were blanketed with Silicon Valley job opportunity flyers and business cards. That night at home, employees weighed their options. They were tired. They had been working long, startup-like hours in a passionate attempt to make a difference—to avoid the impending layoffs and to restore profitability. Their reward was the news that things would get worse.

With morale at such a low, employees came to work with dread. For two months, no one knew who was "on the list." Their salaries were good, but their stock options were underwater. The company looked like a target for takeover. Employees were skeptical about future strategic direction, and the company was virtually executiveless. Employees were also worried about losing what they perceived as a hip, innovative company culture. The perception that the new NT product introduction might be the company's savior—even though it was a year away—echoed in the press and in employees' minds.

SGI's reputation for exceptional employees was attracting competitors' attention. The economy was booming. Jobs were prolific. Silicon Valley was flourishing with pre-IPO internet start-ups. Opportunity seemed to be everywhere except at SGI. Ex-SGI executives who went to head up or start other successful high-technology companies (Jim Clark with Netscape, Tom Jermoluk and @Home, Rob Burgess and Macromedia, among others) were recruiting SGI employees away in droves. Many employees had friends who left the company and made it big.

THE CHALLENGE

SGI found itself in a precarious spot. To remain an independent company, the company must:

- Hire a new executive team. This included the CEO, CFO, CIO, VP of sales, VP of marketing, and VP of corporate communications.

- Create a new business plan and model. This included divesting noncore businesses, drastically reducing the operating expense structure, and realigning business units toward independent profitability.

- Create an integrated product road map merging with supercomputer technologies. Purchasing Cray Research in June 1996 created an integration challenge that spanned the broadest product line in the industry and included desktop workstations and supercomputers.

- Ensure that the new NT product line was successful. This included everything from negotiating contract partnerships with Microsoft and Intel (formerly viewed as "enemies") to ensuring that the new NT products were differentiated in a keen market, to creating new e-commerce distribution channels, to outsourcing such vertically integrated functions as manufacturing (something to which the company was averse), to developing new NT skill sets within a company whose devotion to Unix was nearly religious.

- Maintain focus on other pieces of the product line, and answer customer and market concerns that SGI was cannibalizing its mainstay Unix revenue by focusing on NT.

- Aggressively cut all expenses—not just head count. This meant cutting many programs perceived as perks at SGI, which would be quite a challenge with employees who were already restless.

- Avoid a hostile takeover and protect the company's intellectual capital investment safeguarded in the vaults of employees' minds. Because SGI was a knowledge-based company and had very little process or knowledge infrastructure, employee productivity and retention became a cornerstone objective.

Employees were disillusioned and asking, "Why should we stay?" They felt that executives had lied to or misled them about the company's financial position as well as the strategic direction. A Website posting the names of those exiting the company was heavily trafficked. Productivity ground to a halt. It was no secret that many employees considered leaving. But retaining and motivating the employee base was key to SGI's recovery.

How did communications play a role? A crisis communication team and a few key executives believed that a critical component to productivity and retention was a clear, accurate, honest, insightful, motivating and to-the-minute depiction of the company, its successful future vision, and the steps necessary to achieve this future. In *Beyond Spin*, we explore the SGI worldwide employee communications strategy during this period, as well as other communications challenges at leading corporations such as Arco, Citibank, Federal Express, Qualcomm, Charles Schwab, Levi's, Microsoft, and more.

"Headless Body in Topless Bar!" went beyond spin to sensationalism. Today's organizational communication models must go in the opposite direction: away from sensationalism, hype, and propaganda, which are no longer acceptable to knowledge-rich employees who have as much access to information as organizational communicators do. Control and manipulation are no longer possible. To be effective in today's corporate environment, communications must be open, accurate, timely, and strategically weighted. Combining these communication tenets is not novel; these same hallmarks also guide societal journalism. Adopting journalism inside the corporation is the proposition of this book.

The New World

Taylorism

Macro Sociotechnological Factors

Summary

For a government to serve a populace; for a religion to spread the word; and for a corporation to align its employees with its overarching vision, values, purpose, mission, strategies, and priorities, there is always a need for organizational communication. Alignment for the purpose of directing or changing group behavior has never been easy. Even in the best of circumstances, directing organizational motion is complex. The role communication plays in advancing this alignment is significant and often underestimated.

Organizational communication is the aggregate of all communications within an organization, or the collective communication between two or more individuals within the organization. This includes not only central "corporate" messaging but also divisional communications, team-based communications, hallway conversations, the rumor mill, one-on-one discussions, broadcast e-mail, and more.

If done well, an organizational communication strategy shifts an organization to line up behind a vision. If done very well, the organization passionately adopts it. But if done poorly, the company finds itself immobilized at best. If done very poorly, the organization rebels and most likely turns directly against leadership.

John Kennedy's focusing of the American people on space voyage, Martin Luther King's mobilization of the civil rights movement, Henry Ford's introduction of the manufacturing assembly line, and the implementation of Federal Express CEO Fred Smith's revolutionary overnight delivery are historical examples of large-scale organizational communication performed well. These leaders communicated, passionately and clearly, a vision and the steps necessary to move toward a future place. Despite the complexities of their missions, they aligned broad and disparate communities around complex, never-before-realized objectives.

One can quickly analyze corporate communication effectiveness by asking employees these questions:

1. What are the overarching vision, values, purpose, mission, strategies, and priorities for our organization?

2. How does your role align toward achieving these goals?

Broad inconsistency among answers to the first question and a blank stare in response to the second one signal ineffective organizational communication. This ineffectiveness is likely to have an impact on organizational morale, efficiency, productivity, and retention—all elements that dramatically affect the bottom line.

Companies have long tried to rein in organizational communication. Some organizations attempt to control everything. Some use the 80-20 rule, controlling what they consider "corporate" messages (or what they assume is 80 percent of an organization's overall communication suite) while hoping that all remaining communications fall in line. During the industrial age, in a largely mechanistic society this approach worked for a short while. Its life span was marked.

Why is organizational communication so difficult? Because it cannot be controlled, because many factors affect it, and because unpredictable elements play a role in its success. Many organizations today still believe they can mechanically align employees by controlling certain factors to produce a desired outcome. The levers of communication are no longer easily pulled.

Absolutist mechanistic thought, dating back to the seventeenth-century theories of Newton and Descartes, has often been challenged. In his book *Cosmopolis*, Stephen Toulmin depicts four centuries of increasing obsession with "the delusion that human nature could be fitted into precise and manageable rational categories." This "logical exactitude" has ignored the holism of systems.

A number of macro sociotechnological factors discussed later in this chapter give evidence in support of the idea that systems theory and chaos theory are converging and necessitating a shift from a mechanistic organization to an organic one. Deterministic theory explores the reactive nature of an object acted upon by any force. Applied to business, these theories played out in mechanistic management theory, or Taylorism.

TAYLORISM

Mechanical alignment requires predictability among a limited number of communication variables. Organizational success represented graphically looks like this:

$$A + B + C + D + E + F = Success$$

In this case, C needs to know about and communicate only with B and D. C need not know what drives Success, or how E and F affect Success. As long as there is complete alignment between B and D, C does all that is required to achieve Success.

If the representation shifts to something like

$$A/2 + B^2 + C + 3*D + E - F = Success$$

then C does not need to know all of the changes in the success equation; C only needs to know that B has changed to B^2 and that D has changed to $3*D$. This represents a Taylorist model.

Henry Ford's operations were models of mechanistic industrialization in several ways. As Joseph White reports in *The Wall Street Journal*, "The Model T put America on wheels. But the real revolution was the production technique developed in 1913. Ford Motor Co's moving assembly line, and the rapid spread of its mass-production methods, kicked the industrialization of America into overdrive and profoundly changed the way people work and live world-wide" (p. R25).

When Ford retooled his manufacturing plant to create a new assembly-line process, his communication strategy was probably equally calculated. He might have procured expert advisers, both internal and external, to brainstorm, suggest, craft, and codify the assembly-line design, strategy, and implementation plan. He might have "cascaded" an executive memo outlining the new strategy and a time line for the changes. Perhaps he conducted a set of meetings with management at the various tiers of the Ford organizational hierarchy. To rally the troops, centrally orchestrated factorywide meetings might have followed, with a general message about the new assembly-line methodology and the success it promised. Most likely, he instigated assembly-line training classes and a handbook delineating changes and detailing the specifics of the new methodology. Employees undoubtedly were then methodically informed and taught their role in the greater assembly-line machine. These are classic, straightforward organizational communication elements to achieve alignment in mechanistic environments.

This controlled approach to communication wasn't without challenges. White tells us that "the workers hated the new methods. The men didn't like it, because they had to work harder. Everyone had to learn how to say 'hurry up' in at least four languages. Men quit in droves. Though mass production's aim was to whittle tasks down to simple rote and repetition, the revolving door was undermining productivity" (p. R28). Ford responded with equally reflexive triggers: he doubled wages to five dollars per day and decreased the workday from nine hours per shift to eight. Calling it "profit sharing," he was striking a new kind of bargain with workers. White describes Ford as a "scrappy entrepreneur trying to stay afloat in the Silicon Valley of the early 1900s: Detroit. What Bill Gates is to business celebrity today, Henry Ford was in the 1920s" (p. R25).

Taylor's ideas worked so long as employees' tasks were atomized. They would not work in most environments today because employees now multitask and consciously view their jobs in the context of a larger system. This type of holistic alignment is more organic and not as easily orchestrated because many factors influence the parts, which in turn affect the whole. Such modern management theorists as Peter Senge, Margaret Wheatley, and Myron Kellner-Rogers have popularized this notion of systems thinking and organic, self-governing orders applied to corporations. They talk about organizational shifts from purely mechanistic to organic.

In 1990, Senge's *The Fifth Discipline* pioneered the concept of the "learning organization," a "systems" approach to management. In the book, he makes the case that the whole of an organization is more effective than the sum of its parts. He invites managers and employees to challenge their "mental models"—deeply rooted assumptions and generalizations—and to break down the limits of thinking that blocks the ability to create, adapt, and change reality. Wheatley followed suit, building upon the work of physics theorist David Bohm and others to describe intimate likenesses between organic cell behavior and that of institutions.

In their electronic pamphlet "Eyes That Do Not See," Tom Heuerman and Diane Olson, organizational consultants in Minneapolis, refer to novelist Walker Percy to illustrate the nature of mechanistic and paternalistic organizations: "Percy said that a fish does not reflect on the nature of water. Unable to imagine the absence of water, the fish cannot consider the presence of water. Paternalism is the water of organizations. Paternalism is a system of belief based on control, consistency, and predictability suggestive of a parent-child relationship."

In paternalistic organizations, the leaders are responsible for the organization's success and its members' well-being. "Paternalism cannot give organizations what they need in today's marketplace," Heuerman and Olson continue, "commitment, ownership, and responsibility. What parent trusts a child totally? What child tells a parent the whole truth?"

Karen Stephenson, an anthropologist and management professor at UCLA's Anderson Graduate School of Management, echoes these sentiments and adds an anthropological dimension. In a dialogue with forty-five of the "best brains in the new world of work" (according to *Fast Company* magazine), she said:

> As an anthropologist, I hang out not only in corporate jungles, but also in real jungles. . . . I have degrees in chemistry and in physics; and in those sciences we know that there are underlying patterns in how atoms and molecules behave. It occurred to me that there are underlying patterns of interaction between humans. As I've studied organizations, I've come to conclude that when you see people networking, schmoozing, or fighting, you're seeing underlying patterns that are just as deeply embedded in human principles as is anything in physics or in chemistry. Yet these patterns don't show up in the organizational charts that people draw at work— they're encoded in the relationships of trust that allow us to work together [p. 148].

This shift to a new world of work is gradual. Most organizations today are neither purely mechanistic nor entirely organic; rather, they employ elements of both. In reality, many organizations reveal remnants of the desire to preserve the old forms of power and control even as they speak of change.

In the political world, pure mechanical alignment is dictatorial; pure organic alignment is egalitarian. A democratic, representational society falls somewhere in between. Figure 1.1 depicts the continuum between rigid and fluid information as applied to political structures, organizational structures, and communication models.

In the transition from top-down dictatorial societies to aware, democratic, representational societies, journalism has played the role of a societal alignment tool. Its timely, accurate, open information flow and market-driven speed of delivery translate well into the corporate world, where these communication techniques work in much the same way. General Colin Powell says that "the most effective means of ensuring the government's accountability to the people is an aggressive, free, challenging, untrusting press." *Beyond Spin* argues that to shape a more organic, democratized organization, "accountability to the people" translates into "alignment toward the vision" and is enabled by information flow that is open, accurate, and timely—and provided by a strategic corporate journalism model.

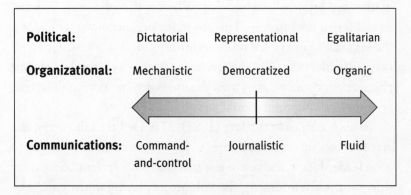

Political:	Dictatorial	Representational	Egalitarian
Organizational:	Mechanistic	Democratized	Organic
Communications:	Command-and-control	Journalistic	Fluid

FIGURE 1.1. Rigid⟨⋯⋯⟩Fluid Continuum

MACRO SOCIOTECHNOLOGICAL FACTORS

Before examining the specifics of strategic corporate journalism, let us examine some macro sociotechnological changes that are caus- ing a shift from the mechanistic model to an organic one. For each factor, we explore the impact on organizational communication:

- Knowledge workforce

- Democratized workforce

- Diversification

  Diverse workforce
  Generational differences
  Globalized economy

- The information age

- Increased pace of change

Knowledge Workforce

Over the past few decades, there has been a shift from a manufac- turing-driven economy to one that is idea driven; consequently, there is a shift from an industrial-age labor workforce to an infor- mation-age knowledge workforce. Whereas the labor-age, Taylorist model relied on automated precision for organizational efficiency, the knowledge workforce relies on intuitive decision making. These two modalities differ just as a precisely notated, well-conducted sym- phonic performance differs from the unknown harmonic results that an integrated improvisational jazz ensemble creates.

In his book *Leadership Jazz* (1992), Max De Pree talks about the art of leadership and summarizes today's organizations: "The key to good leadership, as the key to inspired jazz, is dependent on so many things—the environment, the volunteers playing in the band, the need for everybody to perform as individuals and as a group, the absolute dependence of the leader on the members of the band" (p. 8). Today, organizational communicators must counter the unpredictability of the future by taking full advantage of the wide variety of complementary skills within the organization. This creates the challenge of leveraging the intrinsic interdependence between organizational leaders and the knowledge workforce.

For a knowledge workforce, organizational effectiveness stems more from intellectual adoption than it does from informational alignment. The power has shifted from the organization to the individuals. Communication needs have also shifted. Knowledge workers can't be *told* what to do; they need to *understand* what to do. *Knowledge Management* magazine talks about the new "knowledge ownership": "The wealth-creating capacity of organizations is bound up inside human containers . . . companies are placed at risk by potential departure of key personnel. In the industrial era, value was created by assembling raw materials into finished goods. Now, value derives mainly from ideas, knowledge and competencies" (Dec. 1998, p. 71).

For a knowledge worker to make a "right" decision (one that leads to organizational success and innovation, not just isolated success for the individual), the vision, goals, and strategies of the organization must be so ingrained that making right decisions becomes second nature. In disparate parts of the organization, other knowledge workers with similarly internalized understanding are at the same time making other right decisions. In turn, others improvise upon these decision outcomes in a complementary fashion. The sum of all these catalyzed decisions is far greater than what a programmed, predictable, decision-making machine can accomplish. This unpredictable value-added symbiosis is the essence of the knowledge workforce.

A knowledge workforce therefore demands an enlightened communications approach. Employees want access to relevant information that helps them perform their jobs faster and better. They want connections to data that allow insight. Knowledge workers want not only to thoroughly understand the organization's vision, strategy, philosophy, values, and goals but also to intuitively align themselves with these fundamental elements so that they consistently make good decisions for the organization. As with the jazz ensemble, they also want these decisions to lead to a level of unpredictable, harmonized insight that propels their organization forward.

Force-feeding sophisticated employees the company line does not achieve this kind of alignment. Packaging information in marketing wrappers and giving it the spin of marketingspeak doesn't work either. Jolie Solomon, senior editor for Time Inc.'s business magazines, says that "the recognition of employees as savvy, skeptical adults would lead to more candor, honesty, and irreverence in communicating. This approach would parallel what retailers have learned about retailing to the customer." When it comes to empowering a knowledge workforce, communications must be trusted if they are to be absorbed. Well-educated, rational individuals are more likely to trust communication that is free of spin and that is open, accurate, timely, in context, well reasoned, and evenly presented along with opposing views. If knowledge workers receive this breadth of information and communication, they are more apt to absorb and internalize the organization's messages. Well-rounded reporting equips them with the kind of full informational understanding they need to adjust and make thoroughly weighed work decisions. Knowledge organizations hire smart people to solve complex problems. They hire thinkers, synthesizers. The best organizational communicators leverage this talent by presenting information that is beyond spin.

It used to be enough to simply provide content. Now, the best leverage comes from ingrained context. *Ingraining* is much more challenging than informing; in a Taylorist environment, internalization meant understanding, quite rigidly, what happens directly in front and immediately behind. Organic ingraining means working something indelibly into the natural texture or mental and moral constitution of the knowledge worker. This involves much more than one-dimensional messaging. It requires "branding" messages in highly contextualized ways, whereby every communication carries the backdrop of vision, strategy, philosophy, and cultural values. Ingraining results from organizational communication conveying the essence of what the organization wants to achieve and pointing its workers in that direction.

Democratized Workforce

The shift toward a knowledge workforce has catalyzed a related workforce trend: the move toward a more democratized workforce. With a democratized workforce, decisions are made across the organization, not solely in the executive suite. Decisions incorporate more of people's knowledge; therefore strict hierarchies are no longer necessary or cost-effective and in some cases are even harmful to organizational effectiveness. The proliferation of flat structures, representational organizations, and matrixed relationships creates another set of challenges for organizational communicators.

In a purely hierarchical organization, most organizational communication cascades from executives. The head of the hierarchy is the only one authorized to speak for all the people. If the organization needs to know something, the head of the organization crafts a communiqué and distributes it.

In democratic institutions, many representatives are organizational communicators. The top tier of the democracy no longer controls all elements of organizational communication; instead, the role of central organizational communication is not so much design and control as it is coordination and synthesis. Within the corporation, central orchestration encounters numerous challenges from democratic decision making. Many people are responsible for organizational communication—functional experts, cultural icons, impassioned advocates, and rebels—and each of them may communicate only a piece of a much broader construct. What is even more challenging is that untethered organizational leaders, agenda-driven workers, and mavericks may communicate unaligned or inaccurate messages. In knowledge communities, the unanticipated may come from any direction—internal or external. In some instances, there is no clearly delineated head of the hierarchy. The flatter the organization, the more complex is this dynamic. Some organizations have flattened almost to the point of socialism, with no clearly delineated hierarchical head. This type of organizational structure requires a new set of rules.

These challenges are the bane of many well-intentioned democratic leaders. Only those leaders who anticipate well, understand the pulse of the broader organization, and rapidly adapt are successful. In a democracy, an organizational communication strategy combines context with the messages from these various entities to create a coherent integrated communication, one that strategically reflects and directs the organization.

In crafting multidimensional communication, one must fundamentally know not only the organizational vision, strategies, priorities, and cultural values but also all the formal and informal organization communicators and channels. The democratic communicator must proactively plan for any informal organizational communications and be able to take the pulse, across the organization, of the communication flow along these channels. The democratic organizational communicator must know historic and recent organizational messaging to appropriately position each new piece of communication. Like the pointillist painter Georges Seurat, one must be able to step back from the details of organization communication to verify that as each communication pixel is added it advances the desired gestalt.

There are risks. If done poorly, the communication blurs into a confusing blob—or worse, becomes an inaccurate or misinterpreted blob. But if done well, organizational communication can create a true reflection of the organization that it serves. This accurate reflection helps guide the knowledge workforce toward the internalized understanding that is critical in a flatter decision-making process. Finally, if done well, a system of corporate checks and balances emerges similar to how the U.S. legislative, executive, and judicial branches keep each other aligned in the democratic political process. Employees challenge communications and leaders who are inconsistent, unclear, or unethical whenever the organization's overall vision is in discord. In the best of cases, immediate recalibration ensues.

The transition to a democratized workplace spotlights one of the biggest challenges in crafting a journalistic organizational communication strategy for a democratized, knowledge workforce. Democracies are skeptical of central control. Organizations must beware the *"Pravda* challenge," or a perception of propagandizing. For many years, employees have viewed corporate organizational communication efforts as corporatespeak, or as the work of the "corporate mouthpiece." Because of historical power hierarchies, and perhaps because of individual abuse of this power, such a view of formalized, manipulated corporate communications is understandable. Countering this perspective is the toughest challenge facing organizational communicators today. Since fairness and accuracy are the fundamental tenets of free journalistic reporting, the risk of being viewed overskeptically or cynically increases enormously if communicators adopt a partial journalistic model while still trying to spin or manipulate the message. Chapter Four discusses this challenge further.

Diversification

Throughout most of the twentieth century, corporate societies have been rife with PLUs (people like us). Organizations hired PLUs internally and sold to and partnered with PLUs externally. In the last two decades, however, three parallel trends have minimized PLUism: a diverse workforce, heightened generational differences, and a global economy.

Diverse Workforce

Many of the factors sustaining PLUism in the workforce are identical to those that made Taylorism so compelling. PLUism plays to the comfort zone, to the status quo, and to those who like being in control; it tries to govern by manipulation. Decision making is predictable and one-sided and only allows an organization to move linearly and as one unit.

As with Taylorism, PLUism is doomed because of its myopia. Since the 1970s, organizations have begun to understand the power of a diverse workforce. Different people bring a variety of ways of thinking. Exposure to other cultures introduces multidimensional ideas and thoughts that can lead to creative problem solving. With these benefits also comes a much greater challenge for organizational communicators: consistency of interpretation. People from diverse backgrounds, ages, styles, and cultures communicate, hear, and interpret things differently. One size does not usually fit all. In *On Dialogue*, physicist David Bohm refers to the "microculture," which "purposes that a sampling of an entire culture can exist in a group of twenty or more people, thereby charging it with multiple views and value systems" (p. x). Given this definition, diversification requirements may at their simplest be the need to communicate within an organization made up of many disassociated teams of twenty or more people.

In the *Fast Company* report, anthropologist Stephenson tells of traveling in Guatemala twenty years ago. She and a dozen colleagues were captured at machine gunpoint for no apparent reason. Realizing that the gunmen were not in a negotiating mood, Fred, a colleague, addressed the lead gunman as if he were a friend not seen in some time. Fred went on conversing with him and began moving around naturally and gently. Then he began packing his belongings—all while still under gunpoint. Once past this moment of reckoning, the gunmen let the group go. "I understood then," Stephenson says, "that, while I spoke the language of that country, I didn't speak the culture. Fred spoke the culture. He knew how to use the culture to turn the situation around" (p. 148). Organizational communicators who are as tuned in to these nuances as Fred are able to successfully communicate in this diverse age.

Generational Differences

Successive generations use and adopt information technology differently. To propose a sweeping generality, most people tend to accept, learn, and sometimes passionately pursue new technologies more readily when they are young. A generational resistance can result in a tendency to rely on the technologies from one's youth, while eschewing technologies introduced later in life. Therefore multigenerational organizations may differ in the level of acceptance for various information and how it is presented. In generationally diverse organizations, this challenge can erupt in the form of disconnected communications, especially if generational distinctions map to the organizational hierarchy, or if the executive suite is older than the employee base. In such organizations, the executives may be late to adapt new information technologies.

In the information age, information technologies are introduced to the organization at a staggering pace. A varying rate of technology adoption can affect the ability to blanket the organization with one message. This, in turn, exacerbates the generational disconnect and increases organizational confusion. The cycle can continue if one does not appropriately account for generational diversity.

Globalized Economy

For external audiences such as partners and customers with whom the organization interacts, diversity has also increased. The elimination of geographic boundaries, both metaphorical and literal, allows a globally linked economy to emerge. Consequently, a diverse workforce is no longer just a strategic advantage—it is a necessity. In the *Economist*, Sandy Weill, chairman and co-CEO of Citigroup, calls this "globality—the linkage of events in one part of the world to places far distant" (p. 131). If an organization has not yet realized the limitations of workforce myopia or the strategic benefits to diversity, the necessary shift in perspective from local to global may bring painful lessons. It is not hard to find instances of multimillion dollar international communications gone awry because a company does not understand varying cultural norms. In a famous example, General Motors introduced a new Chevrolet into Spanish-speaking countries—but its U.S. name, Nova, translated as "doesn't go" in Spanish.

To reap the advantages of a diverse workforce interacting within a global economy, an organization can no longer afford PLUistic communication strategies. At best PLUism only engages one faction among diverse audiences; at worst, the differing interpretations of PLUistic communications leave the organization in debilitating confusion. Organizational communicators must understand and incorporate how people of different backgrounds, ages, styles, and cultures communicate and interpret things. With this understanding, they can craft organizational communications that spark diverse, yet still symbiotic, reactions to correctly align the workforce.

Alvie L. Smith remarks in *Innovative Employee Communications* that "the importance of effective internal communication has been intensified because of the dramatic changes that have taken place in our society in the past 10 to 20 years. Nowhere is it more pronounced than in the business and industrial world. Unprecedented global competition has magnified the urgent need to modernize America's aged industrial facilities in order to improve both quality and productivity levels. Equally important is the need to modernize management thinking about the most productive use of people in all aspects of the business" (pp. 1–2).

Information Age

The availability of incomprehensible amounts of global information, with a simple click on a hyperlink, swallows people whole. In 1982, John Naisbitt's *Megatrends* announced the movement from the industrial society to the information society. "We are drowning in information and starved for knowledge," he wrote back then (1990, p. xviii). Today, speaking merely of information overload is passé; most people today are in information shock.

Futurists say society is teetering on the verge of an information revolution. People can't effectively use the information that flows at them, and the information flow will continue—it can't be stopped. It is now inextricably linked to economic performance; a 1998 *BusinessWeek* feature, "The Twenty-First Century Economy," reported "there is growing evidence that the U.S. economy is in the early stages of a powerful new wave of innovation. The leading edge is the information revolution, which permeates every sector of the economy. Over the last year, for example, high tech has taken half a percentage point off inflation and added almost a full point of growth" (Mandel, 1998, p. 60)—growth that is now at a 3.5 percent annual rate in the United States.

The Institute for the Future, a think tank that projects business and societal trends, studies information overload. In a 1998 report, "Beyond Knowledge Management," institute president Bob Johansen says that "some observers predict that humans will reach an absolute attention limit between 2010 and 2020—that they will simply be deluged with more information than they can attend to" (p. 6). Trends in technology and communications data traffic back this up. As C. Michael Armstrong, chairman and CEO of AT&T, reports in the *Economist's* "The World in 1999" issue: "Use of global communications by the world's largest companies is growing by 19 percent a year. . . . Some time in 1999, data will overtake voice traffic on the majority of the world's communications networks" (p. 116). Futurists Stan Davis and Christopher Meyer say that's not so dramatic; more astonishingly yet, they predict that "voice will be less than two percent of the traffic by 2003" (p. 9). Information access is not the issue. People today are information challenged.

What's an organizational communicator to do? The systems theorists point to the need for effective information flow. In *Leadership and the New Science*, Wheatley says, "A well ordered system is defined not by how many brain parts it has, but by how much information it can process. The greater the ability to process information, the greater the level of consciousness" (1992, p. 107). The answer lies not in attempting to control information flow but in being able to give it context as well, and providing clearly organized paths to what people need to know.

Information Quantity

Not long ago, people were limited to the information that was housed by their local libraries, heard over the radio, or broadcast on the nightly news. Organizations had corporate libraries and contracts with information providers such as Dataquest or IDC to provide them with industry news and market research. Now, the once-private doors to information are wide open to anyone who wants to know anything.

What impact has this had on the knowledge-age worker? Can everyone know everything and still be productive? Information overload has quite possibly decreased workplace productivity, rather than increasing it. The organizational communicator has a responsibility not to add to this overload, but instead simplify, set in context, repeat, and synchronize messages that make the information not only bearable but also valuable.

Instantaneous Information Flow

The business world has redefined time by the terms of the Internet. "Internet time" is synonymous with "instantaneous"; in the Internet sphere, one year is squeezed into three months. When Johansen talks about leadership in twenty-first-century organizations, he reminds us that "businesses today move in Internet time—twenty-four hours a day, seven days a week" (1998, p. 180).

With the World Wide Web, news can blanket the globe instantaneously, and any rumor can infiltrate an entire organization in an intranet heartbeat. Brad Whitworth, Hewlett-Packard's Y2K (year 2000) communications manager, envisions an experiment to clock the speed of the intranet rumor mill by planting a faux confidential document beside a copy machine and timing the rumor mill channels to clock how fast the rumor permeates the entire organization (personal interview).

This potentiality creates expectations of immediacy in the minds of organizational communicators. They no longer have the luxury of carefully digging complex communications canals; instead they need a crash course in becoming flood-diversion experts.

Internal-External Transparency

Which information is for internal use only, and which is for external distribution? What used to be a steel wall between confidential and public information is now semipermeable at best and on the way to becoming nonexistent. Employees today often don't understand what *company confidential* means. Nor do they understand the difference between information that is competitive versus what is promotional. This lack of understanding is not new, but information availability and the seamlessness of external communications on the Internet exacerbate the difficulties of this confusion. Such transparency is causing most PR and legal departments consternation.

Some organizations, however, are taking advantage of the opportunity to bring external customers and partners more tightly into the fold. In *CIO Magazine*, the president, CEO, and codirector of research at Meta Group, Dale Kutnick, talks of "the externalization imperative," by which in the past "most enterprises hid their information behind layers of bureaucracy and secrecy"; he predicts that "in the century ahead, companies increasingly will be judged by how well they can 'expose' this information to facilitate the collaboration on products, customer service, marketing, sales, distribution, or manufacturing" (p. 120).

Communication Channel Proliferation

Back when interoffice memos, corporationwide meetings, telephones, pushpin bulletin boards, and the informal rumor mill were the primary organizational communication channels, deciding which one to use for a specific communication was clear. Today one must choose among printed newsletters or papers, electronic bulletin boards, faxes, pagers, cellular phones, voice mail, e-mail, intranet or extranet or Internet sites, newsgroups, chat rooms, collaborative technologies, teleconferencing, videoconferencing, simulcast, multicast . . . the list goes on. Determining which information channel is most appropriate for a message can be like choosing a favorite painting in the Louvre. Sometimes the choices overwhelm.

The channel options, as well as the expectations, add to the complexity of communication. Most organizations have internal communications norms. In some cases—usually with mature enterprises—groups develop communications guidelines or practices that are firmly rooted in the culture. Even when these norms are acculturated, they may not be clear. If a well-delineated set of established communications norms exists, every organizational member can determine exactly how to communicate any message: what language to use or avoid, the channel preferred by different circles of people, the recommended length of the message, the tone, etc.

With so many new and competing communication channels, though, determining the appropriate, acculturated method and tone for an audience may not be easy. In many high-tech organizations, executives use and prefer voice mail as the primary organizational broadcast channel, while the engineering departments prefer e-mail and the human resource department uses the Web. It is critical to understand these norms in order to orchestrate a successful communication. Therefore the organizational communicator must not only differentiate the available suite of communication channels but also select from existing organizational communications norms and craft an appropriate overarching strategy that threads together various audience-specific communication channels. An executive who sends an urgent hardcopy memo by interoffice mail in a voice-mail culture is using an inappropriate channel.

Although crafting the elements of such a strategy is far more challenging than deciding between a memo or a meeting, the outcome of a well-orchestrated, multichannel communication strategy that leverages the inherent differences and purposes of organizationally acculturated communication technologies is powerful. The effect can be dramatic in achieving alignment.

Increased Pace of Change

Are things really moving faster? Or are there just more information and more options than ever before? Do younger generations too feel the increased pace, or is this just another generational difference that has been a part of the human condition since the beginning of time? Societies long before ours claimed things were moving too fast and becoming too complex. But in the past five decades, the pace has definitely shifted into high gear.

In *Blur* (1998), Davis and Meyer talk about the speed of change in the connected economy. They express their main thesis in an equation:

Speed × Connectivity × Intangibles = Blur

The speed element means that "every aspect of business and the connected organization operates and changes in real time." With connectivity, "everything is becoming electronically connected to everything else: products, people, companies, countries, everything." The intangibles are growing fast and affect every aspect of work in the new economy. The resultant blur—or the "trinity of the blur" as they call it—is the new world in which people are coming to live and work. "Connectivity, speed, and intangibles—the derivatives of time, space, and mass—are blurring the rules and redefining our businesses and our lives" (pp. 5–8).

Whatever the reality, the lightning pace of change seems to have created a "life compression" that is blamed for everything from a high divorce rate to lower moral fabric, from poverty to generic societal malaise. In business, this compression plays out in the form of shortened product life cycles, shortened sales cycles, shorter project time lines, and shorter employment commitments on the part of both employer and employee.

Unfortunately, institutional norms and dynamics tend to change much more slowly than the surrounding environment. According to *Fast Company* founder and editor Allan Webber, dramatic technological revolutions can happen as often as every six months, but organizations *evolve*, and they cannot evolve fast enough (1998, Seminar: "The Changing Nature of Competitiveness"). Even the organizations once responsible for monitoring and mastering change now lag. The legal industry is reeling under new requirements for privacy and intellectual property. Legislation affecting the Internet world cannot keep pace with the behaviors that laws are designed to control. Similarly, are our medical institutions ready for the genetic discoveries right around the corner?

Although technologies change at blinding speed, large organizations still change at a relative snail's pace. In "Beyond Knowledge Management," an Institute for the Future report published in 1997, Johansen says that "Moore's Law has us coping with a technology speed cycle that doubles every 18 months. Yet our best examples of technological integration in organizations seem to suggest that it takes about seven years to fully integrate a new way of working. We may be facing a fundamental mismatch between human learning cycles and the speed of technological change," he posits. Organizations that are not as close to the innovative edge are likely to change even more slowly. This is why mechanistic organizations and behaviors are still alive and well, despite the overarching trend toward holistic, organic models.

In today's world, where information can shift in an instant—along with an audience's attention span, and the competitive landscape—organization leaders cannot control information. In the organic view, information is not a "thing." Wheatley (1992) analyzes the catch-all complaint of "communications problems": "The nub of the problem is that we've treated information as a 'thing,' as an inert entity to disseminate" (p. 101). The problem is that communication is not static. "At a young age," she writes, "we knew information for its dynamic qualities, for its constantly changing aliveness. But when we entered organizational life, we left that perspective behind. We expected information to be controllable, stable, and useful for our purposes. We expected to manage it" (p. 102). It is impossible to control information and the speed at which it barrels toward employees. Davis and Meyer say the BLUR and "its constant acceleration are here to stay, and those who miss that point will miss everything. Your job as a manager, as an entrepreneur, as a consumer, and as an individual is to master the blur, to keep the acceleration going, to keep your world changing and off balance" (p. 7).

Regardless, the life span of information and intellectual capital has shortened. It no longer pays to covet information. John Peetz, chief knowledge officer at Ernst and Young, says, "If we try to keep content out of the hands of people in order to keep competitive, we lose." At a knowledge management conference in San Francisco in November 1998, he presented a version of the schema in Figure 1.2 to emphasize that content itself has little intrinsic value. As time passes, the value of information drops significantly.

Not only does information lose its value faster; its value increases as more people know it (Figure 1.3). In *Intellectual Capital*, Thomas Stewart talks about "network externalities." This refers to the fact that the value of knowledge increases because it is widely used. "In industries that depend on communication (not many don't), network externalities are especially powerful, because they create the standards required for communication to occur, just as the utility of English as a language—and the value, therefore, of having the language in your capital stock—increases precisely because so many other people have the same asset" (p. 176).

Therefore information needs to flow faster and more broadly. The organizational communicator must understand, however, that the organizational psyche is overwhelmed and overinformed by the pace of growth. The communicator must send focused, instantaneous messages that capture the audience's attention but do not add

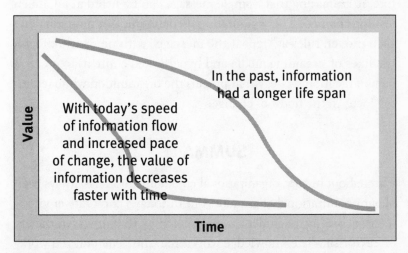

FIGURE 1.2. Decreasing Value of Information over Life Span

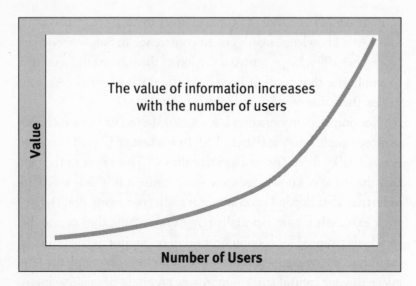

FIGURE 1.3. Increasing Value of Information As It Is Used

to overwhelming information overload. This daunting task haunts most communicators.

In this blazingly fast-paced world, where a collective instant of full audience attention is far more difficult to achieve than ever before, it is amazing that a single message can be heard at all, much less internalized. The organizational communicator must combine such proven rules as "repeat the message" with new technologies the likes of streaming media and hyperlinked context, to create a communication strategy that propels the organization while retaining focus in the midst of change.

SUMMARY

Throughout history, organizational communication has always been about organizational alignment. But in today's corporate environment, achieving alignment is more complex than it was in the era of Taylorism. The knowledge workforce, the democratized workforce, the diverse workforce, diversification of the workforce and economy, generational and gender differences, the global economy, the information age, and the increased pace of change have altered the external landscape in which all organizations operate. The purely hierarchical establishments have given way to institutions that are more representative and organic. Information barrages employees from all sides and challenges them to find what they need— even if they don't know they need it.

Some of these trends (knowledge workforce, democratized workforce, and diverse workforce) affect the organization locally. Others (global economy, information age, and pace of change) are exogenous to the organization. The aggregate of these trends intensifies the need for strategic corporate journalism. Today's organizations can no longer be manipulated with propaganda. Realism is essential. Organizational communications departments need to transition to an open, timely, and weighted free press that facilitates free-flowing information as opposed to the artery-clogging sludge of corporatespeak. It is this free press that is the life support for a knowledge-based, democratized, diverse workforce competing in an information-rich, fast-paced global economy. If applied successfully, journalistic communications within the new corporate structure aid democratized alignment. This formula, summarized mathematically here, is related to the "knowledge equation" that we present in Chapter Four:

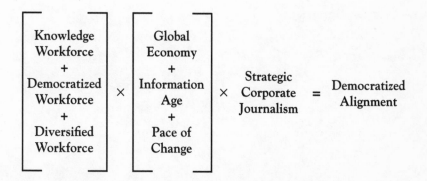

The information age consumes and overshadows the contemporary global, democratized, knowledge workforce. More information is available to and pushed at employees than ever before. Today's organizations have the benefit of instantaneous, global access to information from worldwide adoption of satellite, cellular, and Internet and intranet broadcast technologies. Information flows much faster and more freely than it ever has in history.

As a result, workers feel squeezed by having too much information and by trying to decide what, from among the barrage of data they receive, they absolutely need to know. There is a saying at Hewlett-Packard, "If only HP knew what HP knew." The overwhelming mounds of information available have catalyzed huge trends such as knowledge industries, cognitive architects, avatars, and intelligent agents—all methodologies or tools to help people find data they need.

How has the proliferation of information had an impact on organizational communication? To really understand it, one must first have an elemental grasp of organizational communications. The next chapter attempts to methodically break down organizational communications into its most basic components. This deconstruction, although enlightening, nevertheless demonstrates the challenge of applying mechanistic principles to any system as holistic as organizational communication.

2

Communications Unplugged

George Bernard Shaw once said, "The greatest problem with communication is the illusion that it has been accomplished." How many business failures have been blamed on poor communications? How many organizationwide surveys have identified poor communications as the number one or number two employee concern? In *Leadership and the New Science*, Wheatley notes that in every organization in which Wheatley had worked, poor communications topped the list of major employee issues (1992, p. 101). But ask employees for more specificity about what's wrong, and you're likely to get nowhere. Ask anyone, moreover, about how he perceives his communication skills, and you're likely to get a positive response. What causes this disconnect?

Communicating is easy—it happens all the time. But effective communication is complicated and depends on many interrelated elements. Ed Robertson, employee communications director at Federal Express, has written on five common myths about communication. Myth number three is that "communication comes naturally to us." Roberts says "communication isn't something that just happens as part of the human phenomenon. It takes concentration and effort to develop our communication abilities." He points out that "you can not not communicate, but you can communicate ineffectively." Though true for individual communication, it is even more so within complex organizational communications (personal interview).

This chapter deconstructs and examines basic organizational communication goals, principles, and characteristics. At each turn, we discuss examples and make suggestions for implementing these elements into communication strategies. Although many of our examples happen to come from broad, centrally orchestrated communications, the underlying tenets of each example can be applied to any organizational communication, no matter how modest. We also briefly introduce the importance of corporate journalistic practices here, although strategic corporate journalism—the blending of organizational communication with journalistic principles and practices—is explored in more detail in Chapter Four.

ALIGNED COMMUNICATIONS

As indicated in the previous chapter, organizational communication broadly defined is the aggregate of all communication within an organization. More specifically, it is the collective communication between two or more individuals within an organization. Leaders often take a narrow view of organizational communication, thinking it encompasses only those messages broadcast across the entire organization. Sometimes the perception of organizational communication is even more restricted, including only what is centrally orchestrated by a corporate communications department. Regardless of defining the scope of organizational communication as broad or narrow, the overarching goal likely remains the same: to create alignment.

Whether the communication is a one-on-one discussion; a message to a specific team, department, group, or geography; or a broadcast organizational communication, the communicator strives to ensure positive alignment with the audience. In individual communication, positive alignment may mean anything from simple agreement between strangers to intimate connection between parent and child. In group communications—especially broadcast organizational communication—positive alignment can mean anything from full understanding to complete internalization of organizational values, vision, goals, strategic direction, and operational methods. Senge describes the "synchronicity" of alignment in his Introduction to Joseph Jaworski's book by the same name: "I felt deeply that this phenomenon of alignment was not individualistic at all, but fundamentally collective" (p. 6).

Achieving collective alignment does not mean that the organization loses its uniqueness or ability to respond nimbly to market forces. In *The Power of Alignment*, George Labovitz and Victor Rosansky describe the beauty of alignment: "Aligned organizations capture the best of specialization but are able to respond quickly to change. People in aligned organizations have the capacity to sense change as it happens and the ability to realign themselves rapidly with a minimum of top-down direction. The old, linear approach has given way to one of simultaneity—to alignment" (p. 9).

Alignment is not necessarily positive. As a result of communication, it can fall anywhere on a continuum spanning positive to neutral to negative (Figure 2.1). For individual communication, neutral alignment would be the case of no agreement or no connection, and negative or misalignment would be disagreement or dislike. For organizational communication, neutral alignment might mean organizational ambivalence or apathy, while negative alignment could result in organizational rebellion.

Following alignment, many communicators seek a secondary goal: action. John Gerstner, communications manager at John Deere, points out the "bottom-line: when we communicate about something within an organization, we do it to change minds and attitudes, and ultimately, to elicit action" (personal interview). More than gaining agreement, aligned action is the most powerful result of successful organizational messaging. Examples of aligned action are (in the individual communication realm) a stranger following directions from another stranger, or a mother breastfeeding her infant. For organizational communications, aligned action could be collaborative product development, coordinated branded marketing, or proactive sales calls.

Like alignment, action also falls on a continuum and can be positive, neutral, or negative. There is not always a direct correlation between alignment and action. For example, a communication resulting in complete alignment could nevertheless cause neutral or surprisingly negative actions. The stranger, once understanding the directions, could choose not to follow them. The mother, understanding her infant's nonverbal request for food, could choose to complete another task first. The members of an organization, understanding the strategic direction, could choose to leave the organization.

This fuzzy correlation between alignment and action adds another degree of complexity to the task of the organizational communication strategist who strives for the net effect of all organiza-

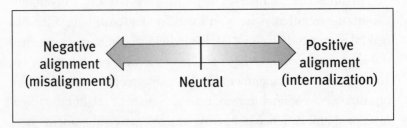

FIGURE 2.1. Alignment

tional communications being positive alignment and positive or aligned action. In the absence of positive alignment and action, an organization is at best unable to fully achieve success; at worst, it can fail completely (Figure 2.2).

Effective organizational communication is much more complex than discrete individual communications. Whereas in individual communications one need only worry about personal effectiveness, in organizational communication the communicator has to consider synchronicity, consistency, and integration across numerous intraorganizational and extraorganizational communication channels. Crafting effective organizational communication requires a much higher degree of orchestration.

Speaking of orchestration, Ben Zander, the conductor of the Boston Philharmonic, often delivers inspirational addresses to corporate leaders on the subject of aligned group action. His partner, Rosamund Stone Zander, says in a *Fast Company* interview with the couple: "The new leader's job is to create a powerful vision that allows room for things to occur that are as yet undreamed of. The

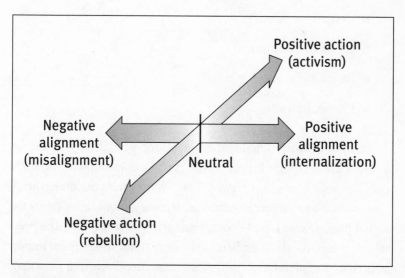

FIGURE 2.2. Alignment and Action

leader must hold the definition of the vision so clearly that all the players involved are able to align with it daily" (p. 112).

ELEMENTS OF AN EFFECTIVE ORGANIZATIONAL COMMUNICATION STRATEGY

There are three basic elements to an effective strategy for organizational communication: content, style, and distribution.

Content

Content is the heart of any good communication strategy. Without appropriate content, there is no foundation upon which to build alignment. Several factors determine whether the content is appropriate:

- Completeness
- Accuracy
- Compellingness
- Consistency
- Contextualization
- Integration
- Personalization

In most organizational communication, all of these factors play a role. However, depending on the specific communication, some may be more important than others. When relaying an external press release to an internal audience, accuracy, consistency (with the actual press release), and contextualization (that is, what the press release means for the members of the organization) are more important than completeness, compellingness, integration, or personalization. For a "fireside chat" by an organizational leader, however, compellingness and personalization may be the most important factors. Confidential communications may focus primarily on accuracy and some component of completeness. Clearly articulating the confidential nature of the message and confidentiality guidelines will aid security. Examining these elements in more detail shows how they play out in a specific organizational communication.

Completeness

In most cases, content that is complete has no elements missing, is coherent, and can stand alone as an independent communication. There are exceptions to this definition of completeness. A communicator might intentionally communicate incomplete or partial information if timeliness of some information is more important than the entire message, or to entice an audience with unanswered questions.

Additionally, completeness may have a broader definition for some communications. For example, in a broadcast written communication, completeness also means that the communication is signed by the communicator, attaches relevant questions and answers or FAQs (frequently asked questions), and lists feedback channels.

In a highly contextualized communication, completeness may mean that salient points of the message are sent to various communicators to help them localize the message before it is communicated to the rest of the organization. An incomplete communication could leave an audience uncertain, with unanswered questions, and possibly more confused than before the communication. Strategic communicators should understand what constitutes completeness for each specific communication.

Accuracy

Accurate content is free from error. It has been spell-checked, grammar-checked, and fact-checked by the communicator and all sources have been referenced in the communication. Accuracy does not necessarily denote honesty (honesty is discussed in the style section, p. 46). President Bill Clinton's statement "I did not have sexual relations with that woman, Miss Lewinsky," may have been legally accurate, but was it honest? The organizational communicator needs to intimately understand this distinction. The communicator who presents accurate, but cautious or spurious, information as being open and honest will, like President Clinton, be labeled manipulative.

Compellingness

Compelling content engages the target audience. Does the content have a hook, a sensational headline, entertainment value, eye or ear media "candy," built-in rewards (such as contests), or an inspired distribution strategy? Some communications may have inherent compellingness based upon the communicator's reputation or the nature of the content. In most organizations, there is no need to create compellingness for positive communications that affect each audience member personally. Communications about pay raises and stock splits need little to make them compelling. Those important but dull policylike messages, or other nonpersonalized announcements such as building consolidations, purchasing guidelines, or desktop standards, may need some sprucing up. If unchecked, manipulated compellingness in a message could lead to hyperbole, hype, and propaganda.

Consistency

Consistency is the most important element in achieving organizational alignment. It does not necessarily mean using exactly the same words over and over. Consistency is about repeating and building from a singular message. It means achieving the desired communication goals for all target audiences without communicating contradictory information. Consistency means leveraging the common basic elements while setting a local context.

In most organizational communication, there are content segments that require exact repetition across all communications channels to all target audiences. But realize that in some broad communications, it is important to have local interpretation of some content. When a company communicates its financial results, the actual numbers need to be repeated verbatim, even though local sales managers and key communicators will want to mold this communication, interpreting how it reflects and affects their specific sales organization. In such instances, it is important that the organizational communicator proactively send consistent message points and standard Q&As to local communicators to help them craft a localized, yet consistent, communication.

Consistency does not involve just content. Sometimes consistency matters in distribution: using consistent distribution channels for similar messages (see the section on distribution later in this chapter). Denoting a primary lead communicator or orchestrator for the communication also bolsters the consistency of the message. In doing so, the voice and tone are the same, and consistency builds the perception of that person as an expert in the subject. It is also a powerful tool to designate a single feedback recipient—if possible, the same person as the lead communicator.

Contextualization

Disregarding context is one of the most frequent and easily avoided mistakes in organizational communication. This often occurs when the communicator is thinking narrowly about the communication (perhaps only as it relates to her own organization) or knows the content so well that she cannot imagine a less-informed perspective. In most cases, the target audience is far less knowledgeable about the subject matter than the communicator is, and the communicator assumes too much from the audience. A quick contextualization—a step backward to provide the broad picture or to explain an interrelationship—almost always strengthens the communication.

Prior to crafting any communication, it is helpful for the communicator to step into the audience's perspective and think broadly about the content. She can ask herself such questions as "What is the goal of this message: sharing information, or enabling insight? Does the audience need to know the big picture? Is there any context that can help clarify this communication?"

There are several reasons why a communicator may want to contextualize a specific message. The communication could be part of a larger communication; there might be metaphorical, analogous, or historical context that helps clarify the message; or the local communicator may want to localize a broad organizational message to a specific audience. For example, an engineering vice president may interpret what the corporate vision means to the engineers in terms of product development cycles and new product releases. Or a country manager in an international office may want to preface the same message with cultural context.

Local contextualization should particularly concern global organizational communicators. As we mentioned in discussing consistency, when a communication has some content that applies to the entire organization and some content that needs to be customized, the wise organizational communicator proactively sends consistent message points and standard Q&As to local communicators prior to, or simultaneously with, the broadcast of the organizationwide communication. In the case of announcing a large corporate merger, there is an obvious organizationwide element to the communication, but there is also a need for localized context that details how the merger affects individual geographies, functions, divisions, or teams. In communicating this message, the organizational communicator synchronizes the external communication of the merger with the internal announcement and distribution of message points and standard Q&As to local communicators. This combination of synchronization, sequencing, and consistency is one of the most difficult communications to orchestrate. This is especially complex if the content is, as in a merger situation, sensitive or confidential.

Integration

Integrated communication is similar to, but slightly different from, contextualized communication. Like a contextualized communication, integrated communication links multiple content components into one unified message. In contextualized communication, the additional context is not required. In integrated communication, however, all components are absolutely necessary for the communication to be complete. For example, successfully communicating a new corporate vision includes integrating the vision with organizational changes, new product strategies, etc.

Complex integrated communications are particularly challenging because the outcomes of the communication can vary dramatically based on how well integrated each component is. If the new corporate vision is communicated and the organizational changes essential to accomplish it are not addressed (even to say that they are forthcoming), employees may ignore or rebel against the new vision because they doubt the organization's ability to succeed.

Although crafting multicomponent integrated messages can be difficult, modern information technologies help the communicator simplify integration. Complex, multiple-link, Web-based communications can be much easier to understand than lengthy, cross-referenced interoffice memos with multiple attachments.

Personalization

The easiest way to get an audience's attention is through charismatic personalization. Like contextualizing, personalizing content requires the author to intimately understand the audience's perspective. With personalization, the goal is not to create logical or metaphorical context, but emotional relevance. Again, some communications, such as stock splits, have an inherently personal appeal, while others are more difficult to personalize. When trying to personalize such communications, ask yourself, *What does this message mean to me? How can I share in a way that adds context?* A leader communicating an impending layoff may say, for example,

"This is very hard for me to share with you because some of my friends have been affected. The company will be reducing head-count. . . ."

Some communicators achieve personalization in their particular delivery style. Others need to determine and include emotional hooks in the content. President Kennedy's commitment to space exploration is an example of a personalized communication achieved through both charismatic delivery style and a strong emotional content hook.

These nuanced layers of content emphasize the importance of the actual message. But even though content is the foundation for any communication, content in a vacuum is useless. Stylistic considerations are integral to crafting content. Communications can be sober, concise, humorous, legalistic, colorful, jazzy, and so on. Style has many shades of gray; myriad communication styles are possible. Although content primarily determines style, other factors may dictate stylistic choices as well.

Style

Incredible content orchestrated and perfectly delivered but lacking style does not resonate with or engage an audience. In fact, if the style is off, the audience might react negatively from the start, perhaps never even acknowledging the communication. Two important determinants of style are *culture* and *audience*.

Culture

The organization's culture may dictate a general communication style that pervades all organizational communication. A command-and-control culture may incorporate a generally authoritarian tone in all organizational communication, while a consensus-building small company opts for a tone that solicits employee input before decisions are made final. It is essential to understand these general organizational stylistic expectations—whether the communicator chooses to incorporate them or not. As an illustration of the latter, intentionally dishonoring the preferred organizational style could be a device to jar employees with a particularly sobering message.

Audience

The target audience can also dictate a certain communication style. For example, an engineering audience may demand an informal, combative, analytical, honest style, while a human resource audience may desire an upbeat, friendly, and professional style. The size of the audience obviously affects style. As with the nature of theater in contrast to film, larger live audiences may demand a more exaggerated style.

Presentation Style

Once the culture, message, and audience are identified, consider the general presentation style. A relaxed, humorous, or upbeat style might be appropriate for certain messages while a serious or staid tone fits another. The delivery channel should compliment the style (see the later discussion of distribution). With its ability to embed dramatic eye candy, video might be perfect for a technology showcase to build motivation or excitement; intimate voice mail may make more sense for an appeal to employees to focus on a new priority. This decision-making process is likely to aid selecting an author and a deliverer of the message.

Some communications, such as corporate videos, don't require authors. But most do. In fact, Chapter Four shows how important named authorship is to strategic corporate journalism. If a communicator is required, then personal stylistic considerations come into play.

Which person or persons should deliver the communication? For some organizational communications, the target communicator is obvious: the CEO, the CFO, a division vice president, etc. But many communications can potentially be delivered by a number of target communicators, and the communications strategist may have to decide who should eventually present the message. Here are some reasons why a choice could be difficult:

- The most appropriate communicator, in terms of relevance to content, has an inappropriate style.

- The communication is urgent and the most appropriate communicator is unavailable.

- The communication is difficult and the most appropriate communicator does not have the credibility to deliver it effectively.

- The most appropriate communicator designates someone else to communicate the message, to build the designee's credibility.

If you are trying to create a perception that a team is aligned and working together, or if the communication is the by-product of a group, the communication can also be delivered by more than one person.

Target Communicator

All of the scenarios in the list just above complicate determining who will be the target communicator. In evaluating this choice, remember to weigh which factors are most important, considering the message's objective. If the appropriate communicator is not the person widely perceived as an obvious choice, an explanation should preface the communication. A division vice president who is standing in for a CEO traveling in Japan might begin a companywide meeting by saying, "As you know, our CEO normally presents the financial results, but since he is in Japan visiting a customer, I've been asked to share this information with you." Being as open and truthful as possible is important, and it requires delicate handling. It might be hard to admit that a particular communicator has an offensive or ineffective style, and this may not be appropriate to share with an audience.

If there is more than one possible target communicator, the communications strategist should consider important personal stylistic qualities of each communicator: *credibility*, *charisma*, *power*, *authenticity*, and *honesty*.

If the communicator doesn't have *credibility* with the audience, it is difficult to reach the goal of the communication. More than other stylistic elements, credibility is about perception. If a communicator has perceived credibility with an audience, his messages are heard. It is possible within a single communication to gain some credibility even if little existed previously, but this is not a common outcome. In reality, credibility is usually gained over time, with repeated, honest, authentic messages.

A communicator can, however, bring a negative impact to credibility with a single communication. A simple slip of the tongue can affect a communicator's perceived credibility for years. In 1992, presidential candidate Ross Perot's "you people" slip in addressing the National Association for the Advancement of Colored People shows how a communicator can instantaneously lose credibility.

If morale is low and messenger scapegoating is high in an organization, credibility is especially hard to maintain and easy to lose. Unfortunately, when times are tough, many communicators respond by communicating less or not at all. Offering no communication counteracts credibility even more than miscommunication does. Effectively communicating during difficult periods can actually be the best way to build credibility. A leader who addresses an audience by saying, "I don't have all the answers, but I do know that . . ." or "This is a difficult time for me too, but . . ." gains huge marks for credibility.

Accountability can also build credibility with an audience. Nancy Hill, former broadcast host of Tandem Corporation's internal television network, describes a specific time when the president and CEO, Jim Treybig, took personal accountability for massive layoffs: "Jimmy had his faults and sometimes he frustrated people. But I remember the day that he announced the layoffs. He stood in front of a companywide managers' meeting with tears in his eyes and said something like, 'I'm sorry that we have to do this; this is my fault . . . not yours. And I'm asking that we all take a pay cut so that we don't have to cut so many people.' Well I'll tell you, I was in awe. We took the pay cut. I was completely converted" (personal interview).

Charisma and *power*, stylistic elements that are often interrelated, greatly affect the success of a communication. Charismatic speakers can completely engage and align an audience almost independently of the content. Such statements as "I don't know what she said, but I'm behind her 100 percent" show the strength of alignment possible from a charismatic communicator.

If a communicator uses power as a stylistic element, the audience aligns out of respect, fear, or acculturation. Power alignment tends to be more rote in nature and is typically found where the audience is likely to require the organizational leaders' approval for decisions and actions. As discussed in Chapter One, although mechanistic organizations still exist, many have evolved into knowledge communities for which a power style is ineffective or even countereffective. This is especially true of fear-based authoritarian power, as opposed to respect-based power derived from expertise or credibility. The organizational communicator must take the pulse of these elements to understand the backdrop against which a communication is delivered.

Respect-based power is more effective in knowledge communities. Witness the rise of subject-matter experts as leaders in modern organizations (for instance, engineers heading up technology companies, academicians running universities, etc.) and the decline of titular authoritarian figureheads. Even in a total command-and-control culture such as the military, a leader must be careful about using fear-based authority because without adequate respect among the troops, credibility may be impossible. Hollywood movies enjoy vilifying leaders whose fear-based authoritarian style backfires catastrophically. But organizational leaders who appropriately and effectively harness charisma or power in their communications reap the benefits of an engaged audience.

Authenticity varies from communicator to communicator, but generally speaking, authenticity means being genuine, real, and not overly staged. Tom Heuerman, a Milwaukee management consultant, offers this definition: "Authenticity is the expression of our beliefs into action—the intrapersonal congruency of ideas and behaviors" (Heuerman, "Authenticity," 1999) Heuerman also reports how Herb Kelleher, president and CEO of Southwest Airlines (one of *Fortune* magazine's best American companies to work for in 1998) says, "I don't have a leadership style except being myself."

This does not mean that one should not plan, prepare, and rehearse organizational communications. In fact, most of the time authenticity comes more naturally if the communicator rehearses and internalizes the content so that a genuine connection with the audience occurs. Unfortunately, some communicators try to achieve authenticity through spontaneous, unprepared communications. Even if this type of unrehearsed organizational communication achieves authenticity, it often looks incomplete, inconsistent, and inaccurate—and it even risks legal exposure. The communicator's goal is to know the content intimately and attempt to let a personal style emerge that engages the audience in a believable way.

Though synergistic to authenticity and accuracy, honesty is slightly different. *Honesty* is a slippery word; it means different things to different people. Honesty implies accuracy, usually requires authenticity, and can include full disclosure. If full disclosure means communication of all known information, then it is almost always impossible, especially in business organizations, where in many cases business fundamentals dictate (and laws regulate) just how disclosing an organizational communicator can be. For example, one cannot broadly communicate information about a planned corporate merger until the merger is consecrated.

Organizations define honesty differently. Those with an acculturated understanding of confidentiality may agree that honesty includes little white lies like "I don't know," whereas other organizations may want complete truthfulness. Truthfulness does not mean communicating confidential information; it simply means changing the response from "I don't know" to "that matter is confidential."

The organizational communicator should understand the organization's definition of honesty. This helps determine how much honesty the target audience expects. In many organizations, accuracy is far more important than honesty. In some cultures, honesty is not important but exposed dishonesty is. In others, people just avoid "dangerous" topics. Or perhaps honesty ranks even higher than accuracy; religious organizations, for example, usually rank honesty very highly.

Matching the appropriate style to the culture, audience, and content helps build a culture of trust. Trust, like honesty, is a somewhat intangible concept. Yet it is a fundamental element of the knowledge equation, which we present at the end of Chapter Four. When talking about communications and technology, communicators often overlook the importance of trust. In a recent *Harvard Business Review* article, "Fair Process: Managing in the Knowledge Economy," authors W. Chan Kim and Renée Mauborgne talk about the foundations of enterprise communications: "Innovation is the key challenge of the knowledge-based economy, and innovation requires the exchange of ideas, which in turn depends on trust" (p. 72).

But can trust be scaled up from a small group to an enterprise? Anthropologist Karen Stephenson talks about the possibilities: "Once you can visualize tacit knowledge, you can do something with it. You find repeating patterns of interaction—hot spots—that define networks of trust and reciprocity. Once you find those hot spots, you know where to find people who are innovating. The next question is, 'How do you scale trust?' Here's the big challenge: technology without people won't work. People without technology won't scale. Particularly in virtual networks, where you are working with people you've never met, you have to find a way to create trust and to scale it across the network" (p. 148).

Physicist David Bohm, whose ideas have been applied to organizational communication (Albert Einstein once said that Bohm was the only person from whom he ever understood quantum theory), says in his book *On Dialogue*, "The notion of 'impersonal fellowship' suggests that authentic trust and openness can emerge in a group context, without its members having shared extensive personal history" (p. x). Although trust can be derived from content and style, dialogue or interaction is usually a prerequisite. (Interactivity is discussed at more length in the next section of this chapter.)

When crafting each communication strategy, you should remember that some of these stylistic variables are more important than others. Sometimes the content is so powerful that it can be stylistically packaged without much emphasis on the communicator. On the other hand, in the overall scheme of an organizational communication strategy, style might dwarf content and delivery. For example, the charisma of an organizational speaker can hide a multitude of orchestrational inadequacies; highly stylized videos can entertain without having much content at all. At other times, style is inconsequential—a bad financial quarter is a bad financial quarter no matter how the message is spun. The content often dictates the communicator's style.

The backdrop of content, style, and distribution affects every organizational communication—be it hallway conversation or a corporationwide announcement. Sometimes the backdrop is subtle; at other times it is more obvious. The organizational communicator must analyze the situation, craft the message, and communicate in the best possible manner to achieve the desired alignment and action. If the knowledge employee comes to understand the organization's vision and her personal role in achieving the vision, and if she acts on that understanding, then the organizational communications strategy has succeeded.

Distribution

First there is content. Then there is style. Distribution technologies follow. Distribution—delivering the message—embraces anything from a simple in-person conversation to sequenced use of multiple communication channels. The three major components of any distribution strategy are channels, media, and production.

In the last three decades, organizational communication delivery channels have proliferated. The section in Chapter One on the information age enumerated the growth of such new channels as voice mail, e-mail, Websites, and so on. Obviously, the choice of appropriate channel depends on many variables (in addition to content and style): culture, audience size, location, and urgency, to name a few. The plethora of target communication options has an impact on both the flexibility and the complexity of distribution.

Choices in media have also expanded. Until recently, organizational communication media mostly consisted of voice and text. Now the communicator must consider two- and three-dimensional graphics, digital photographs, recorded audio and video, and broadcast audio and video. These media are now viable and easily integrated into an organizational communication strategy. Though communicators have a wider set of choices, they also need increased understanding of the media tradeoffs. Virtual meetings are possible with live broadcast video and audio via satellite or an intranet, but are they truly cost-effective?

This channel and media complexity also affects the basic production process in distribution. Sending an organizationwide interoffice mail is one thing; orchestrating an organizationwide virtual meeting replete with broadcast video and live teleconferenced Q&A sessions is quite another. Given such amazing possibilities, how does one weight the value against potentially substantial costs? (Distribution ROI—return on investment—is discussed in Appendix 1, "A Guide to Corporate Journalism.")

Distribution Elements

Repetition, velocity, frequency, synchronization, sequencing, and interaction are terms not used solely in discussing distribution, but they are elements that affect the interrelation of content, distribution, and style. We discuss these elements in this section on distribution because the challenge of achieving the right balance among the elements is really a distribution challenge.

In this age of information overload, an audience's attention span is decreasing along with the life span of most information. *Repeating the message* is more important than ever before. In a business environment that wholeheartedly embraces fundamental branding concepts, organizations don't often connect the value of external brand repetition with the need for internal message repetition. Al and Laura Ries's book *The 22 Immutable Laws of Branding* reminds organizations of the fundamental "communication" elements of branding a company to its customer base. Many of those same elements can be just as easily and effectively applied to internal message branding. According to Francis Duren, manager of employee information corporate public affairs, Caterpillar Inc. takes this concept of consistency so seriously that the company has adopted the attitude that "everything communicates." They have built an extensive internal campaign, "Communicating Caterpillar: One Voice," to ensure a branding level of internal communications consistency.

Repeating is more than simple reiteration. "Finally, tell and retell. Many times leaders of organizations become impatient with repeating the same key messages and desire to move onto the next subject. However, it is imperative that the key messages be restated with creativity and passion. The real challenge for communicators is to breathe new life into key messages and find new variations. About the time communicators are tired of saying the same old things, that is about when the message is beginning to connect with the audience. The trick is to find yet another way to say it so it will take hold" (anonymous quote from large company stategic communication plan).

The *velocity* of communications has increased. Velocity of communications is defined in terms of the time elapsed between an event occurring, or a noteworthy piece of information being generated, and the news being disseminated. Chapter One refers to the Internet-time flow of information nowadays. Couple this speed with shortened audience attention span and you see how the organizational communicator cannot afford to sit on news. Organizational communicators were once able to completely control information, but they now face both internal and external competing news sources. The journalistic goal to "get it first—but get it right" rings true inside the corporation too. An informed knowledge workforce can quickly become disillusioned by the blistering pace of the rumor mill if organizational information is privately withheld or published externally before appearing internally.

The velocity of change is also increasing. Frequent change requires perpetual recalibration, which in turn mandates more *frequent communication*. Kirk Froggatt, former vice president of human resources at SGI, uses the diagram in Figure 2.3 to illustrate the need for constant recalibration during organizational change.

Obviously, if the distance between the calibration points is shortened then less time is spent going down unproductive paths. People inside organizations today expect more frequent calibration

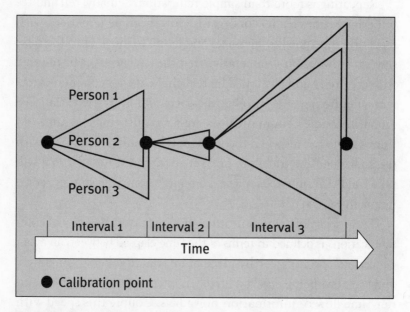

FIGURE 2.3. Frequency of Communication During Change

through heightened frequency of news. The monthly newsletter is no longer adequate. For most organizations, the world changes much faster than monthly, and organizational communications function as midstream course corrections. J.P. Morgan has published a daily news bulletin for as long as Laura Dillon, managing director of Corporate Communication, can remember. "Best we can tell is that it was started before the Second World War, sometime in the 20s or 30s." This bulletin, which was formerly called the *Interdepartmental Reporter* (but known as the "pink sheet" for the paper it was printed on), is now an intranet website called Morgan Today.

Finally, even without the pressures of competing news sources and the need for calibration, employees expect increased velocity of information and *frequency* of communication. They live in a world of frequent, instantaneous information access—and they feel they are entitled to it at work too. Not providing similar access within the organization can well create a perception in the minds of employees—especially younger ones—that the company is woefully behind the times.

The timing of a communication, or *synchronization*, requires a delicate touch, especially considering the increased number of organizational communicators in the democratized workforce and the growth and visibility of external communicators. If one division's employees learn of change within their divisional organization through rumors generated by the leader of another division, mistrust is sure to follow and alignment is eroded. Instantaneous information flow and the blurring of internal and external communication boundaries force organizational communicators to be more "synced up" than ever. It is risky to share financial results with employees before the street gets the figures, but it is also risky to release the results on the street before employees see them. The two actualities might be just moments apart. As a result, synchronizing these communications is critical; unfortunately, because of the number of unknown or unpredictable factors, it is also difficult to perfect.

Similar to synchronization, *sequencing* a communication involves timing. Many organizational communications need to be sequenced in a tiered fashion. The reason for sequencing is often to empower the various organizational leaders with information before the rest of the employees. Sometimes a communicator sequences because the content is more sensitive and relevant to one audience than to others (for example, organizational changes that are first communicated to the affected organization). Whatever the requirement, as with synchronization the challenges of sequencing have increased dramatically with the increased velocity of information flow.

Before the Internet, when information could be more controlled, communications could target different audiences at whatever pace was necessary for each audience to internalize the message. Leaks might occur and the rumor mill churn, but for the most part, the impact of full disclosure could be secured until whatever time the communicator chose.

With the Internet and intranets, leaks are now fully "contexted" and the virtual rumor mill no longer churns—it whirls instantaneously around the globe. As a result, sequenced communication must occur within a tightened time frame. An organizational change that in the past might have taken weeks to fully cascade across the organization must now take place within a matter of days, or even hours.

Organizational *interactivity* is active interchange or dialogue among groups or members of an organization. As we indicated earlier in this chapter, interactivity aids in trust and the internalization of a message. In fact, many organizational communication strategists believe that internalization and alignment are impossible without interactivity (see the Preface). Although interactivity is critical to trust, organic alignment, and the knowledge equation (see Chapter Four), it is impossible without the constancy of open, accurate, and timely information. Since the focus of *Beyond Spin* is this open, accurate, and timely flow of communication, we address interactivity only tangentially in the next few pages.

Most organizational interactivity is among individual employees, individual managers and employees, individual managers and their teams, or small groups of employees. The real power in building better interactivity lies in the age-old challenge of improving manager and employee communication skills. This can be done in several ways, including training, coaching, and influencing organizationwide norms for manager-to-employee communications. Some organizations excel at promoting interaction between managers and employees. Federal Express has long focused on managerial communication, institutionalizing a "Managerial Communications Climate and Competence" process wherein managers learn their role as organizational communicator and hone their skills as communicators (Internal Federal Express Document).

Hewlett-Packard, a Silicon Valley computer systems manufacturer, conducted a comprehensive study (which has since been validated by a variety of studies) to show the importance of interactive manager and employee communication. Y2K communication manager Brad Whitworth offers this conclusion: "The better the managers' communication, the more satisfied the employees are with all aspects of their work life. Most managers, when shown these results, are willing to allow that a more satisfied employee is a more productive employee" (personal interview).

Even though dialogue between managers and employees has by far the most impact on interactivity, there are broader forms: communities of practice, facilitated forums, intracompany "brown bags" or seminars, to name a few. Instead of exploring the multivariate universe of many-to-many interaction, we will limit our analysis to the broadest forms of organizationwide dialogue once the issues associated with these all-inclusive types of interaction are understood. We will also focus our analysis of interaction toward mid- to large-size organizations where enterprise-wide interactions present the most challenges. There are two primary categories of true organizationwide interaction: that between executives and employees, and rapidly growing technology-assisted employee interaction. Although executive-to-employee interaction is powerful, it is also risky, and most broad interactions between executives and employees are overly orchestrated and logistically knotty, with intrusive meeting dynamics often overshadowing true interaction. Interactivity entails being genuine; orchestration often implies acting. Executives are rarely good actors; when they attempt to be actors, they often fail. It is equally hard for executives to be real or authentic in highly staged or produced communications. Knowledge workers can spot executive acting in an instant and immediately erect mental barriers to receiving or buying the message.

With orchestrated communications, employees need to know the explicit goal of the interaction. Is it consensus building? networking? brainstorming? or something else? The fastest way to erode trust is to set inaccurate expectations of executive interactivity. If for example, in a communication about cutting expenses, employees are requested to suggest changes and provide input but the executive team does not respond or listen to the ideas received, employees will view the communication as insincere or manipulative—or even as a pedantic attempt to scold them. If the pattern continues, apathy or cynicism can follow. Every executive-to-employee broadcast communication that invites interaction should clearly set expectations for the nature and use of the interaction.

Obviously, orchestrated communications to all employees are not the only form of executive-to-employee interaction. Executives can engage with an employee more personally and individually. But this type of interaction, although logistically easier, is not risk-free. Executive-to-employee interactions get woven into the folklore of the corporate culture; therefore, one faux pas can have a cultural shelf life of years. Likewise, one brilliant interaction can have incredible mileage. How should an executive proceed? How much interaction is required, and what are the best channels to use?

Executives need to understand the pulse of the organization, the acculturated interactivity channels (for example, some organizations have acculturated the team staff meeting as an interactivity channel or forum), and the level of expected interaction. Many executives come across as out-of-touch simply by using the wrong communications channel—say, interoffice memos in an e-mail culture. Also, executives can underestimate the desire of knowledge employees to interact with their leaders. When Rick Belluzzo joined SGI as CEO, he publicly invited employees to send him e-mail. He expected dozens of responses, but he received hundreds. The fact that Belluzzo responded to every e-mail won him instant trust among the employees. If executives understand expectation setting, the appropriate interactivity channels, and the time commitment required for organizationwide interactivity, then orchestrating executive-to-employee interactivity can quickly increase broadscale trust.

A 1999 *Fortune* article reports that "to build morale, communication has to be two-way." Executive interaction with employees, the article goes on to say, is one way to accomplish this:

> While top management at the 100 Best Companies are doing more delegating than ever, they do see the value in schmoozing with the rank and file. Lawrence Bossidy, AlliedSignal's [no. 80] chairman, gets close to his people each month by sending a two-page communiqué about issues such as medical insurance and diversity. These "Larry Letters" have a 99 percent readership rate. And to soak up ideas from the field, he holds breakfast meeting several times a month with employees selected at random by computer. At Ingram Micro (no. 68), Chairman Jerre Stead maintains his own twenty-four-hour 800 number phone line—yes, he really answers it—to take calls from employees [Branch, 1999, pp. 128–130].

A far easier and less time-intensive way for an executive to secure trust is to create an open environment that invites executive-to-employee interactivity and then walk around offices throughout the company. "Management by walking around" was a popular trend in the 1980s, but it still works—especially for executives or any leaders who tend to be isolated in the corporate tower. Of course, this technique is logistically problematic in the global corporation.

Technology-Assisted Organizationwide Interaction

The influx of technology-assisted employee interaction parallels the rise of the Internet. Newsgroups, chat rooms, e-mail aliases, and even voice mail aliases channel this type of broad organizational interaction. These technologies have definitely increased the amount of all-employee interaction and have highlighted the impossibility of harnessing organizational interaction. Quite possibly, the growth of technology-assisted interactivity has caused the most concern for control-based leaders. These new channels can be used either formally or informally for content that is work-related, important, and confidential—or for content that is none of these. Technology-assisted channels that seamlessly cross the boundaries between internal and external environments create holes in the mechanistic system. But they are fundamental to the instantaneous information flow that is essential in organic systems. They play a critical role in organizations that need to react quickly to change by forming virtual teams and creating global cohesiveness.

This is not to say that organic communications systems don't have boundaries. Boundaries are necessary to avoid chaos. The cells of the human body do not freely communicate with an external virus. Nor should a company's confidential information be freely shared over whatever fluid channels it allows or creates. These new organizational boundaries need to be defined—not for control, but for competitiveness. Bill Gates compares the digital infrastructure of companies to the human nervous system. "Companies need to have that same kind of nervous system—the ability to run smoothly and efficiently, to respond quickly to emergencies and opportunities, to quickly get valuable information to the people in the company who need it" (1999, p. 74).

Boundaries translate differently according to the organization. For those familiar with information sharing, the new channels that encourage information flow may prove easy to accept and leverage. For organizations filled with "Internet free-speech radicals," the company may need to clearly define what *confidential* and *intellectual property* mean so that employees understand and respect the boundaries. Recriminating, creating fear, closing down organic discussions, or trying to eliminate an external communication channel would be counterproductive. Educating employees—not controlling the channels—is the key here. Where does this type of interaction lead: to fragmentation and chaos, or to community and aligned propulsion? Can an organizational communication strategist play a catalytic role to avoid the former and ensure the latter? As indicated in Chapter One, branding the organizational purpose, vision, values, strategies, and priorities is important as a backdrop for organizational interaction. But some corporate communication strategists are also experimenting with remote facilitation, intelligent agents, and virtual avatars. In this new realm of multidimensional networked interaction, the jury is still out on whether such real-time directive techniques can be successful.

With such complexity and the available interaction technologies, it is easy to forget that this type of interaction still pales in importance to face-to-face communication—the most common form of interaction. The rumor mill situated at the water cooler, social interactions, and nonvirtual chat rooms are alive and well.

Developing a Distribution Infrastructure

The set of acculturated communications tools, media, and channels that organizational communicators use to orchestrate communications constitute the communication distribution infrastructure. The members of an organization expect communicators to use specific tools, media, and channels for specific types of communication.

It is as challenging to erect an appropriate distribution infrastructure for one's organization as it is to determine cost-effective media and evaluate stylistic requirements for a message. New distribution channels require organizational adoption. In most organizations, the acculturated communication channels that have been internalized over time are used for different types of communications (voice mail for communications requiring an action; e-mail for those requiring detailed context, etc.). If, in an organization where e-mail is the primary channel for urgent and complex communications, a communicator delivers a specific urgent and complex message via an electronic bulletin board or voice mail, the organizational members might be confused and even ignore the communication. One can't simply introduce an unacculturated communication channel into an organization without attaching a strong benefit to making the switch.

Even with well-articulated benefits, new communication channels must be introduced slowly unless the new channel is inordinately compelling and dramatically easier and more effective than the alternative. An example of quick adoption of a new communication channel was corporate America's embrace of the fax machine. The fax quickly filled a distribution-channel void. Well-understood and pent-up demand for this channel drove the cost of the technology down quickly, and fax technology infiltrated most business organizations as a primary organizational communication channel within a few short years. On the other hand, corporate America has been slow to embrace satellite-based video as a primary communication tool because it is prohibitively costly and difficult to use.

Although multiple distribution channels can add flexibility and enable closer audience targeting, too many distribution channels can disorient and add to information overload. The greater the number of primary channels, the greater the chance for organizational confusion. When it comes to infrastructure, understanding and integrating the most effective mix of distribution channels is the biggest challenge of an organizational communicator's job.

Again, what determines an effective distribution infrastructure depends upon the organization. Organizations that create a well-internalized distribution infrastructure wherein all members of the organization know exactly which channel to use for every type of communication have an enormous advantage in crafting an effective organizational communication strategy. In most cases, the distribution infrastructure consists of a small number of broadly applied primary distribution channels plus a suite of highly targeted secondary distribution channels. To achieve fewer primary channels, many companies actually broaden the use of a channel rather than focus it toward a single use or single audience. For example, in many organizations e-mail has expanded from a one-on-one interactive channel to the primary channel the organization uses for broadcast messages, as well as for formal and informal interaction. Similarly, thanks to hyperlinked, multimedia-enabled Web technologies many companies are using intranets as a primary multiuse channel. Leveraging a single, multiuse broadcast communication channel is a strategy that creates channel clarity.

Push Versus Pull

Communication distribution choices fall along a "push-pull" continuum (Figure 2.4). Some organizations have been acculturated to a push model: communications are pushed at the organization via such channels as e-mail, voice mail, and interoffice memos. Other organizations use pull channels such as the Web to publish information. The pull model is so called because the audience bears the responsibility to go to (is pulled to) the channel and retrieve the information. In the pull model, it is extremely difficult to broadcast information across the organization and be certain that the entire organization hears or reads it. On one extreme of the continuum, if a message is too obscure a pull, the audience can't find it. At the other extreme, in a heavy-push model, pushing communication can become overused, so much so that the result is ignored as "spam." This obviously defeats the communication goal. Figure 2.4 shows a push-pull continuum for various communications channels.

The difference between extreme push and pull communication channels is clear in this figure. In actuality, however, models are rarely pure and communications choices are found along the bulk of the continuum. A channel becomes push once it is so acculturated that it reigns as the default choice. For example, the figure situates e-mail somewhat more toward the push end of the continuum for a typical organization; but for some, e-mail is not a push technology at all because even if everyone has it not everyone reads it regularly. Audience penetration and extent of regular use determine the effectiveness of the push. Chapter Five discusses this in more

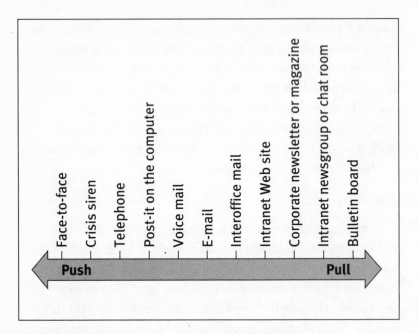

FIGURE 2.4. Push-Pull Distribution Continuum

detail by studying creation of a push mechanism at SGI—its global intranet portal.

It is important to remember that push and pull channels are not mandated; they evolve democratically. Organizations often try to mandate push models by using acculturated push channels for spamming communications. This cry-wolf tactic usually results only in devolving the channel—or hastening evolution of more effective ways of filtering spam. A balanced approach is double-pronged, capitalizes on visible pull channels (those that are close to the center of the continuum) and nudges the organization toward those channels through light pushing. Wheatley (1992) describes the intricacy of push-pull this way: "The intent is not to push and pull, but rather to give form to what is unfolding" (p. 111).

Organizations can influence the evolution of a communication distribution infrastructure that best suits the overarching communication goals, both short- and long-term. This might be easier for young organizations starting with a clean slate. Unfortunately, young organizations tend to focus, justifiably, on short-term success and often don't strategize organizational communications distribution infrastructures; they let them evolve without any nudging. If the organization grows fast, the communications distribution network and practices may not keep pace. In the end, the result is a large organization with deeply ingrained but immature communications practices.

With so many distribution complexities, hiccups are bound to occur. Videoconferencing might be awkward, rude, or annoying. Teleconference operators might disrupt a meeting, or media might be incompatible. People forgive distribution errors far more easily than mistakes in content or style. The technical glitches of a presidential state of the union address slip from the mind much faster than do inappropriate slips of the tongue.

CONSIDERING THE ORGANIZATIONAL LANDSCAPE

After evaluating the key elements of content, style, and distribution, one must then survey external and internal landscape factors. Figure 2.5 depicts the development of a communication strategy.

Even if structured and orchestrated brilliantly, a communications strategy can completely miss the mark if it is crafted in isolation. While examining the elements of an organizational communication strategy, it is essential to understand the complete environment in which communications take place. To gain such understanding, the organizational communicator must analyze the internal and external factors that affect the organizational landscape.

External Factors

Chapter One detailed some of today's exogenous environmental trends (knowledge workforce, democratized workforce, diversification, information age, increased pace of change). The organizational communicator must evaluate which trends are strongest and which most affect the organization. The general economic climate should

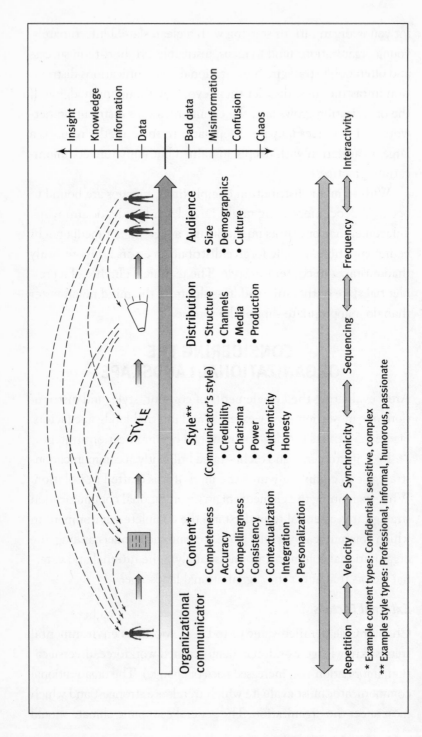

FIGURE 2.5. Developing an Organizational Communication Strategy

Insight
Knowledge
Information
Data

Bad data
Misinformation
Confusion
Chaos

Audience
• Size
• Demographics
• Culture

Distribution
• Structure
• Channels
• Media
• Production

Style**
(Communicator's style)
• Credibility
• Charisma
• Power
• Authenticity
• Honesty

Content*
• Completeness
• Accuracy
• Compellingness
• Consistency
• Contextualization
• Integration
• Personalization

Organizational
communicator

STYLE

Repetition ⟷ Velocity ⟷ Synchronicity ⟷ Sequencing ⟷ Frequency ⟷ Interactivity

* Example content types: Confidential, sensitive, complex
** Example style types: Professional, informal, humorous, passionate

also be evaluated. During a general economic downturn, it might be comparatively easy to communicate difficult expense-control messages even if they have nothing to do with the general economic state. In this case, external information affects the organizational psyche and prepares the audience to hear such a message.

Macro External Climate

In some instances conditions in the macro external climate are so overwhelming that it can be difficult to make any intraorganizational message heard (unless the organization is specifically equipped to deal with the external environmental issues). In wartime, for example, most organizations will have difficulty communicating non-war-related messages to their members, but churches may actually have an easier time communicating (that is, spreading the word) than under normal conditions.

Macro External Factors

Beyond the general external landscape in which a company functions, micro external factors more specific to the organization also come into play. Industry viability, the competitive environment, available talent supply, customer demand, and perceived company viability are examples of immediate external environmental factors that business communicators need to understand. Some of these factors are easy to analyze and quantify, while others are more difficult to assess. An organization's available talent supply can be quantified through statistical analysis, for example, while the perceived organizational viability is much harder to assess. Furthermore, some of these variables may be interrelated or even symbiotic. For instance, a change in perceived viability could dramatically affect an organization's ability to recruit talent. Successful communicators are keenly aware of this shifting landscape, and they even make recommendations to executives and leaders about how a communication may be affected by these details.

From 1997 to 1999, the perceived viability of Silicon Valley Internet startup companies soared. During this time, they had an aura about them—perceived enormous viability made them favorites on Wall Street, which in turn positively affected their ability to recruit top talent.

Once the organizational communicator has surveyed the external landscape, it is time to look within the organizational boundaries and examine the intraorganizational environment.

Internal Factors

External factors are important, but unless they are extreme, understanding and monitoring an organization's internal factors more directly affects an appropriate organizational communication strategy. The combination of general external factors, organization-specific external factors, and internal factors creates the entire landscape within which an organization must operate (Figure 2.6).

Internal organizational factors to consider include:

- Size

- Structure

- Social structure

- Organizational intradependency

- Organizational psyche

- Cultural identity

- Organizational value structure

- Viability

- Business and operational strategy

- Organizational communication infrastructure (charter, organizational structure, resource model)

Size

Organizational size is an obvious factor to consider when evaluating appropriate communication tactics. Communicating in a small

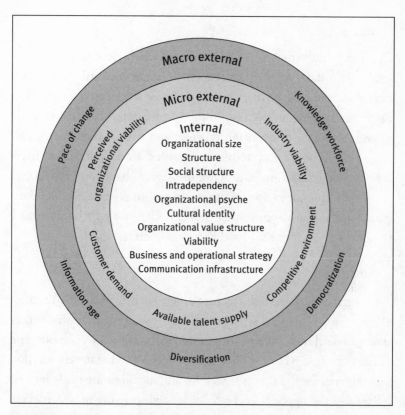

FIGURE 2.6. External and Internal Landscape Factors

business having only one locale might be as simple as standing up in one's cubicle and shouting, "Hey, everybody, Jane just accepted our offer." In a global corporation or one having multiple locations, communicating Jane's acceptance is not that easy. The strategic communicator first determines whether the entire organization needs to know of Jane's acceptance. If so, the communicator also has to evaluate whether the content should change based on the location. For example, some locations might not understand Jane's position, her department, or what value it provides the corporation. This added contextualization may be required for some recipients of the communication.

Structure

Organizational structure—whether centralized, decentralized, hierarchical, or flat—primarily affects the choice of distribution channels. For example, a live meeting might be an effective channel in centralized organizations, but it might be inappropriate or too costly to orchestrate for a decentralized company. Structure might also affect other content and delivery variables. In decentralized, hierarchical organizations, there are usually multiple audiences and possibly even multiple communication groups. To achieve broad organizational consistency and synchronicity, it might be necessary to contextualize content for different audiences.

Social Structure

The organizational social structure differs slightly from organizational structure. The social structure involves the organizational power structure and how organizational decisions are made. On one end of the continuum of possible social structures is dictatorial decision making, where all power is vested in, and decisions are made by, one leader. On the opposite end is a fluid social structure in which every person within the organization is equally responsible for decision making. As indicated in Chapter One, the workplace is flattening from what it was in past hierarchical structures; most organizations today map somewhere in the middle on the representational model and would consider themselves an amalgam in which organizational decision making is tiered. Though a dictatorial social structure might be a simpler one for orchestrating organizational communications, it is inappropriate for a knowledge workforce (recall the discussion earlier in this chapter of style and power in knowledge communities).

Intradependency

The degree of organizational intradependency inherent across departmental boundaries determines how interrelated a communication should be. For example, an organization with independent product silos may not need to communicate product-strategy detail across departments; in a large conglomerate of business units where each is responsible for a piece of the same product line, the entire organization needs to understand the integrated product strategy.

Organizational Psyche

Organizational psyche is similar to morale, but much broader. It refers to an organizational state of mind, but it also includes a psychological predisposition that can affect morale. A parent's message to a teenager who is not in an appropriate state of mind to listen falls on deaf ears. Consider communicating to a low-morale audience that is not ready or willing to hear a message. This is not to say that communicating to high-morale audiences is easier or even the goal; many times, an "up" audience may be characterized by disfocus or arrogance that prohibits a message from penetrating.

The organizational communicator should help create the appropriate organizational psyche so that the message can truly be heard. The organizational communicator may delay a communication until the organizational psyche is better prepared to hear the message. For example, broadcasting a leadership profile story during a company downturn when leadership scapegoating is de rigueur undermines the message. Communicating a generous corporate giving strategy in the midst of layoffs can definitely have negative repercussions among the workforce.

Cultural Identity

The personality of the organization plays out in its cultural identity. Some cultural traits affect organizational communication more than others do. The degree of formality within the organization should affect the content, delivery, and style of an organizational communication, whereas the intensity of the organizational work ethic may affect the communication style but not necessarily the content or delivery.

Value Structure

The organizational value structure is a set of values consciously chosen by the organization. In an ideal world, an organization's cultural identity reflects its values. This is not always the case. Cultures evolve; values are chosen. Organizational values should pervade communication.

Consider integrity. If integrity is an organizational value, it should directly affect the content and style of organizational communication and act as a guidepost for action. Everything an organization does, including communication, should reflect its value structure.

Viability

In the discussion of external variables, we talked about perceived organizational viability. Coupled with it, the actual internal viability of the organization plays a role. These elements, though different, obviously interrelate, and any disconnect between externally perceived viability and actual viability challenges organizational communication. For example, a company losing its employees because of negatively perceived external viability usually mounts an internal campaign to help employees understand the company's actual state. In the converse of this example—perceived external viability is positive while actual viability does not measure up—rarely does the company make efforts to change internal perceptions. There is a danger here. An organization that "believes its own press" can develop an overinflated sense of its accomplishments, begin to focus inwardly, and ignore the external landscape. This myopia can lead to ruin.

Understanding viability means making an honest assessment of the external landscape and the organization's competitive stance. Internal communication of this assessment is where the spin is usually thickest. Breaking through to this level of openness not only engenders employee trust but also arms employees with valuable insight that aids strategic analysis.

Strategy

Most organizations communicate their business and operational strategy internally and externally. This strategy—whether offensive or defensive, leading-edge or late-adopter, customer-oriented or insular, commodity-driven or value-add—affects the content and style of organizational communications. An organization in an offensive, aggressive posture may craft communications that create a negative view of primary competitors. A company with a customer-oriented stance might spend more time educating employees about the customer base and service strategies.

Many other operational strategy variables also affect organizational communications. If a company adopts a comprehensive outsourcing strategy, communication both reinforces organizational core competencies and educates so that organizational members understand when to outsource. A solid organizational communicator clearly understands the business and operational strategy and consequently understands if and how it affects the communication strategy. Mastering this element alone can greatly affect organizational alignment and separate the exceptional communicator from the average one.

Communication Infrastructure

The organizational communication infrastructure—the support structure that enables organizationwide communication—includes everything from technologies (voice mail and e-mail systems, network and information technology or IT architecture, desktop equipment and standards, etc.) to the teams responsible for messaging. For a small company, the organizational communication infrastructure could simply be a telephone system with voice mail. For a large enterprise, the communication infrastructure usually includes one or more central communications departments that determine and implement an overarching organizational communication strategy.

For such complex organizations, one must drill down another layer and understand the composition of central communications departments. The four major components of a central organizational communication infrastructure are the charter, the reporting structure, the resource model, and the communication distribution infrastructure.

Depending on the organization, the prominent organizational communication *charter* could include such goals as motivation, community building, increasing business literacy, accelerating organizational learning, compliance, executive messaging, or synchronizing internal and external communications. All of these can support the broader communication purpose of organizational alignment or action, but the overarching communication strategy shifts depending upon the primary charter of a communications group. For example, if the primary organizational communication goal is community building, the overarching communication strategy may focus on interactive and personalized messaging. If it is business literacy, the strategy may include in-depth business features.

The charter of the central communications function both depends on and influences the *reporting structure*. Responsibilities for organizational communications may reside in many places within the structure. If a large corporation's primary driver is community building, organizational communications are likely to fall under the purview of the human resource organization. If, however, the primary charter emphasizes executive messaging, or synchronized internal and external communications, then organizational communications may report to the CEO or the marketing communications organization respectively.

In theory, the primary charter should dictate where the organizational communications function resides within the overall organizational structure; however, in reality the reverse is often true. If the central organizational communications department falls within the HR organization, it may naturally adopt a community-building or culture-building role.

Whatever the structure, organizational communications goals not naturally associated with the parent organizational function will surely be difficult to achieve. The organizational communication strategist should pay close attention to these dynamics. If the central organizational communications department reports to human resources, it is likely to be harder for a communications department to accomplish, say, business literacy than if it reports to a marketing organization. Subsequently, this requires special focus and might include hiring talent not currently found in the organization. Likewise, if an external communications team is responsible for organizational communications, messages probably adopt a public-relations tone. In this case, internally specific content and authenticity may be difficult to achieve.

The nature of a central organizational communication *resource model* directly affects the breadth of the overarching organizational communication strategy. Videos, virtual meetings, intranet Web development, and contextualized communications all require different skill sets and financial commitments. Ideally, the resource model should be predicated upon a strategy, but—as in many organizational functions—it is often a legacy resource model that drives the strategy instead. For example, if the organizational communication leaders have a background replete with video experience, they may craft an overarching organizational communication strategy using video as a primary medium. Or if the previous year's budget was based on a certain cost-per-employee ratio, then shifting to another cost model to achieve a new strategy may prove difficult.

A central organizational communication department is almost always a corporate cost-center function. Although metrics exist, quantitative benefits of effective communication are hard to detail. As in all such functions—information services, finance, legal, etc.—creating an appropriate resource model can be challenging, especially when budgets get squeezed. Most such functions rely on legacy models, external benchmarking comparisons, and personal influence to create the resource model. Since strategy does not always dictate resources, the organizational communicator must sometimes craft an overarching communications strategy based on a predetermined resource model. (See Appendix 1 for in-depth discussion of developing an appropriate resource model for a central communications department.)

SUMMARY

Considering both the backdrop of macro socioeconomic trends and organizational communication variables, the organizational communicator should craft an overarching strategy, the aggregate of which is positive organizational alignment and action toward the organizational values, vision, goals, strategic direction, and operational methods. Positive alignment means that each organizational communicator delivers the data, information, knowledge, and insight. Consequently, this member acts on the derived awareness, understanding, learning, and creation.

Figure 2.7 details the process of crafting a specific organizational communication strategy.

This chapter deconstructs organizational communication into so many elements that the act of communicating can seem overwhelming. Depending on the situation, this complexity can be very real. At other times, all of the important elements are so ingrained and natural that successfully communicating within an organization is as intuitive as breathing.

To examine a reconstructed view of organizational communication that is likely to be familiar, let's consider crafting a strategy to promote education within a family unit. The organization is the family, the desired communication goal is alignment around education, and the action is to enroll in educational classes.

The macro trend embodied by Generation X in today's information age may affect how the children of the family unit expect or consume information. Micro analysis may reveal a paternal and authoritarian social structure, the insecurity of a pending divorce, and a family living in a neighborhood where education is generally not valued. Given this landscape, the organizational leaders (the

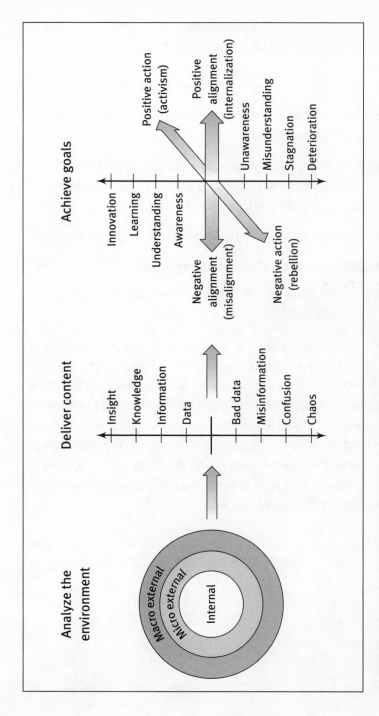

FIGURE 2.7. Crafting an Organizational Communication Strategy

parents) craft a specific organizational communication strategy to promote education, which may include the following:

- Complete information detailing all educational options

- Giving context to the information to show how education leads to success

- Synchronized information delivery to address antieducation sentiments found among some family members and conveyed by neighborhood friends

- Interactivity, to allow the children to ask questions

- Repetition every chance the parents get

- Stylistic elements of honesty and authoritarian power

This is a simple example, but it clearly demonstrates the approach and some elements important in crafting a communication strategy that leads to a specific outcome. In larger organizations, landscape analysis, goal setting, and strategy crafting follow a similar process, but the orchestration is, of course, much more complex.

Now that we've uncovered the elements of corporate communications and the backdrop of macro trends against which organizations perform, let's peek beneath the hood of societal journalism to understand the driving fundamentals.

3

Journalism in the Real World

Why Journalism?
Get It First—But Get It Right
Openness and a Free Press
Weighing News Value
Intrinsic Credibility Challenges
Corporations Resemble Society

D uring a state visit to a southern Soviet republic where Russian literacy was minimal, Mikhail Gorbachev found workers of one state-owned plant had only one request from the central government in Moscow: send more copies of the Communist party's official daily newspaper, *Pravda* (*truth* in English).

Impressed with his comrades' interest in the publication, he asked about their favorite sections of the paper, admitting his voracious appetite for economic news and regular features on the five-year productivity and allocation plans. After a few minutes and more than one blank stare, one of the workers told the president that they did not usually read the newspaper.

"Then why do you want more copies?" asked the premier.

The answer came instantly: "Because there is no toilet paper."

Apocryphal or not, the story has a moral that is clear: a newspaper should be worth more than the paper it is printed on. What gives a newspaper, or any news medium, value is credibility built through active development and diligent application of free journalistic practices and principles.

The Soviet Union was never known for its protection of the press or encouragement of the freedom and independence the press would require to grow and earn credibility. Instead, the state exercised iron-fisted control of even the most insignificant facts and the most innocuous analyses. It is for this reason that during the entire seventy-four years of the Soviet Empire's existence, there was an active effort to repress reports of passenger airline catastrophes. Thanks to the acquiescence of an official, state-owned and state-operated press, Soviet civil aviation had a 100 percent safety record!

WHY JOURNALISM?

In the United States and elsewhere today, corporate employees are now required to understand the larger strategic and long-term reasons for pursuing a course of action and then make critical decisions for their organizations every day. In a democratic society, understanding of and respect for the core vision documents (Constitution, Bill of Rights, etc.) and laws is a value that must be instilled in its citizenry, through civics courses in school, lessons taught at home, and leaders who embody and engender respect for those fundamental guidelines. Absence of respect for the law can lead to the situation currently experienced in many formerly communist countries. In Russia, for example, by 1991 there was little *respect* for authority and the law; as the Soviet regime came to an end, only *fear* of authority and the law existed. After the Communist structure was disassembled, new laws and credible authority did not develop quickly, and the rule of force and power took over as the basis for distributing wealth and meting out justice. This is not a healthy way for societies to develop. It creates great inefficiencies in the system since decisions are a product of inherently restrictive and unjust factors.

The same is true for any corporation wishing to increase its competitive and innovative base. If power and position dictate how decisions are made, and if the organization hoards information as a means to bolster the power of the few versus that of the many, then the decision-making process suffers, as does the morale of the organization. This is why reinforcing the purpose and values of any organization is ultimately important. A clear articulation and consistent expression of purpose and values allows everyone to know what the direction is and what the rules are. This articulation also provides a way to judge and regard those who do not play by the rules and gives any news reporting organization a standard to enforce and a benchmark against which to administer judgment.

Credibility is the only currency of a free press. The press can only increase the absolute worth of this currency through diligently applying journalistic principles and practices: weighing the news value of stories in an informed and responsible way, maintaining an editorially independent voice, pursuing fair and accurate reporting, and providing timely delivery and distribution. Credible gathering and dissemination of news all boils down to timeliness, fairness and accuracy, openness, and news value.

In this chapter, we examine these features of a free press—these principles and practices—and their relevance and application in the world. Free journalistic practices are already found, to varying degrees, in corporations and other institutions, but identifying them makes it clearer which are or should be applied more diligently. The next chapter applies these features specifically to a corporate organizational structure.

The news environment surrounding us is something we take for granted. It is already common to receive real-time quotes on stocks, to watch or hear about Scud missiles as they are about to be intercepted in flight by Patriot missiles, and to see foreign or domestic policy commitments made during live interviews and Sunday morning wonk-talk programs. Not only have we grown accustomed to this reality; we feel entitled to immediacy and express outrage when a technical failure disrupts timely delivery of needed news.

Timeliness is an important feature of credible news. Like fresh fish, the daily newspapers in which they are often wrapped also have a shelf life. The news sections of newspapers are outdated the moment they are printed, because they deal with the ephemeral. As the saying goes, there's nothing older than yesterday's newspaper; this holds even truer today with real-time news delivery over the proliferating electronic media and cyberspace. News story datelines, designed to be reference points and research tools, now function more like expiration dates on milk cartons.

News is dependent on timeliness for its relevance. Waiting until the administration of Boris Yeltsin was in power before the Russian press could delve deeply into Stalinist excesses was an object lesson in tardiness. Although the final verdict on Stalin and his henchmen—printed three decades late—was certainly newsworthy, it was far from timely. If Stalin has turned over in his grave, the fact is hidden by the number of flowers strewn on the grave by faithful old women who still believe the pablum of the Stalinist-era press. A timely rendering of the murderous reality of the 1930s, 1940s, and 1950s to an interested audience might have made Stalin's terrorist reign no less brutal but certainly more visible, and possibly less tolerated.

Timeliness is a greater virtue in a competitive journalistic environment than in a monopolistic one. In fact, although competition is not an explicit journalistic principle or practice, it has become a means for the press to check itself. It is a way for the self-appointed public watchdogs to watch the watchdogs.

When news organizations try to beat each other with the latest information, the techniques and technologies for gathering and disseminating news become all important. Any advantage of timing that can be squeezed out of these processes will be squeezed out.

Beating the competition becomes the paramount concern. Unfortunately, the drawback is that accuracy often suffers.

The lack of timely reporting on the AIDS epidemic in the United States has been criticized widely, notably in Randy Shilts's book *And the Band Played On* (1987). In the early days of the crisis, it was said that not only the government but also the news media failed to focus on the epidemiological reality and the true human costs because the victims were perceived to be on the margins of society—drug addicts, prostitutes, homosexuals. Once it was clear that this disease was far more scurrilous and impartial in selecting victims, the mainstream press picked up the story and offered much wider and timelier reporting. The effect was to focus more resources on preventing and curing the disease while also educating the general public on its inherent dangers. Unfortunately, there are still countries in which timely reporting of AIDS takes a back seat to prejudice and delayed reporting continues to destroy human lives.

During the 1991 Gulf War, Charles Jaco was broadcasting live for CNN from Dhahran International Airbase in Saudi Arabia when, according to Jaco, "a wave of oxidized rocket propellant washed across the camera platform." Jaco and team had just gone live after "three or four airbursts of [Iraqi] SCUDs being intercepted by Patriots blowing up almost directly overhead, 1200–2300 feet above." The rocket propellant added toxicity to the chaos and "nobody could breathe." Jaco said he misjudged the situation and "I yelled 'gas,'" prompting him and others to reach for their gas masks. It was, he said, "a panicked judgment made in combat conditions on live television." The mistake, made under pressure and under fire, did not have any instant military or foreign policy ramifications, even though U.S. administration and Pentagon brass reactions at the time were on a hair-trigger. The question of how—or how deeply—an organization's credibility is affected during snap judgment calls and mistakes is an open one, and Jaco argues that this extreme incident under extreme circumstances did not damage CNN's credibility. The fact is that getting things right is harder when the pressure of the medium allows no time for fact checking, reflecting, and second sourcing. Getting things right is a journalistic priority and lies at the heart of building and maintaining credibility, but the pressure to get the story first and fast remains (personal interview).

Such pressures are likely going to continue to increase. Consumers of news now set their level of satisfaction with news being just in time to the expectation of *real-time news*—in contrast to a time when weekly newsmagazines, or even afternoon newspapers, sufficed. The effect has been to greatly speed up delivery. Whereas the Gulf War was played out on CNN, the early war tragedies of Kosovo were transmitted instantaneously across the world by a young girl who, from her personal computer in a Kosovo home, sent penpal e-mails that were broadcast over the Internet. Next, the news will need to be *ahead of time*. Such news—where events are not only anticipated but predicted, as with weather forecasts—will cut closer to the bone of credibility.

The standard clichés that close most broadcast news pieces today are that "nobody knows for sure if this will happen," or "only time will tell." Suddenly, however, there is no time to tell. "Tomorrow's News Today" could soon supplant "All the News That's Fit to Print" as the motto of the next generation of leading news-oriented media. Anticipatory and analytical skills will need to catch up with the technology-driven advances in timely news capture and delivery. Credibility is further threatened in such an environment.

GET IT FIRST—BUT GET IT RIGHT

The pressure is real. "Get it right," is the editor's request, "—but get it first" is the demand. Invariably, when forced to choose between two opposing imperatives, a responsible editor—perhaps grudgingly—defers and chooses "get it right." Accuracy should, and usually does, win out in any battles confronting timeliness.

Accuracy is a basic principle of free journalism. Spell a name wrong and it is the only thing people will remember. Every time a book goes to print, author and publisher are haunted by fear of inaccuracies or typographic mistakes. "Dewey Defeats Truman" is a newspaper headline hiccup made classic by a photograph of a smiling president-elect Harry Truman holding it up. The paper's editors "got it first" all right, made their deadline, and were able to get the presses rolling—in time to make an egregious mistake. Mark Twain's obituary appeared in a newspaper, while the humorist then claimed that reports of his death had been greatly exaggerated. Film director James Cameron might still be "terminating" Arnold Schwarzenegger and wondering if he'd ever make a really big film if the *Baltimore Evening Sun's* headline on April 15, 1912, had been correct: "All Titanic Passengers are Safe; Transferred in Lifeboats at Sea." The more respectable news organizations usually reserve a space in their news hole for retractions and corrections, allowing them to set the record straight and apologize for their mistakes. Regardless of how well hidden or acknowledged, inaccuracy never helps credibility.

One of the things that separate propaganda from journalistically sound news and feature reporting is the degree of accuracy applied to each genre. Even if often factually correct, propaganda is usually guilty of inaccuracy through omission or commission of other highly relevant facts, or in analyzing the facts. The Cuban newspaper *Granma* is full of factual articles regarding the sugar crop and increases in foreign currency reserves, all indicating slow and steady improvements in the country's economic well-being. What it fails to mention, however, is that health care continues to spiral downward because of deteriorating conditions and lack of medicines (unless it makes mention in directly attributing the problems to the "brutal U.S. economic embargo" on Cuba), factors very much a part of defining a country's economic strength.

To offset the propagandistic barrage that Cubans face, the U.S. government believes it can broadcast news and information into the country using mediumwave and shortwave radio as well as television, given that Cuba is only ninety miles away from Florida. Radio Marti is not an independent news source, but an extension of the foreign policy arm of the U.S. government. It fights bland propaganda with more sophisticated propaganda, using impressive production quality and entertainment values. It is occasionally more accurate, but its real value is entertainment and provision of an opposing viewpoint. The problem is that those who live in Cuba perceive all news and information as equally suspect and inaccurate, and therefore unbelievable. This forces them to figure out where, along the spectrum of "fact," the truth lies. A great critical facility may be a wonderful thing to develop, but not everyone is willing to take the time to do personal editorial work. It may be too much to expect of any general populace or citizenry.

During the Communist leadership control, the Czech media reported regularly about American racial inequality and economic disparity, often showing pictures of the homeless and downtrodden. They laced their reporting with pictures of the Ku Klux Klan and drug-addicted Vietnam veterans. "But we didn't believe them," was a common sentiment, "because we knew the regime was lying to us." People came to America "looking for free love and drugs and freedom"—as they were promised in bootleg rock records. Following the Velvet Revolution that brought down the Communist regime in 1989, Czechs and Slovaks were suddenly able to travel to the United States for the first time in their lives. When they returned, some were upset about what they had seen in America. Not only did they witness racism and poverty but they also found "puritanical" behavior everywhere (people wearing bathing suits at the beach—as opposed to always being nude, which is what they had been told by their state-run media—or not constantly willing to hold hands or kiss in public). This chaste state was a far cry from the decadent love-in and drop-out culture depicted by their state-run media.

The Czech-run media lost its credibility even though there was some truth to its reporting. What may have been timely all right was simply not entirely accurate or a fair telling of the truth. The result? Disbelief.

OPENNESS AND A FREE PRESS

There is a long-standing argument, sometimes espoused in institutions such as the United Nations, that a free press may not be a prerequisite for societal development, and certainly not for survival. That may be true, especially in societies and countries with low literacy levels, high poverty rates, closed borders, and homogeneous cultural and ethnic populations susceptible to the most infantile of propaganda techniques. The main prize in any civil strife in such societies is control of the broadcast centers and their antenna towers.

Where propaganda is the main form of information dissemination and where control of this propaganda is centralized, power and decision making are also centralized and usually hierarchical. Is it any wonder that the first allied attacks of the Gulf War were against Iraq's command-and-control centers and broadcast towers? Contrast this structure with the Internet, developed by the U.S. Defense Advanced Research Projects Agency (DARPA), whose infrastructure was built to withstand nuclear holocaust. Any breakdown in the multitude of system hubs is read as a system failure to be circumvented. Trying to destroy the infrastructure and the resultant data packet switching can be like playing the sorcerer's apprentice and trying to stop the multiplying brooms in the movie *Fantasia*.

The drawbacks of centralization may be clear to those who live in a relatively open society with a mostly free press; it is often harder to see the benefits of such a system since much of its form and function are taken for granted.

In its most romanticized form, a free press provides a further check on power and balances the distribution of that power by spreading its cognate—accurate and timely information—to as broad a citizen base as possible. It functions as an educational medium, keeping the citizenry informed and aware, making sure people have as much news and information as they require to make intelligent decisions. When not abused, it is the form of informational exercise that keeps democracy healthy and a citizenry strong and appropriately influential. It used to be a lot easier to keep a secret in Washington, D.C. Finding out those secrets may not make the citizenry feel any better about its leadership, but it lets the citizens decide whether or not the secrets have any bearing on issues of leadership, governance, or policy.

The battle that the free press needs to fight vigilantly and continuously is one of access. Appropriately classifying information, enforcing sunshine laws that force a ray of public light into otherwise closed meetings and decision-making forums, forcing declassification of documentation through the Freedom of Information Act (FOIA), demanding answers from public officials through use of press conferences and interviews—these all aid in the fight for access.

Of course, access is not everything. Both access and independence are required. And what is the goal of independence? To promote an agenda? In an open, democratic system, the idea is to uphold and align the populace toward the principles that rule the society; in a journalism school tradition, the idea is to pursue the truth and to present it well. In fact, the motto at the Columbia Graduate School of Journalism is "that the people shall know"; outside its front doors is a statue not of William Randolph Hearst or Joseph Pulitzer or Rupert Murdoch, but of Thomas Jefferson. The truths and laws of the free-press-based society he espoused are to be served—not the business interests or competitive media holdings of today's journalism landscape. The foundation is truth, arrived at as impartially as humanly possible.

The legendary Fred Friendly, former president of CBS News and Edward R. Murrow's producer on the program "See It Now," would never leave the house without carrying at least one pocket-sized copy of the U.S. Constitution, a document he could recite verbatim. As a reminder of their responsibilities, many journalists carry Friendly's laminated calling card, the back of which carries a quote from CBS News editor Edward Klauber, who "was the real founder of all broadcast journalism" according to Friendly's book *Due to Circumstances Beyond Our Control*:

What news analysts are entitled to do and should do is to elucidate and illuminate the news out of common knowledge, or special knowledge possessed by them or made available to them by this organization through its sources. They should point out the facts on both sides, show contradictions with the known record, and so on. They should bear in mind that in a democracy it is important that people not only should know but should understand, and it is the analyst's function to help the listener to understand, to weigh, and to judge, but not to do the judging for him [p. 200].

Even in countries where the intelligentsia is treated to material privilege and the general populace lives a good lifestyle, a free press and free exchange of ideas and criticism eventually become demands that need to be met. This was certainly the case in Czechoslovakia, a country with a well-educated and urbane society and an advanced industrial base that survived the destruction of World War II.

The country struggled to open its society, culture, educational institutions, and press while Alexander Dubcek led the nation and the Prague Spring bloomed in 1968. The experiment was rationalized as "socialism with a human face." But the Moscow-led powers interpreted the manifestations as counterrevolutionary heresy and a threat to the Warsaw Pact. They crushed the movement and bloodily reversed its gains.

Once the fear of retaliation and subjugation mainly disappeared, Czechoslovakia—not a materially bankrupt country—rose again in 1989 to overthrow its morally bankrupt and lying rulers in a Velvet Revolution. The system it overthrew provided Czechs with plenty of food for their bellies, but none for their minds or souls.

The Prague Spring experiment became the basis, a generation later, for Gorbachev's *glasnost,* which tried to keep the Soviet system marginally open but succeeded only in creating cognitive dissonance in the society. *Glasnost* provided Soviets with the worst of both worlds: enough openness to allow people to understand better how truly closed the Soviet system and society were and would likely remain, and not enough openness to do anything about it.

WEIGHING NEWS VALUE

The weighing of news value is a difficult process to define. The news should be an open, accurate, and balanced reflection of the community it serves, but this is not always the case. Much like the U.S. Supreme Court's definition of pornography ("I know it when I see it," to paraphrase Justice Stewart), it is easy to know a proper balance in news value weighting when it exists. In fact, there is great lament among the public and many journalism professionals at the end of the twentieth century that commercial and sensational considerations have been outweighing traditional professional journalistic judgment.

Newspapers hold editorial negotiation meetings to fill their news hole as often as publication frequency dictates. Dailies rally at least twice during work hours to determine what stories go where, how prominent they should be, and what angle they should take. The intricacies, glamorized in the movie *The Paper,* show just how much is at stake in making final news-weighted decisions. Public interest, sensationalistic edge, and personal influence are some of the many factors that affect newsworthiness.

Pope John Paul II's historic visit to the island republic of Cuba was at the beginning of 1998. The three major American television networks had invested heavily in the previsit coverage of Cuba and Castro and sent their news anchors to Havana to witness and report on the encounter of the two world leaders. The Pope is often credited with starting the fall of communism in Eastern Europe through his intervention in Poland and the consequent freedom of expression that spread like wildfire. Would his visit to Cuba have the same effect? Maybe, but we may never know—because shortly after the Pope's arrival in Cuba, rumored news of a certain White

House intern and of sex in the Oval Office were overtaking (and overtook for thirteen subsequent months) all other news in nearly every medium.

The competitive market may skew decisions about running a story based on sales and salaciousness. News-value questions about whether a story has relevance and import are often shunted, as is the romantic vision of the role of the press in adding to American society's self-understanding of its underlying democratic values. In today's U.S. media landscape, there is no guarantee, for example, that all the major networks will preempt their prime-time schedules to run contemporaneously a presidential speech; they will surely prefer to relegate that bit of civics to the cable ghetto.

Responsibility for balancing the news falls on the shoulders of publishers, editors, and writers working together in an environment that requires collaboration and compromise. All news organizations are faced with the question of apportioning limited resources: space in print publications, time in broadcasts. Decisions about how to budget their limited resource affect the editorial decisions about what makes it into the news and what does not. For some organizations working in the competitive marketplace, the adage "if it bleeds, it leads" has become the primary deciding factor. For others (often the more venerable media), the questions take on more nuance.

"The MacNeil-Lehrer News Hour," for example, was a paragon of restraint during one of the most recent "trials of the century," devoting almost no time to the coverage of the judicial proceedings surrounding the Nicole Brown Simpson and Ron Goldman murders, despite the prurient and media-driven interest in the accused football star. This news program was the exception to the rule. Driven not by forces intent on getting more market share at the expense of the traditional practice of weighing news values, "MacNeil-Lehrer" instead provided a consistent diet of issues concerning domestic and international affairs. The charge, as the editors saw it, was as much to elucidate the public regarding affairs of state as it was to educate it about its responsibilities in those affairs. While

"The News Hour" is not immune to market pressures, it does seem to have a stronger resistance to them.

Different people and organizations weigh news values differently. This tautological argument is not meant to absolve egregious behavior but to point out that there has been, with a few notable exceptions, a spectrum on which news values are exercised and balanced. This may be less obvious in the post-Monica media madness (where the words *semen* and *oral sex* were uttered by veteran newscaster Ted Koppel and sputtered by congressional members), but taste and restraint can be as much a part of the process as they can sometimes be ignored. *The Wall Street Journal* put it well in a postimpeachment article that referred to Monicagate as "a substitute for soap operas." The article pointed to the weighing of sensationalism versus news value by characterizing this "era that inexorably hollows out the hero into the celebrity (which is another, opposite thing); which devalues news into entertainment; which can transform even an impeachment drama into just another televised spectacle" (Farney and Seib, p. 1).

INTRINSIC CREDIBILITY CHALLENGES

A lot of the straying from the fold regarding what to cover and how to weigh it may be related to the contemporary state of peace and prosperity. Perhaps there is a subconscious belief that regardless of the press's transgression, democracy and society are healthy enough to weather anything. This may be either because society can live in denial of both business and political cycles or because we have indeed come to the conclusion of these cycles. For those less sanguine about the disappearance of cyclical and volatile economic and political fortunes, the press may suffer the consequence of having lost all its credibility and ability to inform and educate a citizenry at the time it needs it most, and whenever that time may come. Maintaining credibility in the defense of a democracy—or any open system—requires continuous diligence, not selective or reactive behavior.

What will happen when the same newsreader who is accustomed to talking about a stained blue dress tries later on to discuss a newly rising red threat in international trade policies, or the greenhouse-gas effects on the borderless global environment? Unlike virginity, credibility can be mostly rebuilt with hard work and convincing, consistent behavior. A common phrase in newsrooms is that "it takes forever to build credibility and only a moment to lose it."

When Ted Turner's CNN network introduced a new magazine program, "NewsStand," to its viewers in 1998, it dangled the carrot of a sensational news story about American troops using toxic poisons in the Vietnam War against defecting GIs. An amazing story, to be sure—so amazing that the network decided not only to use the tease "Valley of Death" and run the story about Operation Tailwind on its initial broadcast but also to write an article on it for *Time* magazine and put a Pulitzer Prize–winning reporter, Peter Arnett, on the story as its correspondent. The problem was that the story seems to have had no basis in truth.

Turmoil and demoralization reigned in the newsroom; the credibility of the network was at stake. Turner did the one thing he knew was necessary to try to salvage what credibility was left. He fell on his sword. He came out publicly, cried "mea culpa," and followed a litany of horrendous personal tragedies with the statement that this was the worst thing that had ever happened to him. Public self-flagellation was a way to say he was sorry, but regardless, the network is under much more scrutiny as a result of this one serious mistake.

Although the CNN "NewsStand" team exercised access and editorial independence, their findings were sensationalized and the end result was calamitous for their credibility. But sensationalization is as much a threat as restraint (or self-censorship, as it is commonly referred to in journalistic circles). The independence of news organizations is constitutionally guaranteed for the most part (with notable exceptions, such as during wartime), but the exercise of that independence varies, often depending on the mood of the nation, the popularity of politicians, and popularly perceived threats to national security.

In the early 1960s, the *New York Times* was on to a big story. The newspaper had come across credibly sourced information that the United States was equipping and preparing to support an invasion force onto Cuba's Bay of Pigs. The editorial decision, made independently—if somewhat influenced by President Kennedy's phone call to kill the story—was to withhold the story lest it jeopardize the lives of those involved in the invasion or the operation as a whole, regardless of the apparent foolhardiness of the action. The invasion was carried out and failed miserably. Kennedy later told the *New York Times* that he wished the paper *had* run the story because, as David Halberstam wrote in his book on journalism, *The Powers That Be*, "it might have saved him a disaster" (p. 625).

Second-guessing a story is second nature to most editors, but they usually err on the side of publishing versus not publishing, partly because of the competitive context in which they work. The question of self-censorship arises as questions of loyalty are raised: When critically reporting on the nuclear power industry in the 1990s, was the journalist employed by NBC or its parent General Electric? By CBS or the network's owner Westinghouse? Does it matter? Questions of this type become ethical ones and need to be asked constantly if journalism is to remain healthy.

During the Vietnam War, American journalists were often taken to task for their reporting and are still blamed in some circles as the ones responsible for losing the war. The question was often asked of individual reporters, "Are you an American first, or a journalist?" For those who believed that the journalist's role was to report the truth as the U.S. government perceived and spun it, the journalist who wrote of inaccurate assessments by the military brass, atrocities, and secret wars being fought in Laos and Cambodia was labeled a traitor. For others, bringing a fiercely fought guerilla war against American and Vietnamese ground troops that was in many camps considered illegal, immoral, and unwinnable was the most patriotic of activities. Because America is still torn by these two viewpoints on the war and its aftermath, the question of the role of journalism, and whether the eventual outcome for which it was a catalyst helped or hurt, is still unanswered. *Only time will tell.*

CORPORATIONS RESEMBLE SOCIETY

Knowledge-based corporations and intellectual-capital-driven corporations of the type described earlier in this book have begun to resemble smaller versions of the societies in which they reside. Their employees are more like members of a community, and certain common values and purposes are often attributed to those cultures. They expect democratized institutions and ready access to information. The next chapter looks at how the practices and principles of free journalism instituted in modern corporations help not only to achieve organic alignment and change management that creates a competitive edge but also to foster an innovative and healthy environment.

4

Strategic Corporate Journalism

Timeliness

Accuracy

Free Press

Weighing News Value

The New Corporation

Strategic Corporate Journalism

The foundation of the journalistic principles and practices outlined in Chapter Three is built upon a news-gathering and disseminating body that is able to weigh the news value of stories in an informed, responsible, and editorially independent way; report the stories fairly and accurately; and deliver them in a timely fashion.

These features of a free press and their relevance and application in the world of both government and corporations are examined in this chapter. Although journalistic manifestations and behaviors are partially apparent in corporations and other institutions today, identifying, isolating, and examining them helps clarify a strategy for their conscious application.

The Drudge Report is a widely read source of gossip and purported news. It is nearly worthless not only because of the rumormongering it pursues but also because (unlike *Pravda*) it is not printed on paper and hence is unsuitable for the water closet. This dubious information source and all-around gossip medium (purportedly referred to as "The Sludge Report" in the Clinton White House) is available only via the World Wide Web. Today nearly anyone can hang a shingle and be a publisher.

In the case of Matt Drudge, the self-styled Walter Winchell (the archetypal "must read" gossip columnist) of the electronic era, he was able to garner attention by beating *Newsweek* to that magazine's exclusive story about a young White House intern who had intimate relations with the president. The one-man news operation sent the entire mass media machine and the White House spin cyclers tumbling, demanding quick reactions, responses, denials, damage control, and fast and furious fact checking. The media mechanism had its already tightly wound spring tensioned further, taking out entirely whatever considered and deliberative editorial judgment existed in a news cycle, and forcing real-time reporting and real-time analysis. This immediacy confronts both publishers and news consumers every day.

This reality affects the survival and success of any organization or corporation that is unprepared. If the Monica Lewinsky matter can command so much attention and gobble up huge amounts of government time and resources, then for an organization not nearly as savvy or ready as the White House when it comes to dealing with information crises the chances are high of becoming roadkill on the information highway—particularly if the organization ignores or fails to respond to hazards along the way.

The pervasive access to news in society has a direct impact on a corporation's communication challenges. Information control is impossible in today's networked world. The demands of the employee base, and the new social and technological realities combined with the rapidly shifting information landscape, all require of these organizations a great deal more openness and transparency both during relative prosperity and—to a much greater extent—during crisis. One of the best ways to achieve this openness is by copying democratic societies and applying journalism to the workings of an organization. Corporations need to create and adopt journalistic principles and practices inside their organizations. Incorporating these standards helps develop the organization's credibility.

As with the free press in this new world, credibility is the only currency a corporation has with its shareholders, customers, suppliers, partners, and employees. The knowledge-based corporation may not go financially bankrupt if it does not follow these principles and practices, but it can lose the intellectual capital that is necessary for innovation and maintenance of a competitive edge.

Societal journalism can teach the corporation some lessons. Czechoslovakia, for example, remained populated during the worst of the repression, the most dishonest of its information dissemination, and the most despicable of foreign policies. The government, however, never had the majority support of its people. It could only gain popular acquiescence through fear and intimidation. In November 1989, following the crack in the Berlin Wall in neighboring Germany, Czechs and Slovaks were able to dissent without the immediate threat of death or imprisonment; as a result they moved quickly to overthrow their corrupt, lying, and bankrupt leadership. They knew of the Communist government's misdeeds, both through daily observation of injustice and to no small degree through the infiltration of information that seeped—and at times flowed—into the country. Contradictory and more credible information came over the radio waves, through fax technology, in *samizdat* underground press, and—once the Berlin Wall fell—directly from an authorized press. This news seepage during crisis changed the government's reporting pattern of deception and propaganda to timely reporting. All of this happened before satellite television was available, travel possible, and e-mail accessible to anyone beyond the political elite or scientific community.

Many knowledge-based corporations, too, maintain a large employee population who may already have "quit" the company without having left it, who believe "Dilbert" best characterizes their daily work life and management, and who would be more than happy to witness the overthrow of leadership they consider clueless and conspiratorial. It is not the commitment or the ideology of these employees that is usually at question, but their need to understand, align, and identify with the purpose, values, and vision of an organization. Also essential are visible signs that the leadership represents and is objectively held accountable to the corporate vision and its purpose and value standards. James Collins and Jerry Porras, in *Built to Last*, write a thoroughly researched argument for corporations to have lasting purpose and values if they are to survive. As they put it, "the only truly reliable source of stability is a strong inner core [purpose and values] and the willingness to change and adapt everything except that core" (p. xx).

To correlate corporate purpose and values to government, one need look no further than a country's constitution and bill of rights. In the United States, the government is held accountable to the Constitution and in check by internal means through balancing the three branches of government: judicial, legislative, and administrative. Additionally, a free press holds it in check.

In industry, a number of checks and balances are also built into the system, with boards of directors, shareholder meetings, ombudsmen, legal departments, employee councils, etc. But an informational check that resembles an independent press is often lacking. In this light, the content and distribution of any corporate mass communication function as an administrative mouthpiece used to extol the corporate virtues and successes while downplaying or polishing up challenges and failures. To achieve higher levels of necessary credibility, therefore, it is in the larger interest of the organization to adopt and apply the journalistic principles and practices in its daily operations.

The argument for corporations is not that they should abandon their efforts to shape the external news through public relations and marketing, but rather that they should couple these efforts with an expanded internal reporting mechanism. This expansion in turn has an impact on the organization's ability to compete, internally and effectively (and sometimes directly), with the external news.

This idea that an internal news organization should compete with the plethora of external and structurally independent information sources is sometimes difficult to accept. But the seamlessness and transparency of information flow today does not label information that arrives as being internal or external; it only allows the recipient to assess the information as either more credible or less credible. If the *New York Times* states that a corporation pollutes, is involved in securities fraud, exploits child labor, threatens national security, is involved in discriminatory hiring practices, or is guilty of any number of equally unappetizing activities, the company's employee population does not care if a discredited or questionable internal department suddenly issues a memo, sends a voice mail, or makes a post to an intranet site declaring the *Times* story as unfair and inaccurate. It does make a difference, however, if that very same memo, voice mail, or intranet site has been serving up a consistent dose of journalistically sound news and information over time. Credibility counts.

TIMELINESS

In free, democratic civil societies, timeliness is driven by competition between news organizations. Their profitability and credibility are defined by their ability to beat the competition in the fight for audience. This competition exists internally with organizational communicators battling confidentiality leaks and the rumor mill. But within today's interconnected world, more competition actually exists with bodies external to the organization, be it a nation-state or a corporation. For this reason, in a sense corporations also need to compete with all news sources so that they can be first to provide information on events and changes that affect the health and status of the corporation itself. If not, credibility suffers. In the long run, the very viability of the knowledge-based corporation is threatened through loss of competitive understanding and timely response; employee defection and distrust; and tardy anticipation of investment, market, and societal trends and events with direct or indirect business impact.

As the Soviet Union began to open up and experience its early days of *glasnost*, a terrible tragedy struck in the Ukraine. In April 1986 a nuclear power plant outside of Kiev, at Chernobyl, experienced a severe problem and as a result released radioactivity into the atmosphere. The severity of the discharge and of the accident were unknown to the populace in the early hours and days of the disaster because none of the Soviet news agencies were allowed to carry the news. Some of the earliest warnings of the event came from Finland, on the northern Soviet border, and were broadcast on international shortwave; other Western broadcast and print news agencies quickly picked up on the story. The rest of the world was alerted to this accident, but those living closest to the burning reactor were clueless unless they listened illicitly to international shortwave broadcasts. Evacuations were slow to occur, and danger alerts and warnings were notably absent. The only timely and credible, if incomplete, information was made available from external sources. Confusion reigned.

Outside the Soviet Union, extreme acts were being recommended. Finnish medical officials suggested that women in the early stages of pregnancy abort their fetuses; the remaining Scandinavian countries warned everyone against ingesting milk and game, most notably the Lapplanders' economic and dietary staple, reindeer. So starved was the outside world for news of Chernobyl that Western television broadcasters jumped at the chance to buy a film clip, purportedly smuggled, showing a grainy and distant image of a burning Chernobyl plant. The expensive hoax turned out to be shots of a cement plant in Italy. The reflexive, defensive denials and "no comments" on the part of the Soviets kept the affected population from taking necessary self-protective action and further weakened whatever faith was left in the system and its propaganda machinery. A discredited system seemed doomed.

In the corporate world, examples abound of affected employee and management populations being left in the dark about negative events or news that bears on the company's competitive status.

For years, American tobacco companies lived the fiction that their product was benign. In fact, they went out of their way to tell not only employees but also the consuming public that cigarettes and other tobacco products provided lifestyle benefits. They actively contradicted medical evidence that showed health risks, including lung cancer and emphysema, and provided their own studies showing that the independent research was "inconclusive." All the while, these companies amassed reams of research, kept secret, that did in fact show conclusive evidence regarding the health risks and how levels of nicotine could be upped to make their product more addictive. This information was withheld within the company, but it was also actively discouraged in the mainstream external press (which counted on much of its advertising revenue from tobacco companies). One hand slimed the other in this instance, and the dirty open secret was popularly obfuscated.

Eventually the truth caught up. The public sued. After years of advertising and marketing campaigns as well as direct denials by tobacco companies executives of the detrimental effects of cigarettes, the industry settled on the largest product-liability claim in U.S. history. Tobacco conglomerates were discredited and punished both in the eyes of the consuming public and within the employee and management ranks. Would timely and encouraged release of established factual information from both the Chernobyl plant and the tobacco companies have saved lives, softened the blow, and conserved the credibility of the responsible institutions? The answer may depend on personal perspective; it is clear, however, that the moratoria and belatedly released information had further deleterious effects on what was already suspect.

Of course, the tobacco companies are not considered to have an intellectual capital base, and the need to be timely can be overlooked more easily than in a knowledge-intensive, non-agriculturally oriented corporation. The more demanding employee base at these latter corporations expects and feels entitled to news regarding their organizations first, and demands it for both personal and competitive reasons. With the fluidity and speed of the news in general, this puts great pressure on these organizations to serve up relevant and accurate news quickly and strategically.

It is no longer acceptable to employees—who are now often motivated and compensated with shares of the company stock and options—to hear, for example, corporate financial news first from external sources. If financial results are released at a certain moment to Wall Street, then they need to be released and distributed contemporaneously to the employee base. Were it not for Securities and Exchange Commission regulations that make such prerelease of results news illegal, employees would demand to get financial results first, before the rest of the world.

If layoffs are being planned or conducted, it is no longer acceptable to employees that they discover this on the radio while driving into work or in their morning paper as they sit down to breakfast. Both of these instances may involve "overnight factors" (say, an after-hours management decision or a leveraged buyout that closes late on Friday) that cause employees to miss the news. But the attempt to get the news to them first—and at the very least have it available as quickly as it is to the rest of the world, if not more quickly—is a minimal expectation in the new corporation. Credibility and morale both suffer if this expectation is not met.

Likewise, industry information about competitors and the company's competitive stance is becoming increasingly relevant and expected. In this new environment, companies can no longer deny or ignore competition or industry trends. The body politic of the new corporation demands well-rounded insight regarding changes in process and strategic direction. If the intellectual-capital-based company motto sounds something like "our employees are our most important asset," then a modicum of timely information needs to be invested in this asset class to keep the enterprise healthy.

The merger mania at the end of the 1990s makes it harder to ensure that employees find out first about such news. A new challenge arises as well: news leaks. As Mike Morrison, the retired executive director of corporate communications at Chrysler, says, it is difficult to prevent leaks "when bankers are involved in the process." And they always are, in such deals. Although his comment (made at a speechwriters' conference) was not meant to be a cruel dig at bankers, it is a poignant reminder that those likely to leak are seldom the interested parties. Because of the players' size or visibility, some mergers are harder to keep from the public eye; unique or primary access does not necessarily nor automatically guarantee that first rights of publication go to an internal news body.

Neither Clinton nor Lewinsky approached the independent prosecutor, the press, or the White House staff with tales of their mutual involvement. A friend and confidante of Lewinsky's felt personally motivated to make public secretly taped recordings of private conversations. As with the events that catalyzed a president's impeachment, third parties involved in and aware of corporate activities often have more to gain from releasing such information than do the organizations immediately involved. For example, looking to build momentum in their industry, advertising agencies may prematurely let out news that a new corporate account has been landed months before any campaign is begun (and sometimes before a contract has been signed). The dollar value of the account, occasionally inflated, usually accompanies such leaked reports.

Layoffs, mergers, acquisitions, spin-offs, stock buybacks, plant shutdowns, organizational changes, strategic redirections, competitive repricing, product road map developments, alteration of benefits, medical outbreaks, board-directed initiatives, leadership crises . . . whatever the news, the employees need to be served first, as much as is legally possible, and following that as quickly as possible. If they are treated as also-rans when it comes to news and information, how can they be expected to perform in a win, place, or even show position?

Being first with the news provides an extra bonus. It allows the corporate entity to frame the news and give it an accurate and appropriate strategic context. This context can provide a general understanding that is harder to achieve once third-party analysis is interjected and colors the interpretation of events and developments. It also allows time for the appropriate actions to be taken: evacuation in the case of Chernobyl, avoiding potentially perjurious testimony in Clinton's grand jury testimony. For a corporation, the time thus gained can, for example, allow recalling and restocking a faulty product.

Does a company want to explain the subtleties, terms, and length of a necessary cut in operating expenses to employees, or does it want the business press to explain it in broad strokes? Is it appropriate that a local newspaper's outside analysis frame a merger for a community as being a monopolistic concern worthy of antitrust scrutiny, or should it first be explained to the people most affected so as to incorporate strategic benefits and synergy? By being first with the news, you can focus some of the debate and keep it fruitful. In a reactive posture, the discussion is likely to lead to defensiveness, fear, and mistrust.

As with all these examples, it is nearly always more important to be first with the bad news than it is with the good news. If news that the company grew unexpectedly by 50 percent in the last fiscal year is a little slow, employees are not likely to care that they find it out from a relative who saw it on CNBC. But let them know that the company experienced an unexpected 5 percent *loss* for the year after it was splashed in the *Wall Street Journal*, and their faith in both the organization and the leadership can be seriously tested.

The popularly applied model of corporate communications—lumping employee communications together with the public-relations and marketing arm of an organization—is often outmoded and ill-suited because it can neither respond contextually and broadly nor deliver timely, strategic, and fair news. This is particularly true if the employee communications function is not able to operate relatively independently but cooperatively, or if it is not allowed to apply the other journalistic principles and practices that complement timeliness.

ACCURACY

As in the world of daily journalism, getting the facts straight and getting them first is not necessarily the same as getting the story right. The context has to be correct. The story needs integrity. "Get it first—but get it right" is even more critical in a competitive business context because it can make a difference to a corporation's survival.

The news on the ground is not always the same news delivered to those in charge. Reported casualties in Vietnam were calculated differently by American foot soldiers and the Pentagon brass. The latter's inflated enemy casualty figures were used as justification to continue the war during President Johnson's administration. This blatant miscalculation and legerdemain by generals and cabinet secretaries was an outright lie intended to give the administration a strong rationale for escalation and against negotiation. In the eyes of the war's defenders, the gravest threat to American national security was in backing out of the war, not in losing it, because losing was not a considered option or calculated risk.

The inaccurate information cost the American people the U.S. servicemen lost in the ensuing years of the war as well as the credibility of American institutions, whose constituents retreated into cynicism and skepticism that linger to this day. The republic withstood the strain on its institutions and has slowly healed the societal divisions riven in that climate, but the incalculable costs of that failed policy are still being paid by all sides.

Less dramatic but more measurable are the costs to businesses and industries where inaccuracy in reporting enjoys de facto encouragement from structural protectionism. Sales figures are the pulse of many organizations—a pulse monitored regularly by management. Despite the attention given to this vital sign, there is often disparity between the sales figures reported to top management and those experienced in the field by the salesforce itself. When this disparity comes to light, people point fingers or management tries to show that things are not as bad as they may actually seem. The use of generally approved accounting procedures (GAAP), for example, provides great latitude but little insight into or reflection of the true inner workings of an enterprise or its overall health.

The results that GAAP allows are easily manipulated, the equivalent of any noninterpretive representation; GAAP is the Greenland of the accounting world. A look at a globe shows Greenland as an enormous, continentlike body in the North Atlantic Ocean, a land mass appearing greater than Alaska, Zaire, or Mexico in size and potential. There is very little that gives away the size distortion that flat Mercator projection counters, much less the relative uninhabitability of the place. Much of the reporting done within companies and with the external financial community is based on facts, guidelines, and regulations derived by GAAP. Even though the globe and GAAP results are factually correct, they are not always accurate depictions.

A corporation functioning in a climate that tolerates inaccuracy operates on perceived reality. For some companies, meeting financial plans and a sales outlook means that they continue to pursue run rates that are no longer appropriate in a more honestly reckoned business climate. Resource allocation in this scenario is based on assumptions that may be spurious at best. If and when a fuller and more contextualized truth is finally revealed later, the results often come more as a surprise than a relief for the interested parties. Credibility is shot with the employee population, investors, members of the board, customers, and partners. Those who were trying to protect themselves by practicing delivery of good news instead of bad, or boosterism instead of criticism, can become the victims of their own obfuscation and prevarication. Although companies are implored to eat their own dog food, they should also avoid believing their own public relations.

One way to promote accuracy is through the journalistic method of by-lines, whereby accountability for truth and accuracy of information is directly assigned. A look at the majority of corporate Websites reveals news and information that has no authorship. This allows the corporate party line to be processed and pasteurized until all the flavor and nutrition have been extracted and its provenance indeterminable. Lack of accountability has proliferated and promoted the faceless, nameless bureaucratic "they" who are to blame for all the world's ills, for government's abuses, and for management's cluelessness. In journalism, writers and reporters fight to get their names on articles, to do a stand-up or sign-off at the end of their broadcast piece, to have their shirt-tail professional description attached at the end of a story. Much of today's organizational communication seems to encourage the opposite: hide the source, fudge the quotes, bland the voice, and exculpate the author.

Strategic corporate journalism demands accuracy extracted through accountability, not anonymity. This does not mean that all the questions a strategic corporate journalist has about a topic need to be answered fully. They just need to be answered. "No comment" or "that is confidential" are indeed acceptable answers under varied circumstances, usually limited to periods of sensitive business negotiation, strategically timed product introductions, or during the SEC-required "quiet period" when news and information that is not material needs to be kept under wraps so as not to affect or unduly influence stock price prior to financial result announcement. No answer, however, is unacceptable when a question begs response and can be reasonably answered.

Reporters in the journalism world are encouraged to get multiple sources for their stories to guarantee accuracy. Bob Woodward and Carl Bernstein, as depicted in the movie *All The President's Men,* were required by the *Washington Post's* Ben Bradlee to "second source" their information before the newspaper ran any allegation. This practice of multiple sourcing and fact checking has suffered a bit with the race to publication and crunch to airtime, but it is still a basic tenet of good reporting. Accuracy, though still not ensured, is more likely under this scenario.

In the corporate realm, stories are all too often produced or published with single sources or single, usually inwardly focused, perspectives. Although a reporter in a corporation may speak with a number of people, the hierarchical nature of the organization can create a virtual single voice. Dissent or differing perspectives become imperceptible. This puts the onus on the reporter to seek out an alternate perspective, even if it is not found within the usual and more comfortable information tracts. It requires an enterprise perspective, editorial support, and a sense of mission to go outside the defined bounds and give the story a viewpoint that is less homogeneous and, at times, challenging to the status quo. Cross-checking engineering, financial, and marketing perspectives, for example, usually uncovers corporate "inaccuracies" that, if published one-dimensionally, lead to spin. Accuracy is the goal and credibility is the reward for this type of corporate reportorial foray.

Recall when one part of IBM's organization in the 1980s made claims that pursuing a personal computer (PC) to compete with the Apple II was a waste of time and effort, and when that viewpoint was widely distributed. Analysis of the personal computer market failed to make progress—especially since conventional wisdom at the conservative, mainframe-computer company supported this belief. It would take a strategic corporate reporter's initiative and drive, as well as a willing and trusting audience, to pursue the opposing (and in the end accurate) viewpoint that a PC could change the company's fortunes for the better. The news and analysis came from the external press and influenced the renegade internal IBM teams. An internal news organization could have used this information in a predictive way to catalyze and align the change more quickly, with this justification: the risk may seem high, but the reward is potentially great because the truth is a great defense, a terrific argument, and sometimes the foundation for a new business model. But only, that is, if the enlightened organization does not feel it necessary to kill the messenger.

A "Deep Throat" communications manager at a Fortune 100 company who wished to remain anonymous talked about how journalism can link knowledge to help make better predictive decisions: "All business is in a sense forecasting . . . we forecast what products people will buy, what we should make, how much we should advertise, etc. Journalism, too is a form of choosing information in context, forecasting what is important, from all possible content." Asking the hard questions and forcing strategy creation by headlining it may, in fact, be forecasting.

FREE PRESS

A reporter only feels as free to pursue a story as the editor encourages and the publisher supports. Break that chain, and the reporter is a lone voice in the void. The editor can only encourage a reporter to go after and round a story that is acceptable or appropriately sold to the publisher. The publisher is answerable to just one entity: the owner. In a liberal, free, and democratic press, the publisher worries mainly about the bottom line. The stories are inconsequential—as long as they hold to the mission of the organization, have the potential to increase circulation or viewership (and therefore revenue), follow general journalistic principles and practices, and are not actionable in terms of libel.

More than any other journalistic element, it is here that the broader corporate world intersects cleanly with corporate journalism since today's media empires closely resemble the modern intellectual-capital-based enterprise. Time Warner, News Corporation, Times-Mirror, and other conglomerates do not measure their profit-to-earnings ratios through the manufacture of goods, but through the generation and distributed sale of ideas and content. Their assets are the people who work for them and their ability to manage content.

As is regularly highlighted by Brill's Content (the self-proclaimed "independent voice of the information age" that acts as an unappointed check on the press and media), the challenge today for media organizations is how to fight the cooption threatened by synergy. How do they maintain editorial control when the corporations they work for have very clear and specific business goals and interests with which there is often conflict? How is an independent editorial voice maintained?

Although the issues of timeliness and accuracy in reporting can be a result of process and personnel development, achieving editorial independence and relative freedom is made up less of functional steps. The first requirement is proven ability and trust between the editorial team and an executive team combined with the strength of editorial personality and political will. Where a corporation's purpose is clear and the publisher is aligned with the purpose, values, and vision, then the publisher needs to be given the freedom and acceptance by management to pursue the independently decided necessary stories. If management is pushing the publisher to do a feel-good piece on something that is irrelevant to the purpose or contrary to the values of the corporation, the publisher needs to have guts, authority, smarts, and editorial clarity to counter the request when appropriate. This is not the exercise of blind power or expressive dictate; it is earned respect and the authority to pursue commonly agreed-upon business objectives.

Madonna is a very newsworthy personage to put on the cover of *Time*. But does the Time-Warner contract with Madonna make it difficult for a publisher or executive editor to suggest a different cover story? Disney is one of the world's great entertainment content providers and has myriad theme parks, some of which have been used by the ABC television network as places from which to broadcast their programs. Would the Universal Studios theme park in Florida, Knott's Berry Farm in Southern California, or Tivoli in Copenhagen be options for similar broadcasts if appropriate? Can a corporate editor refuse to publish a story from an executive, or one that is inconsistent with another executive's message?

Conflicts of interest, real or perceived, do not serve the need for independence; they devalue the currency of credibility. In a nonmedia corporate context, does the news organ promote rather than review? Do editors act sycophantically, or with a level of objectivity? Is the media a strategic tool of corporate policy, or a mediocratic management toy? What does corporate news independence look like, and how is it expressed?

Once again, societal journalism teaches a course. In the 1970s, the Pentagon Papers were published despite enormous pressure from the government's administrative and judicial branches. The strength of the publishers at the *Washington Post* and the *New York Times* afforded them the necessary independence and rectitude to pursue the story and publish the findings. In the corporate arena, it might not yet be the role of the strategic journalist to run exposés or turn investigative pieces into advocacy or management inquisitions. It might, however, be part of the corporate news organization's charge to uncover and appropriately highlight deficiencies affecting operations where they exist, as well as to praise success where it is real. Either by force of personality or strength of position in the corporate hierarchy, the strategic corporate journalist's publisher needs access and buy-in for a relatively independent and fully credible journalistic mission to be successful. In the corporate world, a publisher who is powerful and respected enough enjoys management's support. The publisher in this instance has the visibility necessary to extract information with authority under corporate auspices. The publisher's role and actions in a corporation—in the end not too unlike those of an institutional ombudsman—are understood by all to be both officially sanctioned and encouraged.

Developing and maintaining the independence of the publisher and the news organization require that both apply advanced analytical and critical abilities. These skills need to be exercised intelligently in any news organization to maintain a competitive edge, and for the readership, audience, and the corporate entity to gain insight. The right mix of news stories and information is possible as a result of this understanding and leads to the proper weighing of news values.

WEIGHING NEWS VALUE

Ensuring the right editorial mix for a specific audience is more art than science. Seasoned journalists point to their midsection when asked where the decision is made. The gut plays a more important role than gray matter. Balancing intestinal fortitude with advanced wrenching and experience with instinct is a developable talent. It is only acquired from years of working the details, making the hundreds of little negotiations required daily in assembling a news program. The best editors and publishers are people who are less institutionally or hierarchically oriented, infinitely curious, and broadly read; who have a healthy sense of self (but are not egocentric) and a broad range of life experiences; and who can maintain emotional distance and multiple perspectives, yet have a strong sense of justice without being moralists.

In short, the modern renaissance corporation and information structures call for those who are themselves modern renaissance people. The intersection of business and society, politics and economy, and globalism and locality have created a greater need for the generalists of the world to be able to annotate and harmonize the information noise.

General interest magazines and newspapers have in many ways given up on the challenge of providing this higher standard of analysis. Instead, they have passed the baton to those newspapers continuing to accept the responsibility with gravity. The *New York Times* continues to be the paper of record and employs some of the highest standards in journalism. While others opt to focus on celebrities and the movie of the month, the *Times* takes such news into account but focuses primarily on the political, business, and societal issues of the day and tries to synthesize them into a coherent whole within its pages. The *Times* maintains its foreign bureaus, invests in technology, and generally exploits its access, reputation, and resources in the pursuit of timely and accurate news reporting. It looks at the world holistically and provides a global perspective for an American audience.

In the corporate world, the equivalent of the *New York Times* is hard to find. Which corporations employ the right mix of personnel and policy to allow timely and accurate reporting that consistently maintains a global perspective? Media properties themselves, the best positioned of corporate entities, are notoriously bad at self-examination and reporting. To ferret out the inner workings of the *New York Times*, one was more likely to find it in the regular gossip feature in *Spy* magazine. Letters to the *New Yorker* were also to be found only in *Spy* prior to Tina Brown's reign as editor-in-chief. Likewise, news about the inner workings of some companies is easier to find in chat rooms of the online community The Well, for example, than around the corporation's watercoolers.

Finding the right people, the discipline, and the political will to risk the level of introspection and self-analysis that is brought about in a strategic corporate journalistic organization is more than most companies are currently willing to do. Couple this with the need to move away from intraorganizational myopia and examine and weigh related external news and trends. There is understandable discomfort, and there could also be dramatic resistance from the executive ranks. That is, of course, unless they see that the changes at work in their industries and the global society are demanding a new information infrastructure—one where advanced editorial activities are not just desirable but perhaps necessary to catalyze institutional change, awaken innovation, promote dialogue, challenge assumption, decentralize power, promote flatter hierarchies, manage knowledge, and provide both a framework and running observation of the process. The new corporation is facing a plethora of new challenges; strategic corporate journalism provides a means to deal with them.

THE NEW CORPORATION

Conventional wisdom suggests that a social, cultural, or business trend is no longer a trend once it makes the cover of *Time*. Bearing this in mind, we see a number of trends regarding the new economy and business that have been identified by *Wired*; or more precisely, in a very real advertiser's pitch for the Guinness Flight Wired Index Fund. The ad is a nice, pithy summary of some of the sociotechnological trends that we detail in Chapter One. The pitch goes like this (sans the lime green, electric orange-pink colors of the original):

> The new millennium is dawning, and with it a new economy. As the industrial age is ushered out by this new era, a shift is taking place. Today:
>
> ■ People are working more with their brains, not their hands
>
> ■ More and more companies need to sell and market globally
>
> ■ Innovation, not mass production, is the key to success
>
> ■ Increasingly, industry is fueled by ideas—not machines
>
> ■ Change is the only constant*

These trends have created a new set of expectations and conditions for the modern corporation, which today needs to monitor and compete with external news to keep up with the credible information flow. To meet many of these new information expectations, the corporation has to adopt journalistic principles and practices.

The organization must be more sensitive to the type of information required to keep this new organization running. In the external world of journalism, information is assessed through thorough understanding of the audience and its lifestyle, demographics, habits, hobbies, attention spans, etc. In the best world of journalism, news organizations balance what they perceive as the information demands of their audience with the information needs of that audience.

---

*Used by permission of Investec Guinness Flight.

Public-service journalism is a good example of this type of work. Until the early part of the Reagan administration, the Federal Communications Commission (FCC) required broadcasters to allot and give away free airtime for community and public-service programming. Nonprofit organizations such as San Francisco's Commonwealth Club or the World Affairs Council presented half-hour weekly radio programs to provide public education on current global and domestic political issues. It was one of the few places on the radio dial where commercial audiences could listen to in-depth analysis of the International Monetary Fund or Angolan politics. Of course, the audiences were made up primarily of insomniacs or long-haul truckers, since most of the programming ran in the wee hours of the night. The tradition of public-service journalism survives in print, however, with newspapers running series such as "Great Decisions" or special election outtakes.

This distinction—giving the public what it needs as well as what it wants—may be a bit fuzzy, but it is nonetheless important in a functioning democracy where citizens are responsible to be informed and engaged in the political process. If a news organization serves up only the type of information that people desire as indicated by polls and surveys, then salacious and nutrition-free sex and lifestyle stories will fill the news hole. The most responsible news organizations understand that the news diet needs to include world news roughage and political meat if the body politic is to remain healthy.

So, too, the new corporation needs to understand what is desired and what is needed by the information-consuming employees without overwhelming by adding to information overload or exacerbating the pace of change. In a highly competitive information environment and with easy-to-use Internet browsers, employees can visit any of the myriad financial sites reporting on a company's financial news as easily as they can click to the corporate home page. To attract and service its employee audience better, the corporation should have the more complete and analytical story or combination of stories. This corporate news source can also be responsible for building a sense of community—something that is unavailable, other than virtually, with the external news organization. News about the people within an organization with whom others share a workplace, experience success, develop personal relationships, etc., is a necessary function of the internal news organization, in the same way that local newspapers report on social functions and run birth, engagement, and death notices. The point is a simple one: to service a community of any sort requires alignment with the values of that community, active defense and support of those values and vision, and understanding of the information needs and desires of the community.

For news dissemination in small organizations, the "town crier" method and community meetings can serve this function, but in larger and growing organizations the means to deliver news and information need to replicate those of the mass media. It also means that collecting, editing, and writing the news must more accurately reflect the practices and principles of free journalism.

In the real world, failure on the part of a mass circulation periodical or broadcast station to meet both journalistic standards and the interest of its audience is easy to measure. Circulation figures or viewership ratings are the quantifiable (and often fluctuating) metrics that indicate success. In the corporate world, such metrics are harder to come by, though intranet page hits and the "stickiness" of certain sites can indicate successful messaging. E-mail messages and letters to the editor can also gauge the usefulness and attractiveness of a medium and its message.

As previously mentioned, these new organizations are really more like diverse intellectual communities with the characteristics of democratic society. It is not simply circumstance that many of the high-technology corporations in Silicon Valley, for example, refer to their buildings and offices as part of a larger "campus." Workplaces seek to replicate the intellectual freedom and the type of inquiry encouraged on campuses of higher learning. This intellectual freedom is aided and abetted by credible sources of information about the system itself and the degree to which it is able to compete and remain credible vis-à-vis external news and information sources.

These organizations are also voluntarily developing, and competitively encouraged to become as flat and nonhierarchical as possible, pushing decision making as far down the chain of command as is feasible. By eliminating unnecessary bureaucratic layers in the decision-making process, the organization can function in a quicker and more streamlined fashion, adapting and reacting to change as necessary. But the ability to make good decisions and react appropriately requires a system of informing and aligning that is organic: fast, accurate, compelling, and credible. Pushing decisions down the line is not going to help if the new decision makers are making uninformed decisions, or ones based (in the worst case) on false or misleading information.

Values and vision play an important part in the new organization's community because they are a motivator (if not the primary one) for work in a larger society where labor is fluid and monetary remuneration plays a role but is not always the deciding reason for choosing to work in one place versus another. In fact, where this is the case, the value the new corporation puts on the free flow of information and the respect it shows for its corporate values and vision can attract and keep the most highly desirable and innovative thinkers. Consequently, these workers also tend to be highly demanding individuals. Call it the "America factor," where emigrating individuals worldwide often choose the United States as their ultimate emigration destination, despite the economic challenge the country poses for new arrivals. A healthy respect for the constitutional vision of rule of law, freedom of expression and belief, and the means for individuals to contribute to the health and wellbeing of the nation are basic American tenets. This cannot help but be woven into the corporate fabric. The inherently felt rights and consequent sense of entitlement create even greater demands and expectations of both the political system and the corporate structure. In these diverse, democratized, knowledge-based corporations that are overwhelmed with information and change and compete in a networked global economy, open, accurate, timely, and weighted information flow is critical to survival.

STRATEGIC CORPORATE JOURNALISM

Just as the new corporation has a communal employee population with differing expectations and demands, the new environment in which the corporation exists has a new set of information challenges it must meet head-on.

The first challenge, from a purely defensive posture, is to understand that controlling information is nearly impossible. Perhaps not long ago control over information was possible to a degree, but the proliferation of new technologies has made such control all but impossible today. The hard walls of the corporate environment were rendered semipermeable with the introduction of the telephone into the workplace and then almost fully permeable with the expansion of personal computer and Internet technologies that interconnect individuals and organizations worldwide, instantaneously, and without prejudice. The result is that information regarding competition, markets, economic change, political uncertainty, technological advance, health concerns, and thousands of other issues that can help or hinder the corporate mission are much more readily and quickly available. On the other hand, whatever brings invaluably helpful information can just as easily deliver disruptive information—whether or not it is true. The challenge is to have the informational infrastructure in place not only to deal with arising crises but also to deliver with consistency journalistically sound and credible information that quiets or counters the noise from the outside.

The Berlin Wall was not a metaphoric means for excluding printed materials from highly controlled East Germany. It was a very effective, nearly 100 percent blockade against material contraband of any sort. What it could not stop effectively, however, were the television and radio waves that wafted over the wall amid the clouds and across the antennas of clandestinely tuned receivers. The news regarding Soviet intentions not to interfere militarily in the internal affairs of the East Bloc and Warsaw Pact countries was spread not by East German news organs but by Western journalists and reporters. This news, understood by most analysts as a catalyst for the repressed populace to shed its fear of open organization and protest, was neither preempted nor credibly countered by the propaganda oriented services of the east. As a result, the pre-Internet-browsing days of 1989 heralded the reverse domino effect, where news of one Eastern European country after another toppling its communist government fueled the remaining ones to follow suit.

How does this translate inside the corporate walls? In 1998, Intel Corporation turned to the courts to get a restraining order on a former employee who "spammed" a majority of the company with e-mail regarding alleged corporate wrongdoings and practices. Some of the allegations were rumored to have been fed to the disgruntled former employee by current employees. Corporate leadership was forced to respond quickly to deny and counter the allegations, but some of the assertions had a ring of truth to them and persisted in corporate hallways. Intel chose to create a legal wall to keep out such disruptive information, but the wall can only be as strong as the corporation is forthcoming with its employee population. No amount of technological filters or prior restraint can keep out a credible and just argument.

For this reason, an internal news organization needs to operate with a competitive understanding that information regarding the corporation and its industry should be gathered and delivered before external news entities do it. At times, the best that can be hoped for is contemporaneous release of news and information (for example, SEC-regulated material information that can affect stock price). For the most part, however, an internal news organization should have the one thing unavailable to the external competing news sources: primary access to the news makers and information. This access can be used or abused. There is always the danger that leadership that grants access does not perceive or understand the strategic journalistic use of its information for anything other than propagandistic purposes. If the information is used properly, however, organizational credibility is created and reinforced through timely, fair, and accurate reporting, while alternate, competing news and information sources lose their appeal to the defined audience.

Furthermore, just as there is no longer absolute control over information, distribution can also no longer be totally regulated. The new technologies, much like radio and television waves, are virtually free means of distribution. New technologies no longer require printing presses or copy machines or paper, for that matter. The proliferation of and access to new technologies has let the genie out of the bottle.

Even though China may have been happy that the fax machine increased business efficiency to build its export business, it was less than pleased with the role it played in the democracy movement of 1989, when dissidents alerted the world to their plight and the Tienanmen crackdown. The Chinese leadership is equally disturbed by World Wide Web usage for similar purposes today. In fact, in its attempt to control the political dissidents' use of the Web, the Chinese government convicted and jailed a "Webmaster" who was, he says, trying to improve his business by trading mailing lists with an American. Unfortunately for the Chinese Webmaster, the American exploited the e-mail list blatantly to promote the agenda of the Chinese prodemocracy movement.

Accepting the fact that both information and its dissemination are no longer controllable can create a climate of fear, or one of openness. The argument for strategic corporate journalism favors the latter, despite the default position and natural tendency of many a management team to retrench and defend whenever it feels threatened or under direct attack.

Fostering openness and naturally ensuing dialogue is a healthy way of airing organizational issues. It is also time-honored journalistic practice. Mistakes are often corrected on the pages of newspapers; equal time is often given to opposing viewpoints on the air;

and letters to the editor, opinions, and editorials are frequently available as a feedback and input mechanism. The advent of e-mail has certainly made such a feedback mechanism possible in the new technology landscape.

Andy Grove, the former CEO of Intel, knew that his employees would not necessarily sit idly by if their observations and concerns were not being met by management that would filter up their perspectives. He therefore encouraged e-mail to put the individual employee in direct contact with the CEO, making sure the information he gleaned could function many times more effectively and directly in urgent matters than interactions with a mediator.

The amount of information that can filter up as a result is overwhelming, however. The president of the United States does not read all the country's newspapers or constituents' mail but instead relies on staff to edit and condense this information in news summaries. As a matter of efficiency, this model works for corporations as well and makes the intermediating news organization a perfect candidate for receiving, summarizing, and raising the issues to those in power. If done effectively, this letters-to-the-editor and op-ed function can save time and repetition for a leadership that needs to address many other more pressing and focused issues while still allowing the corporate community members the means for mediated interaction. It also gives the internal news organization another source of information from the grassroots level—a vital pulse taking of the employee base—often spurring new directions to investigate and report. This can only be done, however, if the organization retains credibility and is effective at getting timely, fair, and accurate answers. It is this journalistic approach that leverages the trends and technologies that have led to the new corporation and provides an organizational neural network that enables employees to quickly learn, adapt, and organically align toward the corporate vision and ever-changing nuances of a successful implementation of that vision.

To develop a model of strategic corporate journalism, one would examine the organizational communication elements of content, distribution, and style and overlay them with journalistic principles and practices, within an attempt to create as much organized information fluidity as possible. What would strategic corporate journalism look like in actuality? In Chapter Five, we showcase examples of companies implementing journalistic elements. Before we peer under the hood of different corporate structures, let's first examine these journalistic elements in utopian fashion.

Like the *New York Times* or the *Wall Street Journal,* organizational communication (including executive, managerial, and corporate communication) should be trusted and respected. "Corporatespeak" should not be used or accepted.

In the (ideal) corporate world, a free press means that communication flows openly. "Marketingspeak" or any other spun news can be challenged without fear of retribution. Like gossip columns, rumor mills become formalized and used as a metric of the organization's pulse. With such mechanisms as letters to the editor, questions are asked and a nonmanipulative, reflective answer expected. External press—both positive and negative—are available and contextualized so that organizational myopia can be avoided. As with the Clinton impeachment, leaders can be openly challenged and held accountable for their leadership decisions. Cross-company distribution channels prevail. Targeted distribution channels for confidential information flow are broadly understood and respected as critical to organizational success. Leaders' communication styles are open and personal and invite dialogue. Primary organizational communications channels all have an interactive component. All feedback channels are clearly articulated; all messages are authored, indicate recipients, and set response-time expectations. In global organizations, worldwide distribution channels send messages out seamlessly.

All managers within the (optimal) organization understand their role as organizational communicators and the ultimate goal of alignment and action toward the corporate vision, objectives, and operational strategies. Managers do not communicate out of internal competitiveness or to promote a personal agenda but instead strive for timely and frequent communication to synchronize, integrate, contextualize, clarify, repeat, inform, and interact.

Even in difficult times, information flows openly in this utopian organization. Poor economic forecasts are not hidden, and turbulence is predicted like weather reports, enabling the knowledge workforce to plan recoupment strategies. Even layoff situations are handled openly and honestly. Employees use the word *we* more, and *they* less. This kind of openness engenders intraorganizational trust and thus disables barriers to information absorption such as confusion, apathy, and blame.

As these tenets play out in the idealized corporate world, accuracy is not questioned or challenged. Editorial standards such as those presented by the Associated Press (AP) or the *Chicago Manual of Style* are adopted. Research and editorial review become standard practice. Inaccuracies are highlighted, published, and retracted. Contextualization is not skewed or hyped. Communication is not fragmentary; it is consistent, complete, and integrated. Unbiased analyses blend internal strategies, external trends, and competitive threats to paint an accurate reflection of the operating landscape. All communications are well researched, multisourced, and authored, and they have feedback channels so that accuracy can be challenged. Multimedia channels are more common since additional graphical representation, audio, and video create a more accurate reflection than text alone.

Vague references and descriptions are clarified and qualified. Empty promises are not tolerated. For truly legal, sensitive, or confidential matters, answers like "that matter is confidential" are used instead of "I don't know." Executives do not need to become actors, and words do not need to be spun.

Weighing news value means that corporate vision and strategies are clearly understood by all organizational communicators and content is weighed and contextualized for diverse audiences and against success factors. Communicators vigilantly distinguish between strategic weighting and manipulation; checks and balances clarify this distinction. Broadly agreed-upon editorial goals and audience feedback ensure that weighting doesn't become a hype tool. Metrics monitor usage and indicate when stories need to be refreshed. Formal editorial responsibilities are no longer limited to policies, procedures, and legalese but instead become common throughout the organization. Important messages are repeated until they are branded into the organizational psyche. Thematic series are used to achieve focus. Contextualization of important messages takes a broad focus, including historical and external trends.

In this best of corporate worlds, communications departments create a balance between forward-looking strategic pieces, current external news and trends, and incoming organizational messages. Metrics, executive access, and feedback channels are used to correct the course of organizational behavior. Undue bias toward corporate headquarters does not survive. Rather, equal distribution across all organizational audiences reigns.

Executive influence helps achieve strategic weighting. "Owners" of push or broadcast channels police them to ensure appropriate weighting. These channels should not be coopted for individual exploitation—even by executives. This policing may take the form of strict guidelines around organizationwide e-mail, voice mail, and intranet portals, yet it should not restrict use of these channels based solely on the position of the communicator. The content should dictate this weighting process. In a perfect organic corporate system, this policing is not necessary; knowledge workers know when to push information and when not to. Savvy editors with a combination of business, communication, and cultural acumen make decisions according to editorial goals and processes.

———

Internet response time now sets the standard for timeliness. Organizations cannot turn back to the days of timely preparedness and careful orchestration. Writing, production, approval, editing, distribution, and cross-organizational synchronization processes must all be geared for reactive, nearly immediate response. An elastic and acculturated distribution network should enable the full, complex range of communications, from instantaneous push or crisis to orchestrated pull (for example, a forward-looking feature); from time-sensitive messages requiring action (benefits enrollment) to heads-up reminders requiring planning (companywide meetings); from important company announcements (financial results) to detailed information that needs companywide attention (area code change); or from companywide interaction (rumor mill) to one-on-one dialogue (project management). This network should also inform and not overwhelm. Communicators must balance the network's various push and pull channels to achieve target coverage without information overload.

In addition to an effective distribution network, central communications departments need to have reliable informants and a network of communications contacts to quickly get the information and blanket a global audience. Messages also have to be synchronized across a variety of internal and external channels.

Corporate organizations should not directly compete with external efficiencies of information dissemination, but rather operate with expectations set across the organization about which messages are to be as timely as the external media and which are to be more broadly contextualized and internally synchronized. As long as these expectations are set, external channels need not be censored. The most personally sensitive messages are distributed first internally, and employees understand the realities of resource constraints. Organizational trust, alignment, and action ensue.

Strategic corporate journalism—or the open, accurate, timely, and weighted flow of information—is fundamental to success within the knowledge economy. Figure 2.7 (in Chapter Two) depicts the development of a communication strategy that, at its best, leads to action toward aligned innovation. The *knowledge equation* below represents the same goal by supplanting communication strategy with strategic corporate journalism (SCJ) plus interaction:

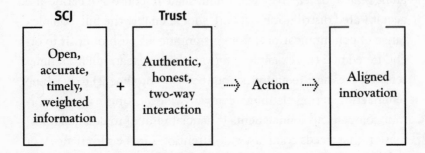

Does this sound far-fetched or impossible? Let's take a look at some examples of corporate journalism in action.

5

Corporate Journalism in Action

Brief History

Examples of Corporate Journalism

Progress—and Room to Grow

I n Chapter Four, we introduced strategic corporate journalism, the blending of journalistic principles with a corporate communication model. In this chapter, expect to see some of these ideas played out in real, live corporate situations. First, a brief historical perspective of corporate journalism.

BRIEF HISTORY

The concept of corporate journalism is not entirely new. In fact, the origins of organizational communication are rooted in journalistic elements. For example, the International Association of Business Communicators (IABC), an association for employee communications professionals, was formed out of a merger of the American Association of Industrial Editors (founded in 1910) and the International Council of Industrial Editors (established in 1944), both organizations with journalistic underpinnings.

Today most communications groups, including corporate communications organizations, use language rife with journalistic references: *newsflash, senior editor, company magazine,* etc. The corporate newsletter, a concept pulled from journalistic news and adapted for corporate communication needs, has been a part of many organizational communication strategies since the early 1940s. This journalistic legacy is not new, but the heightened focus on journalistic principles and practices coupled with other key elements make corporate journalism more powerful than the promises of a simple corporate newsletter.

As established in Chapter Three, credibility is the foundation for journalism. Simply using journalistic principles and practices does not necessarily mean that credibility follows. What makes community newsletters different from the *New York Times* or the *Wall Street Journal?* The breadth of focus; the writing quality; the variety of content, resources, and independence as a primary information source all play a part. These differentiating elements that identify superior journalistic approaches translate directly into the corporate world.

The difference between strategic corporate journalism and other organizational communication models is the relative importance of specific communication elements, namely frequency and openness (see Chapter Two). An incredibly reputable journalistic publication distributed once a year will not influence ongoing corporate alignment the way daily journalistic communications can.

Ethical and accurate reporting of past and current events in and of itself—no matter how contextualized, integrated, and consistent—is not adequate to achieve the alignment essential to organizational success. The two greatest relative differences are the degree of openness and bias. Corporate spin results from closed, myopic, and hyped communications. Because of the natural ivory-tower tendencies of organizations, corporate journalism (like societal journalism) should continuously challenge the boundaries of openness and bias.

Yet, as indicated in Chapter Four, there are also points of divergence between corporate journalism and societal journalism. They stem from the differences in goals of societal alignment and organizational alignment. Societal alignment is a much more fluid concept than organizational journalism. Societal journalism plays almost purely to the pulse of the people, against the background of the guiding principles and tenets of the society. Organizational journalism focuses on the organization's specific vision and goals. This level of specificity details the difference. It requires more contextualization. Within the wide landscape of societal tenets, societal journalists do not need to provide focused context. General references to constitutional rights and cultural value systems are enough. The corporate journalist must point toward, and subsequently contextualize, a specific vision.

Societal journalists don't necessarily strive for broad message sequencing or synchronicity. In fact, they strive for just the opposite: to be first out of the chute. This is true even though, interestingly enough, tightly knit journalistic relationships and common market forces drive what is "hot news" and seem to create synchronicity. A quick look at a current magazine stand reveals dramatic thematic similarities. Again due to the specificity under which an organization needs to align, organizational synchronization must be much more precise.

To achieve sequencing or synchronicity, a corporate journalism model must be integrated with all the communication factions within the organization: employee communications, investor relations, public relations, marketing communications, and industry relations. Since this broadscale interaction and reporting cannot be achieved single-handedly from a central corporate communications organization, those who centrally coordinate broadscale organizational communications must also educate all organizational communicators about how to collaborate, synchronize, and sequence their communications to achieve organizationwide alignment.

Another variance from societal journalism is the frequency of change regarding the direction of overarching alignment. Most societies don't alter their guiding tenets frequently; for example, in the 220-some years of U.S. independence, only twenty-seven amendments have been added to the Constitution (including the ten amendments of the Bill of Rights included when the Constitution was adopted by the states). Most organizations, however, do make fundamental shifts during their life span. This fluctuating specificity means that corporate journalism must keep pace and corporate journalists must learn to stay abreast of transformed vision, changing goals, and reinvented strategies.

EXAMPLES OF CORPORATE JOURNALISM

Though standard corporate newsletters and magazines did not necessarily constitute corporate journalism, some companies have effected change with these tools. Through its evolution, the corporate newsletter has functioned to hype the organization from an internal perspective; over the years corporate communicators have begun to integrate journalistic publishing disciplines into these newsletters.

John Gerstner, manager of electronic communications at John Deere, has worked in the corporate realm since 1968. He describes the concept of corporate journalism with an illustration:

> I would offer you *JD Journal*, the corporate magazine of John Deere, which I launched in 1972 and edited until 1998. In my final editor's note, I wrote:
>
> "I am leaving the world of print to focus on the Internet, becoming Deere's first manager of corporate electronic communication. I won't miss the deadlines (or those wiseacres who find typos in our printed haystack). But I will miss the daunting—though very rewarding— challenge of translating the heartbeat and spirit of this incredibly huge and fast-paced 158-year-old organization into words and pictures in a magazine.
>
> "I once wrote in a communications journal that the

best corporate magazines 'move minds, raise sights and spirits, and make waves on distant shores.' I think we've done some of that. Thank you, John Deere people world-wide, for all your great stories."

So . . . have I been a corporate journalist all these years? I definitely think so [personal interview].

Moving minds, raising sights and spirits, and making waves on distant shores. This is the domain of the corporate communicator, the place where the seeds of corporate journalism find fertile ground.

Some companies migrated from text into the audiovisual jour-nalistic production. For over ten years, Citibank's Consumer Bank in the United States ran an internal audio show offering toll-free access, with journalistically reported features central to its content. Citibank also incorporated a video series, "Bank Beat," that "used documentary journalistic approaches to bring people and events alive," says Judith Binney, director of international communications at Citicorp's North America Consumer Bank (personal interview).

Other companies have advanced to broadcast video. When Tan-dem Corporation realized how much money they were spending on the creation and distribution of videos to their employees, "they de-cided to create Tandem Television Network (TTN) and produce 'First Friday,' a monthly worldwide broadcast to all Tandem offices," according to Nancy Hill, one of the original cohosts and former human resources manager at Tandem. "Although modeled after 'Saturday Night Live,' with entertaining skits and financial forecasts from 'Buck Profit,' the news portion of the show adhered to jour-nalistic practices."

Hill remembers her training for the show: "We hired a profes-sional anchor trainer who coached me in everything from appro-priate facial expressions to prompt monitor reading." She and her cohosts would interview Tandem executives, broadcast-news-style, on tough or complex issues such as strategy, operational effective-ness, and restructuring. "The restructuring show was the hardest show I did," she says; "I asked edgy questions. We had to surface the real issues." Prior to the broadcast, employees submitted questions and the anchors also fielded live questions from listeners—no questions were censored. "'First Friday' was special. When we did our sign-off show ('First Friday' ran for four years), everybody burst out crying. Ten years later, people in the supermarket still tell me how wonderful I was and what a difference I made. It was a lot of fun, but it was the journalistic approach that made the difference," says Hill (personal interview).

In addition to strict journalistic production standards (Hill jokes about how similar it was to a live news show in the way that her director called her and the others "Talent A" or "Talent B"), Tandem tried to create openness with the show's content and tone. Hill describes the nature of "First Friday's" impact: "It created a sense of community with an open flow of communication, warts and all. It created commitment. Seeing Jim Treybig [the CEO] and the executives telling it straight kept employees bought in."

Although "First Friday" was open, it was not unbiased. It remained totally inwardly focused. Even the tag line, "It's Real World," conveyed a sense of isolation, self-containment, and impermeability.

This insularity is not uncommon. Many internal communicators feel a need to "protect" employees from the damage of bad external press. In fact, some companies only acknowledge external information if it becomes so visible that it can't be ignored. When forced to acknowledge the news, companies often manipulate the message, demonize the external media, or falsely contextualize the information. In 1997 BusinessWeek published a cover story about SGI titled "The Sad Saga of Silicon Graphics." At first, SGI executives did not want to acknowledge the article in a companywide meeting held that very week. They were naturally uncomfortable and concerned that highlighting negative press might demotivate employees. As the day of the meeting approached, the rumor mill was distractingly thick. Upon reevaluation, CEO Ed McKracken did mention the article but (perhaps because the article personally attacked him) did so disparagingly, challenging BusinessWeek as having an ax to grind and "not having the real story."

Some companies, whether understanding the need for external checks and balances or feeling forced by the unbounded nature of the Internet, have begun to eliminate corporate barriers to external information access. Mario Juarez, communications manager at Microsoft, provides intranet links directly to external press coverage—both good and bad:

> We offer a set of daily e-mail and Web-based news distribution services (with stories from a multitude of external print and online sources) that we edit based on straightforward journalistic criteria. We run stories from the major media about the DOJ [Department of Justice] trial, and many are high-profile, negative, and very contrary to the company's version of the situation. We published a big *Seattle Times* report ["Microsoft Aims to Enhance Agility as Internet Landscape Shifts"] about a major [reorganization] that had in no way been announced internally. Not only did this become a big national story that we also represented in subsequent postings, it cast the company and certain executives in a very unflattering light [personal interview].

Insularity, or this desire to keep employees focused on the positive internal story, causes many corporations to sin by omission. Because of the ubiquity of information inside and outside the organization, employees are not likely to be protected from the message. If management attempts to do so, the corporation falls into the propaganda trap, and accuracy suffers. Employees can sense the corporate spin. Credibility dives, and alignment is impossible. Avoiding this rose-colored-glasses syndrome in organizational communications is as onerous for most CEOs as it was for Nikita Khrushchev with *Pravda*. Some companies, like Microsoft, have begun to understand the value of not censoring this information from the corporate networks.

It is one thing to provide easy access to the external press during the good times. If under attack or if performance is down, this communication takes on quite a different flavor. An external article predicting a company's downfall may be more than a bit uncomfortable for a CEO to speak to. Many organizations close down communications during times of crisis.

Organizations that openly address difficult situations earn credibility and create informed ambassadors. Shel Holtz, former communications representative for Arco and current president of Holtz Communication and Technology, a consulting firm in California, recalls how Arco dealt with negative external press that was reporting a highly publicized mishap. "When I was at Arco, Pump Station 8 on the Alaska pipeline blew up; a number of people were killed. Our reporting educated employees about the cause, the people who were lost, and a host of other issues. We also reported immediately whenever Arco was the subject of, say, a Department of Energy lawsuit or other issues. As a result, employees always felt informed; nothing ever came as a surprise" (personal interview).

Mergers and acquisitions—like arranged marriages and divorces—are fraught with communications challenges that are inherent in any combination of communication styles and expectations. After Travelers announced its merger with Citicorp in April 1998, communication became sporadic and uneven. On the eve of Citibank's normal round of review-and-appraisal meetings in February 1999, Citibank employees learned about an eighteen-month salary increase postponement—via the *Wall Street Journal*. It is probably an understatement to say that senior management took a credibility hit for this incident.

Open and accurate communication is also surprisingly important when communicating seemingly positive news. A 1997 *Harvard Business Review* article explored the importance of including employees in the decision-making process even for good decisions. Regarding a labor agreement in 1992 between Volkswagen management and the union, the article states:

The accord VW [Volkswagen] signed with the union's secretary-general included a generous 20 percent pay raise for employees. VW thought the workers would be pleased. But the union's leaders had not involved the employees in discussions about the contract's terms; they did a poor job of communicating what the new agreement would mean to employees and why a number of work-rule changes were necessary. Workers did not understand the basis for the decisions their leaders had taken. They felt betrayed. VW's management was completely caught off guard . . . when the employees started a massive walkout that cost the company as much as an estimated $10 million per day [Kim and Mauborgne, p. 68].

What does information openness achieve for an organization? The same thing that open communication leads to in any relationship or in effective societal journalism: buy-in, trust, commitment, and alignment. This translates to bottom-line competitiveness.

Other corporate communicators have not only exposed external information but boldly invited external news coverage inside corporate castle walls. Melissa Jones, communications director for MIPS Technologies Inc., a chip manufacturer, advocates exposing the external perspective because of what she believes is the symbiotic nature between external press and internal alignment. Formerly responsible for worldwide communications at Philips Semiconductors, Jones experimented with what she calls "managed journalism." In 1995, the boundaries were more rigid between internal and external news. Jones recalls attempts that year to openly develop relationships with external press and industry analysts: "Philips Semiconductors had not started opening up with information after a major turnaround effort that took several years to complete. Thus, people knew little about us and wanted to know a good deal more. I suggested a Press Day where we would invite members of the press for a managed showcasing of our company and our products. The first reaction was, 'We don't do that kind of a thing!' But we worked through it. It was a great success because Philips ended up getting a lot of external visibility, and we got a chance to understand clearly what the press and industry analysts thought of our strategies, technologies, and products" (personal interview).

Nothing sharpens internal strategies and operations like external checks and balances. Whether or not a company formalizes internal access to external press coverage, the membrane between internal and external news grows more porous with each passing day. Companies that realize this and provide unbiased, contextualized, external information can actually gain credibility with employees for what might at first seem to be negativity.

Some organizations have also created internal checks and balances by openly presenting uncomfortable internal trends. Jay Coleman, communications manager at Hewlett-Packard, published an article by Jim Haberkorn titled "I'm Losing My Job" in the corporate news magazine, *Measure*. The article examines trends in globalization toward overseas production and presents a case study in which an employee, facing the challenges of such a climate, understands that he will probably be forced out of the company. More than simply presenting external trends, the article showcases an individual who feels a personal impact from the trend.

Acknowledging that HP was expanding production offshore rather than in the United States could have made many executive and production employees uncomfortable, or it could have relieved tensions by simply acknowledging the corporate elephant in the boardroom.

Although checks and balances help achieve equilibrium, organizational alignment is not predictive. Many executives pretend that the Tayloristic organization, in which alignment to the organizational vision is not necessary and coglike employees produce results that mechanically add up to success, is still alive. In *Working with Emotional Intelligence*, Daniel Goleman, a communications consultant in northern California, recounts an analysis of Volvo by business consultant Carl Frost during an intensely competitive period. Employees remained apathetic and seemingly unconscious of the crisis at hand. "The blasé attitude, Frost felt, was a sign of troubling communication, one that let workers at Volvo ignore any link between their situation and the larger fate of the company." This lack of connection, Frost claims, "meant employees took little responsibility for helping their company become more competitive" (p. 285). In this case, lack of openness had an adverse impact on employee alignment and organizational effectiveness.

To Levi Strauss & Co. (LS&CO.), this concept of open communications is so important that it is embedded into their corporate values. Former internal communications director Katherine Woodall (currently a business performance communications practice leader, West Region, Towers Perrin) describes LS&CO.'s aspirations, or core values, which are branded internally from day one. One of them is communications that are "actively shared." Every new employee, from the chief executive to a sewing machine operator, attends leadership training where they discuss the corporate aspirations at length. "Employees discuss how this aspiration aligns with their own personal values," Woodall says; "this dialogue leads to a personal internalization of the values" (personal interview). This alignment toward core aspirations helps achieve alignment toward the corporate vision.

Although Microsoft's Juarez understands the concept of alignment and tries to be very clear about what is aligning with what, "Let's be clear about what exactly is the dog here and what exactly is the tail," he says. "Communication is the tail. If the big dog is a bozo, there's no amount of tail wagging that's going to keep it from getting hit by a truck" (personal interview). If the organizational vision and strategy are faulty, all corporate journalism can hope to do is expose the faults earlier rather than later.

A potentially dangerous by-product of strategic weighting in a closed system is propaganda. Although opening up the communications system helps create checks and balances, it doesn't ensure totally unbiased weighting because ultimately someone—the CEO, an editor, the board of directors, the magazine publisher, a communications manager—always decides what should be communicated. Allegiance to an executive, feelings of responsibility or duty toward an owner, or fear of an ownership structure that distributes paychecks all have an impact on those decisions. The age-old question "Who owns the presses?" resounds loudly in the corporate world too. At any given time, it may feel as though various people make final editorial decisions. An executive, the legal department, employee communications, or marketing communications can all perform that function; what's more confusing, the many departments could make widely varying decisions of their own based on the final message.

Two kinds of propaganda—corporatespeak and marketing-speak—poison effective organizational communication. The former represents the corporate position in only positive and sometimes one-sided ways. The latter, designed to generate leads and sell product, can sound equally lopsided to an internal audience that knows the dirty laundry and wants it to be honestly acknowledged. The languages of both corporate and marketing serve valuable purposes. However, they do not line up identically with internal communication objectives. Of course, functionally specific tones can also be a result of where the central internal communications departments report. Overly smarmy HRspeak, overly technical engineeringspeak, overly controlling ISspeak, and overly quantitative financespeak are equally problematic.

Mickey Georges, managing editor of the *Junction* intranet portal at SGI, spends much of her time "pushing back" on corporate-speak, including executivespeak:

> Most people need help tailoring their message to their target audience. The "shotgun" approach is not going to get results.
>
> Evangelizing a global focus and promoting a balanced perspective are my premier skill sets, as it were. Employees, including executives, tend to be headquarters-centric as well as source-centric. In other words, if it's happening at headquarters and the material came from "me" [or someone or somewhere proximate to me], it is obviously the most important story at the moment. And executives seem to specialize in last-minute, critical,

pull-out-all-the-stops communication. Throw it up, see where it sticks. We need to quickly contextualize these messages with other current and/or historical communications. Investor relations and the PR group help us to filter appropriately, and then we publish as soon as possible. Normally the next business day. Sometimes sooner [personal interview].

To maintain a strategic focus, organizational communicators must stay clued in to organization vision, values, and operational strategies. In a world of blurringly fast change, this is not a once-a-year invitation to an executive strategy session; it is an intimate, executive-level relationship.

As corporate journalists struggle with openness, accuracy, and strategic weighting, the Internet muddies the waters with regard to timeliness. On the one hand, communicators have the technical ability to publish content in a moment's notice. On the other hand, many other publishers also have the same ability. As information from so many publishers proliferates, employees can access it. This ready access exacerbates the organizational communicator's responsibility to publish accurate, synchronized information in context. The pressure squeezes the time available for publishing and corporate communicators to try to keep up with the pace: quarterly corporate magazines have birthed monthly newsletters, which have led to weekly broadcast voice mails, which have begotten daily broadcast e-mail, which is now being replaced with real-time intranet news. . . .

Steve Maita, a partner with Maita/Saviano Public Relations, previous director of employee communications at Pacific Bell, attributes their shift from a top-down, traditional style of communications to a more inclusive style to a variety of reasons, including the pervasiveness of the Internet. The growth of the Internet has made objective and even critical news and information about a company, its competitors, and its industry easily and instantly available to a company's employees, he says. To catalyze more fluid commications,

Pacific Bell created an internal communications council that consisted of representatives from each business unit. "Each council member determined the best way to communicate company news, objectives, and issues to their specific business unit in a way that personalized it based on their jobs and roles in the company. Conversely, council members were able to bring back feedback, ideas, and issues that were bubbling up from those business units. We found through organizational surveys that business units with more participation in the council scored higher in terms of knowledge of the products and knowledge of the business" (personal interview).

It might seem easy to ignore this blur, to stay in a comfort zone, or idealize the long-gone, slower-paced days. Many companies—in fact, entire industries—have done so. Some American manufacturing companies close their eyes to the globalization trend. Some service businesses ignore the onslaught of e-commerce (although stock market Internet indicators are starting to convince many to hop on the e-bandwagon). In late 1998, Sandy Weill, cochairman of Citibank, was rumored to have said, "I will *never* use the Internet"—which sent the e-commerce department of his company into something of a tailspin. Citibank, who had been ahead of the e-banking curve, began to lose ground to other financial institutions that quickly adjusted to the new e-commerce space and prioritized e-banking as business critical (personal interview).

Ignoring trends is not the answer. Futurists Davis and Meyer warn, in *Blur*: "Don't think you'll ever slow down Blur, let alone bring it to a halt. Its constant acceleration is here to stay, and those who miss that point will miss everything" (1998, p. 7). The Charles Schwab company understands keeping up. Schwab blazed the way in electronic financial brokerage and real-time internal communications. Schwab's intranet portal, the "Schweb," learned from its early internal development and eventually leveraged development for their commercially successful external site.

In addition to openness, accuracy, strategic weighting, and timeliness, other elements are important in creating a strategic corporate journalism model. Accountability is critical. Most organizational communications should be authored (there are some exceptions, such as corporate videos), and difficult messages shouldn't come from an unnamed "they" (that is, the executive team).

Journalistic interactivity with a constituency is also necessary for a communication vehicle to be viable. Most publications welcome letters to the editor. Corporate journalistic communications should also have an editorial feedback mechanism. Feedback does not necessarily mean live dialogue; any feedback channel such as letters to the editor can provide selective response. In Tandem's "First Friday," questions were collected over the course of each month and categorized, and then a representative sampling of them was addressed live on each show. If a communicator chooses a selective-response feedback model, then either the person responding (who may be someone other than the author of the initial feature) or else editorial guidelines should explain how and why responses are chosen or published.

A well-defined taxonomy (the study of general principles of scientific classification), like a clearly organized table of contents, can greatly enhance the fluidity of information transfer across the organization. Organizational complexity has forced taxonomy onto center stage in the quest for knowledge management. Intranets provide both the opportunity and the challenge of classifying all organizational information. Unfortunately, an organizational index is much more diffuse and layered than a newspaper or magazine index. This creates a substantial challenge for the corporate intranet librarian. Getting it right requires multidimensional approaches and reshaping according to user feedback. Schwab's "Schweb" is a good example of "intricate and intuitive taxonomic classification system based upon extensive usability testing," according to Michelle Volpe, former communications manager at Schwab and current internal communications manager at Barclays.

Archiving and effective searching also strengthen the information backbone, providing context and history for both organizational communicators members. Some organizations boast a rich library from which to pull historical context. Susan Burks, an art consultant working with AT&T, has used archival imagery, footage, and sound from AT&T's Archives as a decorative element within the corporate environment. She believes that this type of rich audio and visual media can provide employees with historical context often needed to counter balance today's short term focus (personal interview).

Chapter Two mentions that for corporate journalism to be consumed, it must be disseminated over an acculturated communications network. When trying to acculturate a journalistic broadcast communication channel, organizations should use traditional branding techniques. The most important branding concept is frequent and consistent repetition. Monthly newsletters, weekly Monday morning executive voice mail, and daily news e-mail are examples of branding communication channels through consistency and repetition. Naming plays an important role in this acculturation (Schwab's "Schweb," Citibank's "Bank Beat," Tandem's "First Friday"). Compelling vocal qualities, eye-candy graphics (not necessarily large ones), memorable mastheads, and headline "eyebrows" also reinforce a communication channel's identity. (See Appendix 2 for a glossary of terms.)

PROGRESS—AND ROOM TO GROW

Although some companies have successfully merged journalistic elements into corporate communications, from a broader perspective progress has been measured. Attempts at controlled communication such as this are common even in enlightened companies. Qualcomm, a communications technology company, is known for its entrepreneurial culture and its employee base rich with Ph.D.s, where ideas are freely exchanged across company boundaries. Eileen Brennan was recruited from the local broadcast news ABC affiliate to bring journalism to the corporate environment. She relates her initial reaction: "It was a shock. I was used to asking the hard questions, and suddenly I felt like I had to walk a political tightrope." But Brennan's manager, Tamar Elkeles, vice president of learning and communications, encouraged her to push her journalistic integrity to the limits. Now with a daily news Web page in place,

Brennan is making journalistic headway by posting external Qual-comm press coverage, positive and negative. "When I first started linking negative pieces, executives called my boss and said, 'Do you know what she's doing? Are you OK with that?'" The retort was simple: employees already know about the negative press, and elim-inating it from view feels like censorship and contradicts the attempt at fostering principles of open communication.

Companies can fool themselves into believing that they have open, honest, strategically weighted, and timely communications, but bringing in an experienced societal journalist can provide a reality check. Though Qualcomm incorporates some advanced journalistic elements, the eyes of a societal journalist still see a long way to go.

The shift toward a corporate journalism model inside a company is incremental and arduous; it must be approached with vigor and discipline. Credibility, the foundation for successful journalism, is born slowly and is difficult to maintain. And as with societal jour-nalism, credibility can disintegrate with one untoward incident in-side the corporate journalistic world.

Although the executive ranks are getting more comfortable with opening up (J.P. Morgan's intranet-based daily news source, Morgan Today, is another example of the early adoption of a non-censorship publishing model), some management theorists believe that leaders should push harder—and even charge forward into prickly briar patches. Communications should be open to negativ-ity; organizations can learn from it. SGI's "bad attitude" newsgroup is infamous for its clever, biting, and well-articulated electronic ban-ter. Some readers view this as a useless, time-wasting gripe forum, while others try to identify and correct issues that lie beneath the surface criticism. Wheatley takes this concept even further: "We also create order when we invite conflicts and contradictions to rise to the surface, when we search them out, highlight them, even allow them to grow large and worrisome. We need to support people in the hunt for unsettling or discomforting information, and provide them with resources of time, colleagues, and opportunities for processing the information" (1992, p. 116).

By combining reality checks from societal journalists and the thinking of cutting-edge management theorists, organizations can begin to move toward a strategic corporate journalism model that prepares them for the fluid and boundaryless future. Jim Wolfensohn, president of the World Bank, says in the *Economist's* predictive "The World in 1999" article: "Business leaders need to realize that a vital element in a modern democracy is modern corporate governance. Just [like] governments, firms must be run transparently; management must be accountable. Corporate governance has both internal and external dimensions. Internally, it refers to the checks and balances of power within a corporation; in particular between management, employees, the board of directors, shareholders and debt holders" (p. 78). Fluid information flow and sound journalistic practices aid this democratic governance.

Governance in this new world ushers in new ethical dilemmas. Earlier in this chapter, Nancy Hill, formerly at Tandem, said she saw the executives "telling it straight" during the broadcasts about widespread layoffs. There are those communicators who are certain that open, timely, accurate communication keeps employees bought in. Is it possible that they keep employees bought in for too long? Is it possible that a lack of external checks and balances can keep employees lined up for longer than they should, given a corporation's true state? Is it possible that an effective and compelling internal communication strategy can keep employees committed to a sinking ship? Is it possible that the communication system can act like a life-support system, keeping a company artificially alive? Is it also possible that the synthetic life dupes the inwardly focused executives into believing their strategies and operations will adequately solve the company's problems? These are the new questions facing internal communicators today.

In the next chapter, an in-depth profile of one company's corporate journalism evolution (including a highlighted crisis period there) sheds light on how strategic corporate journalism aided the company during turnaround and potential recovery.

6

Corporate Journalism: A Case Study

**Stages in the History of SGI
(formerly Silicon Graphics)**

**Endnotes: Worldwide Employee
Communications FAQ**

In the last chapter we presented glimpses of isolated journalistic elements found inside corporate walls. In this chapter we delve deeply into one company. We examine different stages in the history of computer manufacturer SGI as the company grows from a small start-up to a global enterprise (Figure 6.1). At each phase, we present a broad sweep of the business strategy coupled with the communication strategy at the time. Corresponding external news reporting and feature coverage about the company are also referred to when available.

The observations made regarding SGI reflect the personal opinions of the authors.

FY End Revenue	Employee Count		
	6	11/81	Date founded
$5.3M	n.a.	5/84	CEO McCracken joins
		7/86	First profitable year
$41.5M	442	10/86	Silicon Graphics (SGI) goes public
$166M[1]	1,100	4/88	Bifurcation: ASD and ESD formed
$521M[1]	2,200	1/90	First million-dollar quarter
		1/92	2 for 1 stock split
$907M[1,2]	3,200	7/92	MIPS merger
		2/93	Clinton and Gore visit Mountain View campus
		6/93	*Jurassic Park*
$1.13B[2]	3,600	12/93	2 for 1 stock split
		1/94	McCracken appointed to Clinton's NII
		2/94	Founder Jim Clark leaves
$1.54B[2]	4,200	7/94	*BusinessWeek* "Gee Whiz" cover
		2/95	Alias|Wavefront merger
		7/95	FY '95 year-end event with Huey Lewis; Tag Watch gifts
$2.23B[2]	6,300	8/95	Stock at 45.625
		1/96	*WSJ* "Silicon Graphics Loses . . . Luster" article
		2/96	SGI acquires Cray Research
$2.92B[3]	10,500	7/96	COO "T. J." leaves
		8/97	*BusinessWeek* "Sad Saga . . ." cover
$3.66B	11,000	11/97	McCracken resigns; 10% employee layoff
		1/98	CEO Belluzzo joins
$3.1B	9,500	10/98	Stock at 7.375
		1/99	Release of NT "comeback" product
		4/99	Change of corporate identity from Silicon Graphics, Inc. to SGI
		When?	SGI turnaround?

FIGURE 6.1. SGI Time Line

Financial and employee numbers reflect fiscal year end results. SGI's fiscal year ends June 30.

(1) These periods have been restated to reflect the merger of Silicon Graphics, Inc. and MIPS Computer Systems, Inc. in fiscal year 1992, which has been accounted for on a pooling of interests basis.

(2) These periods reflect the mergers of Silicon Graphics, Inc., Alias Research, Inc., and Wavefront Technologies, Inc., which have been accounted for in a pooling of interests.

(3) Amounts reflect the April 2, 1996 acquisition of Cray Research, which was accounted for as a purchase.

STAGES IN THE HISTORY OF SGI (FORMERLY SILICON GRAPHICS)

1981–1986: A Premature Infant

In 1980, Jim Clark, a Stanford University engineering professor, predicted that the ability to manipulate three-dimensional graphics would revolutionize the computer industry. Clark convinced six of his top students and research associates to join him in starting a graphics hardware company. In 1981, Silicon Graphics was incorporated. SGI was premature on two counts, with its freshly conceived integrated 3D graphics vision and its underdeveloped business skills. Despite the company's early birth, the team's passion and vision for digital graphics enticed both customers and top engineering talent to the company. From 1981 to 1985, SGI remained a small company (fewer than 500 employees) focused on developing and producing graphics workstations.

The friendships and academic nature of the original team, their tightly focused goal, the lack of any real competition, and the deliberately maintained small organization created an organizational communication environment that was very intimate, inwardly focused, and highly interactive. For the first few years, organizational communication meant everyone sitting together in a conference room and debating issues until consensus emerged. Many of the company's hallmark traits—an innovative, hip attitude; the heavy value placed on openness and creativity; and an autonomy that sometimes led to combativeness—still exist today. During this era, the "Spirit of SGI," a culture mantra that has remained unchanged over the years, was codified to capture and emblazon the essence of what makes SGI tick.

Like an infant on the edge of survival, in 1984 SGI teetered on the brink of bankruptcy. But the board, quickly assessing the situation, realized that the company needed business expertise and hired CEO Ed McCracken, an up-and-coming management star at nearby office equipment manufacturer Hewlett-Packard. McCracken took swift actions to bring the company into the black. In July 1986, two years later, SGI posted its first profitable year.

McCracken and his team strongly believed that personal relationships led to fast decision making and all-around efficiency. They reinforced the already embedded personalized, interactive organizational communication culture at SGI by institutionalizing an open cube, community-focused facilities environment that encouraged people to interact freely and regularly. They also began to hold quarterly "all hands" meetings—corporationwide, interactive organizational communication sessions hosted by the executive team.

In those early days, the informality was laced with zaniness. In addition to the standard Silicon Valley beer busts, SGI celebrated inaugural roller skating parties on the freshly poured foundations of new SGI buildings and held "lip sync" competitions, outlandishly staged in the twenty-thousand-seat Mountain View, California Shoreline amphitheater.

As the company grew, divisions retained the personal, interactive flavor. During this time, though a technologically savvy firm, the company adopted voice mail as the primary one-on-one communication medium. Even in the mid-eighties, when most engineering companies inculcated e-mail as the preferred personal communication tool, the SGI culture opted for voice mail because of its personal nature, intimacy, interactivity, and the additional information relayed via vocal modulation, pace, and tone. The engineering crowd may have used e-mail more regularly, but the dominant enterprisewide media was acknowledged to be voice mail.

Because of the company's clear, singular focus, static market, relationship-based culture, and relatively small size, there were no barriers to fluidity of information and therefore no need for corporate journalistic support. Since SGI was virtually alone in the 3D workstation market space, insularity could exist without repercussions. Formalized communications—both internal and external—had not yet developed.

1986–1991: The Hyperactive Child

In October 1986, SGI went public and emerged from this premature infancy as a healthy organization. It was a company finding and defining the niche market of 3D graphics workstations that enabled leading-edge "lighthouse" customers in graphics-intense industries to innovate. During this growth spurt, passion about 3D graphics soared, and SGI predicted that the need for computer 3D graphics would become pervasive and mainstream. Consequently, SGI bifurcated its business units, creating both the Entry Systems Division (ESD), chartered to create less expensive graphics workstations for this broader graphics marketplace, and the Advanced Systems Division (ASD), the umbrella organization for the existing high-end business.

Despite these organizational shifts, the internal and external landscape variables changed very little during this time. In 1987, SGI was still relatively small (611 employees, $86 million in annual revenues). It still maintained a singular focus on graphics hardware, external competitors had not yet emerged, and the company was still focused inwardly. SGI's financial results started to soar dramatically.

In early 1989 (1,700 employees, $299 million in annual revenues), many landscape variables changed at once, notably the company's focus and size. The decision to fish in uncharted waters (low-end graphics hardware) added complexity to the organization. As a result, the organizational communication model changed as well. Within the human resource organization, an employee communications function was created, staffed with one manager. The primary goal of employee communications (EC) was to help the new, double-headed SGI align toward a larger singular vision of success.

From 1989 to 1991, the interactive communications model continued, not only from an EC perspective but also in organic, fluid ways. Although team meetings, telephone conversations, voice mail, e-mail, Usenet newsgroups, and hallway chit-chat were the primary channels of organizational communications, informal small-group interaction began to appear in universitylike, guru-hosted brown bags, "chalk talks," and seminars. Dialoguing and brainstorming, rather than agenda-driven business meetings, dominated these forums.

Even organizationwide communications channels took a personal or interactive approach. Gatherings and events such as the quarterly All Hands meetings, the Spirit trip (a peer-nominated employee recognition event), the corporate winter holiday festival, and a company picnic were all centrally orchestrated to achieve interaction among all employees. Broadcast print channels such as *All Hands*, a monthly companywide newsletter, were developed to communicate company successes in a personalized way. In *All Hands*, employees authored first-person stories, and even McCracken had an informal column, "Ed's Corner," in which he shared what was on his mind. Informal corporate videos and unauthorized "bandit" videos were developed to personally share corporate vision, successes, or financial summary messages. One infamous bandit video was produced by the "skinny hackers," a notorious group of jogging-obsessed engineers (two of whom were company founders). Designed to introduce internally a new software product called Showcase, the video is memorable because all of the employee actors, including several executives, touted the benefits of the product while, on camera, appearing to be nude.

SGI outpaced its earnings predictions. In 1990 (2,200 employees, $521 million in annual revenues), McCracken called SGI the most unknown Fortune 500 secret in Silicon Valley. Wall Street began to raise its eyebrows. The external world began to notice. In a 1990 *Forbes* article titled "The Third Dimension," Richard Shaffer reported that "three dimensional computer graphics . . . is turning into a real business mainly through the efforts of one company, Silicon Graphics" (p. 266). Passionate teams of employees could do no wrong. Strategy often followed successful ideas, and energy shot through the roof. SGI continued to grow. In early 1991, succeeding on all fronts, SGI achieved its first $100 million dollar quarter.

From 1986 to 1991 the three primary factors complicating organizational communications were bifurcation of the business, growth and dispersion, and the emergence of competitors. Although organizational communications had been stepped up with a central employee communication department, a corporate newsletter and increased use of voice mail, e-mail, and Usenet newsgroups could not fully adapt to this new environment. The business unit separation (ASD and ESD) and global dispersion (by the end of FY91, SGI had grown to include fifty-five North American and thirty-six international sales and support offices, one domestic manufacturing site, and two manufacturing sites overseas) began to clog information flow. Even though competitors had just started thinking about the 3D workstation space, Shaffer noted in his *Forbes* piece: "Now the fun begins. The heavyweights in workstations, as well as some important newcomers, are starting to make up for years of neglecting the 3D opportunity." Unfortunately, because SGI no longer felt the need for external validation to acquire venture capital, it became more inwardly focused than ever.

1991–1995: Popular Youth

In 1991 (2,900 employees, $736 million annual revenues), with its industry-leading technology and a growing presence in the entertainment industry, SGI leaped to popularity with financial analysts, industry analysts, and the commercial media. SGI was the homecoming queen—at a prom where they were playing Hollywood's *Jurassic Park* theme music. The company reveled in success, and both external and internal communications played upon it.

In 1991, an *Economist* article highlighted SGI as "one of the fastest growing firms ever to hit Silicon Valley," noting McCracken's "3D vision" and predicting that "within five years most personal computers will offer three-dimensional graphics as flashy as those now found in Hollywood movies or high-tech engineering studios" (1991, pp. 72–74). A short time later, *Fortune* listed SGI in an article about the "best investment strategy for 1993" (Kuhn, Neumeier, and Sheeline, 1993, pp. 25–26).

With the release of the feature film *Jurassic Park* in 1993, SGI became known outside market analyst and investment banker circles.

SGI was widely promoted as the juice behind the movies—the manufacturer of the systems used to create eye-popping special effects. The company, proud of its newfound tinsel-town PR and favorable nods in the entertainment business, rented a local movie theater so that Mountain View employees could preview the film.

The external attention sparked some internal factors that affected SGI's organizational communication. SGI did not pay close attention to the emerging external competitive environment but instead fostered internal competition. A rivalry emerged between ESD and ASD, and the two divisional leaders openly challenged their respective divisions to outperform the other. The divisions became fierce competitors. They withdrew into their silos. They created boundaries and people communicated only within their own division.

Meanwhile, back at corporate communication headquarters, employee communications focused not on business strategy but on corporate success, history, and culture. The EC team created a highly polished printed corporate showpiece called *Spirit*, a magazine that focused solely on the elements unique to SGI's organizational culture. *Spirit* became a forum for corporate storytelling and myth. This led to embellished portraits and increased deference to corporate folklore cornerstones—the personalities and the traditions—of the SGI culture. The bimonthly *All Hands* published employee-written, homespun pieces with little journalistic flair, while the quarterly *Spirit* enjoyed enough budget and reverence to hire professional writers. In essence, journalism at SGI had its genesis with *Spirit* in 1994.

With capable divisional leaders in place, McCracken explored leading-edge strategies and concepts that could propel SGI's growth. Wanting to avoid the "bureaucracy creep" that commonly stifles the innovative edge in a growing company, he and his executive team clung to the company's personal-relationship orientation. In trying to build a medium-sized company that was both innovative and relationship-centered, the leaders found that the culture reacted instinctively, as if it had a mind of its own. The antibureaucratic sentiment was so extreme that "the three P words"—*policies, process,* and *procedures*—were considered "un-SGI," and their mention could get one booed out of a meeting.

Late in 1993, Steven Prokesch interviewed McCracken for the *Harvard Business Review*; in a sidebar called "Battling Bigness," the author described SGI as experiencing uncomfortable growing pains. SGI was struggling to accept "the fact that it is no longer a start-up."

Out in the ranks, the divisional leaders' power grew. With this, divisional business focus also grew ever more detached from executive strategy. Interestingly, dramatic differences developed among executive personalities. McCracken, a natural introvert, wore his conceptual, reflective posture well. In 1994, a *BusinessWeek* cover story, "The Gee-Whiz Company," claimed that "not since Apple dazzled the market with the trend-setting Macintosh has a computer company so captured the public imagination or promised so much for the future" (Hof, p. 56). The article also quoted Steven Milunovich of Morgan Stanley as labeling SGI "the Microsoft of computer graphics."

SGI and McCracken attracted President Clinton and Vice President Gore's attention (both visited SGI in February 1993, just after their first election), and in 1994 (when the company had 4,200 employees and $1.54 billion in annual revenues) McCracken was appointed cochair of the U.S. Advisory Council on the National Information Infrastructure, a widely publicized committee created to address the challenges presented by the embryonic Internet phenomenon. *Vanity Fair* listed McCracken as number twenty-eight and Jim Clark (SGI and Netscape founder) as number eighteen of the top fifty leaders in the information age in 1995 ("The New Establishment . . .," Parry, 1995). Hollywood film studios started touring SGI's campus headquarters.

Internally, McCracken seemed to have a gurulike, mystic aura. The leader of the ASD division, Tom Jermoluk, had a visible, hyperactive style and pulled frat-boy antics that were both admired and disliked throughout the organization. He became the SGI model executive, representing the youthful, innovative, passionate elements of the SGI culture. By contrast, Mike Ramsay, who was

ESD's chief and possibly even more introverted than McCracken, began to take a back seat to Jermoluk. For a time, McCracken and Jermoluk drove the SGI culture. It was the "Ed and T. J. Show."

For the most part, McCracken and Jermoluk drove organizational communications. The corporate structure was creating a broad middle-management layer, but the expectations for managers were different from those in more mature companies. In general, SGI middle managers were judged and rewarded not on their management ability but on their individual contributions. The "lone ranger culture" ran wild, and heroic individual effort attracted attention and promotions. As a result, managers frequently had no management experience and did not view communication as their responsibility. Most employees looked to the top of the organization for organizational communication.

In late 1993 (3,600 employees, $1.13 billion in revenues), engineers browsing the Internet discovered XMosaic, a new technology that enabled hyperlinking of various digital text and media. SGI engineers began to publish their information via that browser and the Web. One engineer even single-handedly aggregated a corporationwide technical reference information Website, called the SGI Data Warehouse.

The browser technology caught the attention of the employee communications team. At this time, they had no way to broadcast timely communications. SGI had a cultural block against sending companywide e-mail and, unlike many other companies in Silicon Valley, had not yet implemented groupware technology such as Lotus Notes. XMosaic's user-friendly, immediately intuitive interface had the answers. The EC team pulled together some employees to evaluate it. In less than a year and without formal executive sanction, this group created *Junction*, the corporate gateway to SGI Web reference information. Employee communications and corporate information systems (IS) jointly shared this function.

The site evolved over a year, and in 1994 the team released *Junction 2.0*. The front page of this website now drew employees nearly everyday. By creating a news metaphor interface, the team inadvertently paved the way for both broadcast communication as well as a journalistic publishing model. Because the IS organization supported the cause, the default home page for all employee browsers (Netscape by this time) was set to *Junction*. Its easy access to all global Web reference information further enhanced the broadcast potential of this portal.

The two most critical organizational communication decisions made during the evolution of *Junction* happened accidentally. When the team created *Junction 1.0*, no one understood the power of a single corporate portal. As fortune would have it, the grassroots Junction team consisted of representatives from corporate functions (corporate IS, corporate HR, and corporate communications) who, because of their roles, thought about centralization. This cross-boundary collaboration naturally led to the single portal.

Secondly, and even more accidentally, the *Junction* front-page newspaper metaphor for organizational communication was created at the last minute in a redesign. The worn-down team could not finalize the front-page online design. In a fit of exhaustion, the team manager told the contract graphic designer that if she wanted a permanent job, she must create something that needed daily graphic design. Twelve hours later, *Junction 2.0* was born—complete with a corporate "newspaper" look and feel and front-page artwork with "big picture" headlines. The front cover could change any time the news called for it. With *Junction 2.0*, the communications capabilities included one headline main story and three bulleted substories.

These two elements enabled SGI to broadcast organizational communication over the intranet in journalistic fashion. Partly because the default browser pointed to *Junction*, and partly because of the culture that had evolved, the communications team could track at least 80 percent of the organization hitting or consuming the communication within hours of its publication. *Junction* was naturally becoming "all things Web" at SGI.

At this time (in late 1994), although SGI had created a powerful vehicle for broadcast organizational communication, *Junction* at first was not used for broadcasting strategic journalism. Stories broadcast over *Junction* were first-come, first-served, unweighted stories in no context, submitted from all over the organization. New-product launches followed such local team announcements as the "SGI Pet Page." Internal Website promotions preceded critical messages from executives or quarterly earnings. The tool was solid from a technology perspective, but clearly news creation and dissemination followed no strategy.

Soon other internal organizations were using the intranet similarly and building upon the technology. In an attempt to satisfy the information needs of the salesforce, the field organization created *sales.corp*, an audience-specific portal site with organized communication and tools meeting the needs of a niche audience. Although this communication channel was needle-focused and tightly orchestrated, most of the content presented on *sales.corp* was written by the product division or information owner in marketingspeak.

As SGI's global business grew, so did organizational communications. Yet three of the four primary organizationwide communications vehicles—corporate All Hands meetings, the *All Hands* newsletter, and *Junction*—primarily addressed a Mountain View employee base. Only the culture-focused *Spirit* magazine covered global topics. A sales communication department, distinct from the employee communications department, was formed, though little coordination existed between the two functions. Communications fragmented between sales and marketing messages and all-employee corporate messaging.

Company success brought arrogance, unlimited spending, and obsessive insularity to SGI. The outside world did not exist and was not allowed in—unless friends were invited to events like the theatrically extravagant lip sync contests (*BusinessWeek* once reported that SGI's lip sync had "taken 'The Gong Show' to new lows" Hof, 1994, p. 63) or the annual winter festivals that included such headliners as the Pointer Sisters, Patty LaBelle, and Kenny G.

1995–1997: The Difficult Coming of Age

In the mid-nineties, Clark was gone (he left in 1994 to head up browser start-up Netscape), but his vision of a world demanding 3D computer graphics was alive and well. Poised to capitalize on the new world, SGI was high on its success and not prepared for the different environment that this future would create. A cadre of competitors entered the 3D computer graphics game, and the ground shifted beneath SGI's feet. From 1995 to 1998, the company experienced more growing pains and wrestled with self-realization as to how to compete in the new world.

On January 3, 1996, the *Wall Street Journal* posted the company's preannouncement of disappointing quarterly financial results in an article headlined, "Silicon Graphics Loses Some of Its Luster." In the article, ChicagoCorp analyst David Wu said, "This is what happens when management starts to believe it walks on water" (Hill, p. B4). He softened the blow slightly, however, by concluding that "things aren't falling apart."

The next month, *Forbes* ran an article (Darlin, 1996) that compared SGI's problems with Apple Computer's apparent demise. The reporter claimed that both companies had hoisted themselves with their own petards by naïvely and shortsightedly believing in a proprietary operating system. SGI scoffed at such reporting. But the internal obsession and avoidance of external factors continued.

Then *Financial World* rebuked SGI for not entering the mainstream, lower-margin PC market. The article was titled, "I Won't Dance. Don't Ask Me," and the tag ("Don't talk mass market to Silicon Graphics. Don't even think about it") left no doubt about that reporter's viewpoint (Ward, 1996).

In 1996 (10,500 employees, annual revenues of $2.92 billion), SGI acquired Cray Research. SGI had successfully completed three past mergers, but Cray was a whole different matter. Its product line and business model were much more complicated. Cray was a twenty-four-year-old company of four thousand employees located in the Midwest. The age disparity (that is, both the companies' lifetimes and the age of the employees, with Cray's average significantly higher than SGI's), geographic cultural differences, and product-line divergence made for a bumpy marriage. Since this integration exacerbated SGI's downward spiral, fingers pointed in all directions.

During this difficult period, McCracken spent a lot of time inside the Washington, D.C. beltway; he left all business operations to Jermoluk. Employees shifted their focus from the quieter meditative guru to the hyperactive frat boy.

In these years, on the employee communications front both the team and the journalistic model were evolving. In 1995 (6,300 employees; $2.23 billion in revenues) a young, energetic journalist was hired by EC. Just before the fateful "Tag Heuer watch year" and the October 1997 All Hands meeting (see the Prelude in this book), the team began to incorporate the journalistic writing style of *Spirit* into the *All Hands* newsletter and the information communicated over *Junction*. *Junction's* news stories were characteristically reports and updates, showcasing nearly instantaneous stories whereas *All Hands* published the month's best summary pieces and duplicated features.

When SGI acquired Cray, the Midwestern company's community had a twenty-year history of using e-mail as a controlled broadcast communication channel. Cray's embryonic intranet Web presence was used as a repository for reference information. SGI jump-started the transition to the Web by using a tough-love strategy: certain business-critical applications (such as benefits enrollment) were only available through the intranet. A key element in this forced transition was the fact that although the familiar option was eliminated, the replacement was more efficient on all fronts. This approach was at first painful for the new Cray/SGI employees, but once complete it paved the way for broad and integrated organizational communications.

This new journalistic direction and the broader coverage ignited sparks of business credibility for the employee communications team. But it did not have advanced journalistic skills, nor did its members completely own the *Junction* publishing process. Corporate IS managed the back-end infrastructure that made intranet publishing possible, and by default IS still owned the daily editorial publishing process. These two factors prohibited corporate journalism from advancing.

In late 1996 and early 1997, the new EC team made some swift moves that invigorated the journalistic model. The entire functionality of the Web portal—including the technological publishing infrastructure—was moved into the EC organization. The EC team created a communications model predicated upon access to McCracken and the executive team, one that would help focus the company. A junior beat reporter, a senior writer, and an executive editor were hired and the team began to report and write strategic reflections of the company.

The corporation struggled; the business model crumbled. Competitors stole market share. Times were tough, and spun communications backfired. Employees wanted to know the truth. In August 1997, the *BusinessWeek* cover story, "The Sad Saga of Silicon Graphics," exposed a company that had "lost touch with basic business practices" (p. 68). To support this assertion, the article documented personal behaviors of executives, including alleged indiscreet activities during a sales conference in Mallorca, Spain, where "managers and executives had too much to drink and caroused late into the morning" (Hof, with Sager and Himelstein, p. 71). Because of the personal nature of the article, both executives and employees responded angrily and defensively.

Oct. 1997–June 1998: The Headless Period

During the period between McCracken's resignation and installation of Rick Belluzzo as the new CEO; between the worst quarter in eleven years and a plan to return to profitability; between the time of a fat company with no strategy and that of steps toward a more focused, lean, competitive enterprise; between the first broad-based layoffs and an attempt to renew employee security, the company spun.

The new *Junction* intranet publishing infrastructure, coupled with advanced journalistic skills, allowed employee communications to create a crisis communication plan designed to keep employees well informed throughout SGI's most precarious period, October 1997 through March 1998. At the core of this plan was a journalistic communication model that delivered timely, accurate, synchronized, consistent, contextualized, and up-to-date communications to employees. The media used at this time included alert e-mails, headline voice mail news, manager talking points, and Web-broadcast contextualized messages.

Four critical changes in employee communications in mid–1997 (when the company had 11,000 employees and $3.66 billion in revenues) created a foundation that has propelled the corporate journalism model ever since.

Team Skills

The team consciously acquired more journalistic skills. A former *Newsweek* foreign reporter, a college journalism graduate, and a former business magazine and newspaper publisher joined the EC team. Roles modeled after journalistic functions were created: executive editor, executive-beat writer, employee-pulse beat writer, community editor, managing editor, assignment editor, copy editor, production manager, etc. Current team members were trained with editorial skills. The team built a solid set of business news publishing experience, Web development, and marketing acumen that has since allowed them to strategically transform SGI's primary communication medium.

Organization Structure

Worldwide employee communications took over the entire *Junction* publishing process from corporate IS. Instead of a first-come, first-publish news diet, this organizational move allowed *Junction* to be run like a newspaper, with consciously chosen and selectively weighted information critical for strategic focus, global representation, and alignment.

Focus

Employee communications eliminated *Spirit* and the *All Hands* news-letter in 1998 and focused all resources on highly integrated Web publishing for *Junction*. For the year prior to its phase-out, *All Hands* primarily targeted audiences with intranet access challenges (such as manufacturing, small sales offices, etc.) and served as a reminder or reinforcement of the *Junction* news features. Also at this time, the team consciously focused more broadly on global news needs and delivery and changed their name to worldwide employee communications.

Cross-Functional Communication Linkages

During this period, leaders from the primary organizationwide communications functions (employee communications, investor relations, industry relations, public relations, and marketing communications) began to meet regularly and discuss consistent, synchronized internal and external communications, a common organizationwide integrated publishing process, and an organizationwide urgent communications alert system. Content creators from all over the company also began meetings and regular newsgroup dialogue to share content plans and eliminate duplication.

Also at this point, the worldwide employee communications team continued to refine and develop the strategic corporate journalism model. The members launched a new *Junction* that enabled flexible story weighting and front-page teaser content introductions modeled after the *Wall Street Journal*. A new, highly visible intranet site, "In the News," provided links to the external press, and both positive and negative press were posted; only speculative articles were censored or introduced with an editor's note. They hired an assignment editor to build and manage a pool of journalistically skilled contract writers who would create business feature stories. They refined the editorial planning process to handle incoming news items, executive messaging, article "sponsorship," and strategic reflections of the company. They expanded the roles of executive speech-writing and communications consulting to allow broader and more immediate access to information as well as influence upon communicators throughout the company. They worked toward a mission of improving business literacy and insight for employees worldwide.

Junction became the primary integrated channel of organization-wide communications for executive messages, for highlighting external press, for real-time announcements, and for contextualizing in-depth business features. It was also the portal to SGI's intranet on which the company had built internal reference sites, workflow transaction tools, data mining engines, and distributed learning courses critical to employees' daily operations. Junction was thus quite unlike *All Hands* or *Spirit*, which were second-tier, nice-to-have media. *Junction* was critical to an employee's success and daily performance. It was read—or at least scanned—by most employees around the world every day.

July 1998 to the Present: Beginning Maturation

Can SGI do it? Apple seems to have achieved at least a partial recovery with the iMac product line, and many are waiting to see if SGI will follow the ascent. Reporters tentatively use the word *comeback* now (even *BusinessWeek* ran a fairly middle-of-the-road article, "What Makes Rick Belluzzo Run?" about why the "heir apparent left the catbird seat at Hewlett-Packard for beleaguered SGI"; Burrows, with Reinhardt, 1999, online version).

During the crisis period, the worldwide employee communications team transformed the corporate news publishing model. There's nothing like dramatic intensity to light the fuel of journalism's fire. Armed with the skill set, the strategic mind-set, critical links to other communicators, and the technical infrastructure necessary to advance a corporate journalism model, the team made changes and built and refined a corporate news source. They structured themselves like a startup publication. They tracked demographics. They built a content plan and managed it with a strategic editorial calendar. They developed process and publishing guidelines. Credibility rose.

Since mid-1997, strategic corporate journalism at SGI has advanced rapidly. Further management changes added experience to a team that now synthesizes technology, strategy, business development, marketing, and publishing. Since then, a calculated progression toward a corporate journalistic model has been under way.

Does the model work? Yes, but no model is perfect. Because worldwide employee communications is not the only internal communications organization, and because communication organizations are not functionally related, synchronization and consistency across the enterprise can be bumpy. Because EC reports to human resources, there is a tendency to overhighlight HR-related stories. Because EC contracts with external writers who lack familiarity with SGI's culture, it is sometimes hard to quickly acclimate new writers as to content sensitivities, and sometimes communications can come across as too polished. Because EC does not report directly to the executive level, access to information is sometimes challenging and orchestrating global communication is sometimes more reactive than is otherwise necessary. Couple tight resources with increased reliance (as a result of the credibility, groups all over the company—including executives—request communication advice and support, often urgently) and you get long hours, enormous deadlines, and team burnout. Also, middle managers are still struggling with their new role as organizational communicators. So because of resource constraints EC has moved away from organizationwide interaction (with the exceptions of quarterly corporate All Hands meetings, *Junction* letters to the editor, and some ad hoc events). As yet, organizational leaders have not fully stepped in to fill the interaction void.

Despite the growth toward open, organic communication, both the EC team and executives still periodically struggle with how to balance openness and honesty. Some of SGI's employees may criticize *Junction* as overly positive, too polished, censored, and still biased toward corporate or marketingspeak. Some SGI executives may say *Junction* exposes too much dirty laundry or information that could damage the company's competitiveness. How much openness is enough without damaging the competitive stance? Are there diminishing returns, or even a negative impact, if an organization pushes openness and honesty too far? Did the model help retain top talent during an economic boom and an explosion of Internet startups in Silicon Valley? Did the model aid in aligning employees around the world behind a new vision and strategic direction?

It is difficult to know with certainty. At the time this book is being published, SGI is halfway through the tunnel. Neither the light behind nor that ahead is entirely visible. Only time will tell whether the tunnel they are in is even the right one. Will they follow Tandem's steps, getting smaller and smaller until another company buys them? Will they have a prolonged turnaround, in Apple fashion? In March 1999, it seemed as though SGI had turned a critical corner; expenses and headcount were under control, the company had met financial projections for two subsequent quarters, and the stock price crept over 20 for the first time in two years. But how many corners are there to turn? Only time will tell.

ENDNOTES: WORLDWIDE EMPLOYEE COMMUNICATIONS FAQ

As we write this, worldwide employee communications (EC) is SGI's central internal communications organization. Below are a few facts about EC.

Charter

Since its inception in 1989, EC has handled corporationwide communication to employees about major events and organizational culture. For most of the company's history, the bulk of employees worked at corporate headquarters in Mountain View, California. Because of this, much of EC's focus through the first ten years (1981–1991) focused on Mountain View, including executive messaging, local culture-related communications, and Mountain View–

based corporate events. More recently, a number of factors have forced EC to adopt a broader corporate charter.

SGI's four acquisitions in 1995 and 1996 added another manufacturing facility in Wisconsin and expanded the corporate employee base to Eagan (Minnesota), Toronto, and Santa Barbara (California). Prior to these acquisitions, 70 percent of SGI's employee base worked in Mountain View. After the acquisitions, the employee base at headquarters hovered at 40 percent. This shift forced the company into a more global—or at least a broader national—posture. In 1998 (9,500 employees; $3.1 billion in revenues), EC eliminated all print communications and focused solely on global messaging on the Web and central communication coordination across the enterprise.

Organizational Structure

EC's reporting relationship within SGI has changed once, and only slightly, in years. The function has always reported through the human resource organization, and since 1993 it has reported to the vice president of HR. For a short time it reported to the corporate learning organization. As discussed in Chapter Three, the primary internal communication organization can fall under many functions within an organization. If the reporting structure is designed to achieve synergies most important to the success of the organization, communication success often follows. Since the primary reporting relationship invariably has an impact on the vision and strategy of organizational communications, the internal communications team must also strive for organizational synergies not provided by this reporting relationship.

In the case of SGI, EC's position in the human resource organization helped the team communicate about culture and, to some extent, broad business issues (unlike many HR organizations, SGI's was closely linked to and consequently knowledgeable about the core corporate business). Although cultural and business alignment have not been problematic, proactive access to executive messages and synchronicity with external communication organizations has been challenging. As SGI has grown and other internal communication organizations have formed to aid specific internal audiences, coordinating among these internal organizations has been complex and problematic. This difficulty coordinating between internal and external communications organizations has been exacerbated by SGI's decentralized, independent culture.

Resource Model

Since the initial 1989 budget stabilization, the employee communications resource model (based on cost per employee) has not varied much. Even the creation and adoption of *Junction* as the primary organizational communication tool did not cause the figure per head to change (in fact, during this decision the dollars per head dropped slightly and continues to drop as the team streamlines the publishing process). When the hard-copy *All Hands* newsletter and *Spirit* magazine were eliminated, the resources from these media fueled the heavier Web focus on *Junction*.

Currently the employee communications team consists of one half-time director, one half-time administrator, three full-time employees and two part-timers (editors, writers, and Web production artists), an external contract assignment editor, and external contract writers. This list summarizes the roles and responsibilities of the current team:

- Publishing

    Executive editor, function manager, and communications consultant (part-time)

    Managing editor, Webmaster, consultant (full-time)

    External contract assignment editor (part-time)

    Production expert (full-time)

- Writing

    Executive writer, senior consultant (part-time)

    Staff writer, consultant (full-time)

    Suite of external contract writers (all part-time)

■ Consulting

Events and orchestrated, sequenced messaging manager, senior consultant (full-time)

Channels

Throughout its history, the formal media produced by the EC
team have included the monthly printed companywide *All Hands*
newsletter; the quarterly printed corporationwide magazine *Spirit*;
an annual fiscal year-end videotape; and *Junction*, the corporate intranet gateway. Informal and ad hoc channels have included interoffice hard-copy memos, posters, voice mail, e-mail, Usenet
newsgroups and electronic chat rooms, and corporate videotapes.

Formal events have included quarterly All Hands meetings
(mostly Mountain View–based but virtually broadcast); and the
annual corporate Mountain View–based holiday party, Mountain
View Thanksgiving luncheon, Mountain View employee picnic,
and Spirit trip to recognize peer-selected employee leaders. Informal and ad hoc events included an annual lip sync competition;
specific corporate celebrations, contests, and giveaways; and high-
profile customer visits. In the past, T-shirt communication strategies proliferated. (SGI once promoted an internal slogan: "It's not
just a job; it's a wardrobe.")

Currently the only formal broadcast channel used by employee
communications is daily news on the corporate intranet *Junction*.
This includes executive messages, features, updates, and announcements. *Junction* has truly become acculturated and is the primary
worldwide communication channel for the organization. Depending upon the urgency of the communication, stronger push channels such as e-mail and voice mail aliases, Usenet newsgroups, and
target audience intranet sites are used to push employees to *Junction* for faster and more pervasive communication distribution.

Periodically, the more intimate channels such as videos, executive e-mails, and executive voice mails are used as part of a sequenced messaging strategy to boost morale and reiterate focus

areas, or as broad, personalized exposure for the executive team. Sometimes, if an urgent message requires very little context, e-mail may be used alone. In the late 1990s, e-mail replaced voice mail as the push medium of choice, although in some suborganizations voice mail aliases are still used depending upon the size of the suborganization, people's acceptance of broad-based voice mail, and the content being delivered.

Currently, formal corporate events include quarterly, virtually broadcast, All Hands meetings and the annual Spirit forum. At this time, informal or ad hoc events are rare.

Future World

Futuring is tricky business. No one knows for sure what lies ahead, and there is no Undo key. Like that e-mail you wish you could unsend, once you offer a prediction its highlights remain vivid in the minds of those who hear or read it. If events unfold differently at a later date, those same people can forever remind you that your crystal ball was cracked. We are not so much making predictions as we are hoping to question, provoke, elicit, inspire, and challenge. Picasso once said, "Everything you can imagine is real." This may hold true on a painter's canvas, but it is less true in artfully combining technology, business, organizational development, and communications trends to imagine what lies ahead.

Will employees ever be adequately informed without feeling overwhelmed? Can an organization ever really manage knowledge?

173

Is utopian organizational communication purely organic and egalitarian? Will a human organization ever have perfect synchronicity and consistency in organizational communication? Will organizations create the alignment mechanisms that are necessary to meet the fluidity of the future? These difficult questions force us to peer into territories unknown. The trends now apparent provide at least a looking glass to these future places.

MACRO SOCIOTECHNOLOGICAL TRENDS

In Chapter One we talked about the knowledge workforce, a democratized workforce, diversification, information overload, and the increased pace of change. Will a knowledge workforce supply the information and technological needs of the future, and will employees get the information they need to perform their jobs well? Will the pace of the information age slow down? Will Moore's Law (the amount of available memory storage on a microchip doubles every eighteen months) ever hit a ceiling that constrains the advances of information technology? If Moore's Law does hit a ceiling, that would reinforce what Paul Saffo of the Institute of the Future noted, in an institute "Outlook Exchange" in San Francisco in March 1999, about the idealistic vision of infinite bandwidth: "What looks like abundance at first blush may in fact be scarcity." Basically, we fill whatever pipes they give us.

Reliance on a knowledge workforce is increasing faster than the availability of knowledge workers. Alan Webber, publisher of *Fast Company*, says that in the next ten years the eligible talent field of people thirty-five to forty-five years old will shrink by 20 percent (1998, Seminar: "The Changing Nature of Competiveness"). This will create an extremely competitive talent economy where knowledge workers have more leverage in the organization. Federal Reserve Chairman Alan Greenspan echoes the prediction that the future may see a shortage of talent. In a 1998 *BusinessWeek* article called "The 21st Century Economy," he says, "At current growth rates . . . the economy will eventually run out of workers" (Foust, 1998, p. 70).

Because of this shortage of talent and the changing corporate climate, and also because of the challenge that workers see, maintaining talent becomes critical. Michelle Wolpe, internal communications manager at Barclays Global Investors, says, "With employees more cynical about long-term stability of companies and/or the potential of being laid off in a merger or acquisition, they are less likely to feel company loyalty; consequently companies need to be working to constantly rerecruit employees if they want to keep them."

Greenspan also talked about the environment these workers face: "Times of intense technological change are often volatile, as corporations and workers try to adjust to new technologies" (Foust, p. 70). What communication needs do these knowledge employees have? How do they stay motivated?

In his book *Communicating for Change*, Roger D'Aprix describes communication needs modeled after Abraham Maslow's hierarchy of needs. Employees are increasingly motivated as their communication needs are met at ever deeper levels. The questions "What is my job? How am I doing? Does anyone care? How is my unit doing? Where is the company headed?" need to be addressed before employees become motivated enough to kick in with "How can I help?" (p. 98).

Generally speaking, knowledge workers have fulfilled the needs at Maslow's physiological, security, and social levels. They are confident in their ability to make a difference. Why do people with talent join a company? Webber of *Fast Company* said (at a consortium discussion in Santa Clara in 1998 on the changing nature of competitiveness) they "go where the message is 'we are a winner,' where there is a big risk and reward, to a company that has a 'save-the-world' mentality, and where they can do great work and their life will not be crazy."

Now the manager plays less a role of parental expert and more that of business expert. The manager in a knowledge enterprise needs to be much more familiar with overall company and business unit strategies and must work collaboratively with employees to "architect" roles and responsibilities that help their employees achieve the greatest impact.

A 1999 gathering of what *Fast Company* called "forty-five of the best brains in the new world of work" debated the new knowledge economy. For two days, business leaders, change agents, economists, educators, doctors, technologists, political activists, and public policy advocates compared notes and synthesized worlds to see what the future might hold. The bottom line: as in democracies, individuals are in charge now. People decide the news. This is new thinking.

John Patrick explains, in *Fast Company*. As vice president of Internet technology at IBM he leads IBM's effort to Web-enable computer users worldwide:

> Big and small companies, old and new companies, established companies and start-ups, are all facing the same challenge. But it's not really about how you organize your company; there are a lot of organizational models that can work. And it's not about whether you're centralized or decentralized; I think the world is moving in both directions at the same time. What's really important is recognizing that, because of the Net, individuals are in charge now.
>
> The companies that understand this, and act on it, will win. Take the news business, for example. Editors and publishers no longer decide for us what we're interested in, when we're interested in it, and the depth or degree to which we're interested. We decide. *We* choose what we want to explore, and when and how we want to explore it [pp. 142–143].

The flattening of the workforce may be cyclical. In the past few years, middle management has enjoyed a resurgence and once again become key to today's organizations. If hierarchy does make a comeback, and if the channel consists mostly of knowledge workers, then the ranks will define tactical responsibility and communication boundaries. This means that the communications challenges become more complex because more people will be responsible for communicating. Consequently more people need to articulate the corporate vision and strategy and require well-honed organizational communication skills.

The organization continues to diversify both in terms of the workforce and the customer base. How will diversity manifest through communications among future workforces? Global distribution actually pushes localization technology to speed up too. Soon a Web message in one language will automatically translate into the language the user chooses. The *Economist's* "The World in 1999" feature prepares us to "watch out for simultaneous-translation software, enabling two politicians, one speaking English and the other Arabic, to argue with each other fluently" (p. 85).

Will technology and communication needs create even more generational differences? The Institute for the Future, in a recent "outlook" discussion, predicted that uses of technology are going to shift from satisfying productivity needs to providing a social impact. Adults use technology for work; kids use computers for more than efficiency. It is part of their socialization. In schools, computers are part of the social context. As these kids enter the workforce, this bias affects communication and socialization in corporations.

The global economic boom of the 1990s tops the list of predictives in *Megatrends 2000,* by John Naisbitt and Patricia Aburdene (1990). The 1990s saw emerging European unification and the global scare caused by the Asian economic crisis (it was such a financial imbalance that for a time the whole world focused on the fragile Brazilian economy to see if the global dominoes would fall). Such economic interdependence increases as information networks become the global neural network, and global e-commerce becomes the heartbeat of the next century's economic activity.

Will the information age have an end? If innovation lags actualization, what will today's innovations be transformed into tomorrow? Business forecasters uniformly say that innovation takes thirty years to become a product. The *BusinessWeek* "21st Century Economy" issue reminds us that though the Internet barged onto the business scene and was a commercial proposition in the mid–1990s, it was a "direct descendent of ARPANet, which was based on research funded by the Defense Department in the 1960s" (p. 62). Who knows what today's cellular technologies, personal digital handhelds, laser research, e-commerce frenzy, or Y2K obsession will bring thirty years from now?

What about the more frightful side of information dependence and global fluidity? How will our society cope with information systems that could wage wars? In his book *The Next World War* (1998), James Adams warns of information warfare, in which national infrastructures can be wiped out in one push of a button.

Even without worrying about global information warfare, how much more information can we take? How will information overload look and feel with unlimited bandwidth and more powerful computer brains? In a recent *San Jose Mercury News* article, "The Future of Technology," Paul Horn, senior vice president and director of IBM research, explained his "pervasive computing" concept: "Two decades from now the local devices will probably store anywhere from 10 to 100 terabytes of data" (p. 5E). "Certainly the human brain can't just take in all that data and use it sensibly. You need a computer to filter through all the information and get the really key important nuggets" (p. 1E). This is deep computing.

Indeed, information seems to adopt a personality of its own as it continues to surround us, swallow us, and spit us out. Bob Johansen, president of the Institute for the Future, has interviewed many corporate leaders concerning twenty-first-century organizations. In conversations with Ellen Knapp, chief knowledge officer for PricewaterhouseCoopers, she distinguishes between information "gluttons" and information "gourmets": "Gluttons want everything they see and try futilely to keep up with it all. They confuse quantity with quality. Gourmets, on the other hand, show more discernment. They have a clear idea of what is important to them and make intentional choices regarding what to read and what to avoid, when to attend and when to stay home, what sources to value and what sources to ignore" ("Leadership in 21st Century Organizations," 1999, p. 180). Indeed, communicators in the new world will aid information digestion.

Despite gourmet information editing, indigestion and fragmentation are likely to continue as information keeps barraging people. Physicist David Bohm applies quantum principles to organizational dynamics and offers insight about what happens when an individual experiences overload. In *Wholeness and the Implicate Order*, he says, "Fragmentation is now very widespread, not only throughout society, but also in each individual; and this is leading to a kind of general confusion of the mind, which creates an endless series of problems and [which] interferes with our clarity of perception so seriously as to prevent us from being able to solve most of them" (1980, p. 1). Is it possible that information paralysis is around the corner?

If not paralysis, information overload could at least cause more dislocation. *BusinessWeek* addressed this in its "21st Century Economy" feature article: "Major dislocations and uncertainty for workers and businesses will be inevitable as new technologies are adopted" (Mandel, p. 63). Planning for fluidity and creating universitylike environments are two antidotes to the displacement that so much information promises.

Will the disparity of information access—and therefore of knowledge—diminish, or continue to widen? Information is not only power, though; it also translates to wealth. If the gap between the "knows" and the "know nots" continues, worldwide stability could be at risk. Throughout history, trends toward enlarging the gulf between those who have and those who do not repeatedly lead to rebellion. If information repositories continue to grow, then expanded access to them must at a minimum keep in step. This same disparity translates inside the corporate walls. If the gap between knows and know-nots grows wider, it will debilitate organizations.

CIO magazine describes the "externalization imperative" regarding information flow: "In the century ahead, companies will. . .

be judged and even valued by how well they can 'expose' information to facilitate collaboration on products, customer service, marketing, sales, distribution, or manufacturing" (Kutnick, p. 120). This redefines exposure, in a way, as a positive imperative and one founded on open and honest communication. "Success in the twenty-first century will require new levels of corporate candor," reports Dale Kutnick in the December 1998 issue of the magazine (p. 120). "Enterprises have always had to communicate beyond their borders, but relationships and feedback loops have been erratic at best." This has to change.

Too much information has birthed many new industries and will continue to do so well into the first decade of the twenty-first century. At the moment, projects described as "knowledge management" (KM) or e-commerce initiatives tend to get funded more readily. Technologies that promise to manage information, context resources, or tailor data also headline many organizational initiative PowerPoint slides. Because many businesses are interested in capitalizing on helping people manage the information they have, all kinds of technologies, concepts, and products have been tossed into the ring. Though still difficult to define exactly, knowledge management is already big business. In *Knowledge Management* magazine (October 1998b, p. 15), writer Geof Petch's article "Leadership Challenge in KM's Deep Water" reports that KM as a new category of business thought and technology is registering 84 percent annual growth rates and is projected to reach $2 billion in revenues by the year 2000.

Knowledge is not limited to what is found inside an organization. In the future, good ideas will not just come from the corner office, says *Fast Company*'s Webber; they will come from "customers and the people in the trenches doing the real work" (1998, Seminar: "The Changing Nature of Competiveness"). As knowledge managers, we must learn to tap this reservoir.

Knowledge management "experts" predict a time when information is captured and communicated in the course of our daily routine. Will human beings ever communicate prolifically and seamlessly, like cells in the body? There are sure to be advances in that direction.

In an environment of accelerating change, how will businesses compete? What does Internet time do to competitiveness? If Internet technology continues to advance at the current pace, within a few years we will nostalgically recall today's Internet in much the same way we now remember black and white television. Saffo of the Institute for the Future says, "The Web at 10X is a new experience; the Web at 100X is something unlike [what] we know." The boundaries that now limit our communications will not exist. There will be new boundaries, but technologies will continue to offer more, better, faster.

With countless technologies speeding to market and boundaries continuing to blur, information *in context* is essential to understanding the competitive landscape. Partners are sometimes partners and sometimes competitors. Customers are also vendors. Media, employees, enemies, partners, competitors—what is the new order? Everyone seems to be doing business with everyone else. Once-distinct lines shift and disappear. How do companies play competitively in this environment?

What is internal information? What is external? Answering these questions is becoming more and more difficult. Organizations that adapt to, leverage, and even exacerbate this new environment will succeed. Emerging Internet and e-business organizations are exploring and capitalizing on this transparency. There are many schools of thought on boundaries, among them classic Newtonian mechanism and chaos and systems theories. The most promising approaches are those that merge both chaos and order. Dee Hock, the founder and former CEO of Visa International, describes the "chaordic" organization as one that holds a few principles tightly but, once the principles are defined, allows chaos to rule. Such combination theories are compelling and map directly to characteristics that make strategic corporate journalism effective. A defined vision, clear purpose and values, an operational strategy, and message weighting all combine to clearly brand these elements into the organizational psyche. This creates an environment, then, that is ripe for journalistic reporting. It creates an open and accurate information flow that coexists and weaves in and around the natural chaos of the new world.

"The fact that technology is so fast prompts us to prize speed as an end in itself. The data computers make so available to us moves us sometimes to crave information more than we have the capacity to make sense of it." In the January 1999 issue of *Wired*, some technologists ponder whether the Internet and all the stuff it throws at us is an antidote to loneliness (pp. 97–135). Yes, we may have bandwidth to burn, but no matter how you slice it, unless we decipher ways to add more capacity to the brain's hard drive, information will just spill off the plate.

THE KNOWLEDGE ECONOMY

Intellectual capital is knowledge or information that can be legally owned. The roots of knowledge management are in intellectual capital. A recent Institute for the Future Outlook Project focused on knowledge management. Knowledge is what walks out the door every night in your employees—you cannot own it, cannot control it by patents, and certainly cannot manage it. Companies today are investigating structures and knowledge economies, as opposed to technologies and point solutions.

In *Intellectual Capital*, Stewart describes a shift in the value of information: "In today's wired world of commerce, information beats inventory. The plummeting cost of information and its associated technology is dropping faster than Wile E. Coyote and has changed the economics of organizations" (p. 25). Stewart offers ten principles for organizations to manage intellectual capital, one of which is to focus on information flow, not the flow of materials. Will information really become more important than inventory in the new economy?

Virtual work will also grow thanks to technological advancements, the power of the knowledge workforce, and the mobility of the global company. "The virtual firm," as Michael Dell, CEO of Dell Computers, calls it in the *Economist*, "is one that will enable management, ever more reliant on information, to migrate to the ether. . . . The linkage of personal computers with network servers will change the very nature of our corporations" (1999, p. 124). Witness the evolution of the Internet, which grew organically from the seeds of users' combined efforts. The Internet was self-managed, with no central management. Consequently, its structure now ushers in new ways to stay linked. "The Internet makes it possible to create true information partnerships," Dell says. "These partnerships, formed around information assets, will transform traditional notions of economic value. Instead, both suppliers and customers will come to be treated as information partners."

How else does the rise of the network—both in technology and concept—affect the new knowledge economy? It ushers in a kind of "temporary company," and with it new communications challenges. "The Dawn of the E-Lance Economy," a 1998 *Harvard Business Review* article, describes how the evolution of organic networks over the years provides insight into the coming networked world. The authors of the article write:

> The Linux community [Linux is an open-source version of the UNIX operating system], a temporary, self-managed gathering of diverse individuals engaged in a common task, is a model for a new kind of business organization that could form the basis for a new kind of economy. . . . Despite all the recent talk of decentralized management, empowered employees; and horizontal processes, the large, industrial organization continues to dominate the economy today. We remain in the age of multinational megacompanies. Yet beneath the surface

of all the megamergers and acquisitions activity, we
see signs of a counterphenomenon: the disintegration of
the large corporation. People are leaving big companies
and either joining much smaller companies or going
into business for themselves—e-lancers [Malone and
Laubacher, 1998, pp. 146–147].

Electronic networks allow information to be shared instantly
and inexpensively among many people in many locations. This de-
creases both expensive bureaucracies and centralized decision making. "Electronic networks," the same authors write, "enable these
microbusinesses to tap into the global reservoirs of information,
expertise, and financing. Individuals can manage themselves, coordinating their efforts through electronic links with other independent parties" (pp. 147–148).

They predict further that, in the wake of the Internet's combined,
decentralized, self-managed growth and in the steps taken by Linus
Torvalds, originator of Linux, "we will enter the age of the temporary company." This technology provides fertile ground for self-orga-
nized systems. Groups come together as needed; workers have
less-permanent offices and more-mobile docking environments.
Likewise, people linked by networks come together, form "companies," and then disband once the project ends.

These new companies and the new Web order also give rise to
the enterprise entrepreneur. *Knowledge Management* talks about
those workers who, in large organizations, not only mine and har-
vest knowledge but also manage projects entrepreneurially and effectively will be more successful (p. 71).

Chris Newell, executive director of the Lotus Institute, says in
Fast Company the real challenge is to get people to think in new
ways. The institute, a part of Lotus Corporation that he founded in
1994, explores how technology and human issues intersect. The
new mission for Lotus, he says: "to inspire innovative solutions that
transform communication and knowledge into value. And our value

is both in connecting communities in a way that shrinks the world and in providing access to ideas that will expand the world. That's what it takes to stay entrepreneurial—whether you're a startup or you're trying to reinvent yourself" (Feb–March 1999, p. 142).

John Patrick, vice president of Internet technology at IBM, describes some of the challenges in Web-enabling computer users everywhere. The shift to Internet time is happening everywhere, he says in the same conversation. "Companies that still think that they're open only Monday through Friday, from 9:00 A.M. to 5:00 P.M., are operating on a totally obsolete notion. You can see the shift happening industry by industry: the Net turns everyone into a startup. It's a radical shift—it really does mean power to the people. And you have to evolve if you're going to survive" (p. 143).

What about governance in this new modern democracy? Will anarchy rule? The *Economist* addresses the question as the "battle for corporate honesty." Wolfensohn of the World Bank asserts that "the proper governance of companies will become as crucial to the world economy as the proper governing of countries" (p. 78). Is his thesis, that "accountable business leadership is a vital element of modern democracy," enough? "As the battered economies of the emerging markets piece themselves back together in 1999," Wolfensohn writes, "one lesson will not be forgotten: rotten national economies spring from rotten corporations; if business life is not run on open and honest lines, there is little chance that the wider economy can be" (p. 78).

Self-governance and peer governance also play a role. Though the Internet evolved through self-management, standards and protocols ensured its survival. Similarly, the immediate future will be heralded as "the era of standards" as templates, protocols, and guidelines make a resurgence within organic environments. They do not hinder innovation but will in fact inspire it.

The breakdown of fully predictable Newtonian order has created a desire for some constancy amid the chaos. Hock's chaordic theories describe unpredictable human systems that require some inviolable principles. Call these principles standards, tenets, guidelines, values, commandments, or laws—they are the foundation for order within chaos.

Adhering to these principles yields organic order and also trust, community, and corporate spirit. Like societies and religions that have principles to which they adhere, all organizations must have the same foundation. Organizations that focus solely on sterile visions, soulless environments, or ethically soft behaviors will lose employees in the future. Expect a reinvigoration of spirituality not only in society but also in the workplace.

Corporate spiritualists aren't the only ones talking about corporate trust. Think-tank discussions and futurist conversations all seem eventually to migrate back toward these issues. *Fast Company's* orchestrated gathering of thinkers in the new world of work included leaders, business thinkers and strategists, change agents, educators, and activists (from small, large, young, old, unknown, and well-regarded business, political, and academic institutions). Their dialogue, edited and presented in the February 1999 issue, touches on these issues as well.

Karen Stephenson asks, "How do we create *networks of trust* that allow for diversity? As an anthropologist, I've learned that, primordially, trust is formed around the campfire. Trust is all about homogeneity: you look like me, you dress like me, you talk like me—I can trust you. But today, if I'm going to learn something new, I've got to trust people who are different from me—and that means diversity. Not diversity for reasons of political correctness, but for reasons of innovation. The challenge today is to build networks of diversity that fuel innovation, even when our primordial instincts tell us otherwise" (1999, p. 148).

The Outlook Project discussions sponsored by the Institute for the Future reach similar conclusions. In one such dialogue, the comment was made that "trust, control, privacy . . . are defined by each generation—they don't pass from generation to generation with technology." Organizations must find ways to scale trust that is defined as each generation sees it and uses it across the network.

COMMUNICATIONS TRENDS

Saffo predicts that "by 2010, less than one-quarter of one percent of all communication will be human communication" (presentation of the Institute for the Future, November 1998, in Santa Clara). Instead, he postulates, communication will mostly occur device-to-device, as in chips in cars or remote-controlled machines or agent-to-computer messages. How will this affect the social patterns of communication within which we operate now?

In managing relationships, new codes of conduct may develop. Even now, we e-mail people or leave voice mail messages for those we would rather not talk to, or for efficiencies that are difficult to retain in live conversation. Years ago, workers used to have meetings for everything. How will this electronic climate affect the social fabric in the corporation? In the high-tech home of the future, kids will drive the household "communication space," creating a community "zone" with communication continuity. Who will drive this space in the corporation?

The trends described above have ushered in challenges. What can organizations do to operate better within this new environment? How can complex contextualization become part of a corporation's communication strategy? How can webs provide information architecture that leads to valuable insight? What role will journalism play?

Reinforcing the new dynamics of information-based economics, Johansen advocates "digital storytelling" for organizations as a way to contextualize information, build community and trust, and chart an organization's future path: "If we are interested in creating new knowledge—and not just more information—we need to create 'stories' in the medium of the twenty-first century—digitally excellent and interactive. The company of the future must master this art and foster tools that help workers easily and quickly translate their experiences into compelling stories that can be shared interactively" (Johansen, 1997b, pp. iii–v). This kind of storytelling, he says, could extend democracy both inside a company and as part of the extended social fabric.

Tom Gruber, chief technical officer of Intraspect Software (business intelligence software), talks about "group memory" in *Knowledge Management*: "Group memory is at the intersection of what humans and computers respectively do best. Humans do knowledge work. Computers remember it, in context, and then communicate it when called on. It's an organizational intelligence plus a memory for the enterprise" (Petch, 1998a, p. 48). Products and organizational processes that focus on the importance of collective context and create a common repository will be able to create what he calls a "sweet spot of enterprise knowledge."

Not only must organizations create ways to capture knowledge, they must also figure out how to pass the learning on to more and more people. In the future, the distinction between learning and communicating will diminish. Organizational theorist Peter Senge talks about this in his book *The Fifth Discipline*, which detailed the learning-organization concept in 1990. "Newsletters, electronic networks, and meetings of many types will all be important to nurture the continuing development of the community of practitioners of learning organizations," Senge says (p. xx). He addresses the complexity of communicating in learning organizations as well: "As the world becomes more interconnected and business becomes more complex and dynamic, work must become more 'learningful'" (p. 4).

John Coné, vice president of Dell University, agrees that the boundaries of learning and communications are continuing to blur. In fact, in an article in *Fast Company* he talks about new models for learning, and how business educators and communicators are one and the same person: "On-demand learning—the ideal 'learning event' at Dell has a class size of one, lasts five to ten minutes, and takes place within ten minutes of when someone recognizes that he or she needs to know something" (Dahle, 1998, p. 180). Dell is simply bypassing the old front-end model of learning. "Now we're into continuous learning—you learn what you need to know as you go. . . . There's going to be a radical shift from the importance of knowing something to the importance of knowing how to find out," says Coné (Dahle, 1998, p. 184).

Diane Gayeski, Ph.D., professor of organizational communication and learning at Ithaca College and principal of OmniCom Associates, takes this concept of training and communications merging to an even more organic level. In a book she is writing, titled *Mindshare,* she says, "The lines between training and communication are blurring and probably should dissolve. We need journalistic skills more in the training-and-learning realm than we do in writing about company news" (personal interview). Reported, contextualized information delivered in broadcast fashion is an example of how good journalistic skills have been exceedingly valuable in developing training programs.

If the lines between communication and learning are blurring, what about the lines between organizational communication and corporate dialogue? For years organizational communication trends have centered on proactive, orchestrated communications that enable interactivity. Though these are laudable goals, they ignore the fact that communications technologies are getting faster and more effective. Today, reactive, extemporaneous communications are critical. Being prepared helps, but being an expert at reactive communications provides much more value. Journalism shines in a reactive environment. Corporate journalism skills—especially the ability to get information fast, contextualize it well, and report it accurately—are becoming core competencies of central communicators. These reactive skills, coupled with the ability to synthesize and set context well, propel organizational communication forward and provide the only hope of being proactive in the Internet age.

Corporate dialogue will continue to enjoy the spotlight, but most of the attention here is on what occurs between more intimate manager and employee interaction, peer-to-peer sharing, or communities of interest and practice levels rather than corporationwide interactivity.

LEGAL TRENDS

How will information laws affect the open and global flow of information? The legal industry continues to tackle privacy, free speech, and intellectual property issues. Will laws effectively constrain information flow? Information, as always, weaves its way around legal boundaries. Dams are erected, dikes are dug, but the overwhelming pressure of worldwide information cannot be constrained for long. In a global economy, laws affecting information flow need to be more global. This requirement almost guarantees their ineffectiveness.

Will global monopolies surface, squelching the requirement for efficient information flow? This is one area where legal boundaries are likely to be effective. Otherwise, dominating and cancerlike institutions could cripple information flow and eventually kill the host (that is, capitalism).

SOCIETAL JOURNALISM AND STRATEGIC CORPORATE JOURNALISM

Will trends in societal journalism affect the fundamentals of strategic corporate journalism? As corporate journalists try harder to "free" the internal presses, will societal journalism continue down the path in the opposite direction—away from independence and toward publishers who over influence toward the public's lowest common denominator appetite? Will current trends toward sensationalism and the competitive frenzy to get the story first affect journalism in the workplace? Can strategic corporate journalism affect societal journalism? Will the differences between alignment and partnership in corporate journalism make their way into societal journalism? Since one model pulls its fundamental tenets from the other, changes in one continue to affect the other. Many journalistic publications that are creating Internet vehicles glean ideas from organizational intranets. Intranet journalistic headlines have been pulled not just from the fundamentals of journalism but also from sensational headlining trends. As more organizations adopt strategic corporate journalism, this two-pronged influence continues.

SOME CLOSING THOUGHTS

All of the movement and convergence of trends we've identified indicate that organizations will continue to move away from the mechanistic end of the continuum toward the systems-thinking, chaos-theory, and organic-alignment end. Information, and effective communication of it, is the most critical element in this transition. If open and accurate information does not flow (with some restraints), systems malfunction, chaos disrupts, and the organism dies. A strategic corporate organizational communication model is essential to enable this information flow.

The utopian organization of the future has determined its chaordic boundaries. Legal definitions of confidentiality and intellectual property are now utterly internalized and static. Seamless and unobtrusive knowledge management systems capture and distribute data, information, knowledge, and insight in the course of daily routine. Organizations are operating more and more organically. Perhaps one day in the future an organization will not need a strategic mapping of journalism to guide information flow. Perhaps then strategic content management will be so embedded in the culture and cocreated by all constituents that orchestrating it is unnecessary. Although that socialistic science-fiction future is a distant possibility, organizational metabolisms continue to increase exponentially, requiring faster, more reliable, and more differentiated information flow. Until the day when this flow is intrically woven and "dazzling" (as Wheatley and Kellner-Rogers describe the instantaneous, holistic ecosystem communication in *A Simpler Way*), strategic corporate journalism is required to keep up with ever-increasing organizational demand for open, accurate, timely, and strategically weighted information.

A Guide to Corporate Journalism

Part One: Surveying the Landscape

Part Two: Requirements for Corporate Journalism

Part Three: Return on Investment (ROI)

Part Four: Transition Plan

Part Five: Getting Support for the New Model

Part Six: The Transition

Part Seven: Metrics

How does an organization get started integrating strategic corporate journalism as the core of an organizational communication strategy? This appendix provides guidance for organizational communication strategists to survey their existing internal and external environment. It helps them evaluate the gap analysis for implementation and then structure a team and process to begin journalistic practices within the corporate environment.

This guide evaluates the climate from three angles: publishing, journalism, and corporate communications. We have structured this appendix like a workbook chapter, with questions and templated sections. Consider this set of questions a "communications plan template for corporate journalism." If you answer the questions presented here in their order, you will have a well-structured communication tool that identifies the feasibility and practicality of introducing or refining corporate journalism within your organization, whether large or small. Further, this tool helps you examine the interrelationship between publishing, journalism, and corporate communications.

The essence of strategic corporate journalism is timely transmission of open, accurate, strategically weighted information. Although this book proposes that to achieve organizational alignment most organizations, especially larger ones, need to employ a strategic corporate journalism model at the core of the organizational communications strategy, some organizations may achieve alignment through other means. Strategic corporate journalism works best in organizations that seek a less command-and-control, more democratic organizational alignment.

PART ONE: SURVEYING THE LANDSCAPE

I. Industry Dynamics and Company Vision and Mission

How important and how challenging is it to achieve organizational alignment?

Before creating any strategic or operational communication model, you must first analyze the dynamics of the industry and the goals of the organization.

❑ Does your organization require alignment of its members? For example, if the organization is dismantling or selling off parts and doesn't require or desire employee retention, alignment may not be necessary.

❑ What is the corporate vision and mission? What is the business model? What are the key products? Which markets do you serve? How much information flow does the business model or industry incur? For example, a consumer market focus within a dynamic industry requires more information flow than a niche market in a static industry.

❑ Are your organization's vision and goals, and the information that affects organizational success, simple enough that they are easily understood and articulated by all members?

❑ Does your organization often (or rarely) change its priorities, goals, product road map, or strategic direction? Static organizations that do not change these focuses often may already have a deeply internalized understanding and alignment; therefore, they may not benefit as much from strategic corporate journalism.

❑ Is your organization purposefully monopolistic, insular, or myopically focused? Does your organization need a broad understanding of the competitive landscape, or not?

❑ Is chaotic freedom more important than alignment (as with think tanks, some creative design firms, certain start-ups, etc.)?

❑ Are there organizational legal or practical constraints on how open organizational communication can be (for example, in a weapons research firm)?

II. "State of the Company"

How difficult is employee attraction, retention, and motivation?

❑ Which phase is the company experiencing: growth, maturation, or decline?

❑ Is the company seen externally as hot, an industry darling, an enterprise of the moment, an up-and-comer, a best place to work—or just another place to work?

❑ Do the employees have a large stake in the company's success (unvested options and the like) that affect the retention strategy?

❑ What is the organizational pulse or state of morale?

❏ Is the company in a state of crisis? Are employees looking for signs of turnaround?

III. Company and Workforce Makeup

How complex is your organization?

❏ How many employees does your organization have? What is your annual revenue? What is your current growth rate? Are there resources to fund a central organizational communication department?

❏ How hierarchical is decision making in your organization? Is it clear who decides what?

❏ How decentralized is the organization? Is it clear which decisions are made centrally and which are made locally?

❏ How interdependent are your business units? For organizational success, is it necessary to have fluid information flow between different parts of the organization?

❏ How global is your organization? Does your company just do business or have offices internationally, or does it really think and perform on a global basis? That is, do you have an international organizational and technological infrastructure, fluid financial transactions, considerations of language localization, etc.?

❏ What are the demographics of the employees in your organization? How many employees are located where? What is the gender and age breakdown? Is the workforce a knowledge or a labor workforce? How educated are the employees? What ethnicity and cultural heritage do they represent? How technologically savvy are they?

❏ How mechanistic is your organization? Is there a conscious attempt to shift toward a more organic model?

❏ What is the fluidity of your workforce? Is your workforce easily recruited away because they possess desirable skill sets or are proximate to local competition? Or is your organization the only game in town?

IV. Communication Norms

How does organizational communication occur within your company?

❏ Can your organization have an organizationwide interactive communication meeting easily and often in one room? Some start-ups, for example, can do so; yet the amount and complexity of information affecting the success of most companies makes this level of natural and efficient information flow almost impossible even for small companies.

❏ Describe the organizational dynamics and fluidity of communication of the current environment. How does your company educate its employees? Describe the interactivity dynamics. Does your organization have broadscale interactivity? Does your organization encourage or expect one-on-one interactivity?

❏ Is communication at all closed or manipulative? Is it open and fluid? Are organizational leaders idolized?

❏ Do people believe organizational communications?

❏ How timely are communications? What is the frequency of standard organizational publications? Does organizational communication lag behind external communication? How far is the rumor mill ahead of organizational communication?

❏ Are communications appropriately weighted? Do employees understand the priority of communications?

❑ What is the tone and style of most organizational communications: formal or informal? jazzy or staid?

❑ Are communications set in appropriate context? Do employees understand the essence and relevance of communications?

❑ Are communications consistent? Does inconsistency ever cause confusion?

❑ What is the current organizational communication model?

❑ Detail your organizational communication channels and norms. What are the channels for broadcast communications? for dialogue? learning? collaboration? Do these norms evolve without guidance?

❑ Is there a primary broadcast communication channel? Who "owns" it? Where do organizational members currently look for broad corporate messaging? Are there target channels for specific audiences? Do employees know exactly where to go for particular types of messages? Do organizational communicators know which channels to use for which types of communications?

❑ Do you have one or more central communications organizations (or at least one)?

❑ Is there one primary organization responsible for broadcast communications, or are there several broadcast organizations (perhaps public relations, employee communications, investor relations, marketing communication, etc.)? If there are several broadcast communications organizations, is one responsible for integrating all broadcast communications, or does one organization create the primary communications model that sets the tone for the others?

❑ Who are the primary organizational communicators? Are the executives the only ones who communicate broadly across the organization, or is broadcast communication more decentralized?

❏ Are executives accessible to employees? Do managers cascade messages openly and in prioritized fashion? Are broad company messages consistent with divisional messages? Do managers provide additional context to their teams when necessary, for broad communications?

❏ What are the communication skill sets of organizational leaders? Of organizational communicators?

V. Central Organizational Communication

How is your company structured to enable organizational communications?

If you have one or more central communications departments:

❏ What are the primary goals of these departments: motivation? awareness? business literacy? What are the secondary goals? What is the communications model? What communications vehicles are used? Is organizational alignment sought toward an overarching vision, purpose, values, operational strategy, company priorities, or something else? Does the charter of these teams include external focus?

❏ Where do these departments report? Are they structured so that they can have an organizationwide focus? Are they overly influenced by the goals of their parent organizations? For example, if positioned within the marketing organization, are they overly influenced by PR?

❏ Do the central communication organizations thoroughly understand the aggregate of business elements with which the employees need to align?

❏ Do central communications organizations have access to the executives? How does this team determine focus areas, direction of alignment, or the elements that need to be internalized by the entire organization? These elements should be prioritized according to target audience. (For example: a sales organization may prioritize the sales strategy and product offerings as the two most critical elements with which to align, while finance may focus on financial targets and corporate investment priorities.)

VI. Partnerships

How well integrated are your communications department(s)?

Building and nurturing communication partnerships means more than having contacts and sources. Successful communication partnerships entail building relationships where both partners strive for the same organizational alignment goals. Communications intended for the entire organization are not all generated from one communications department; in larger organizations even centralized organizational communications may be orchestrated by different departments. For an organizational communication system to work, the primary departments responsible for orchestration must work in close partnership. If these departments are not aligned, there is no way to achieve organizational alignment. If you are responsible for a central communications department, you must ask yourself:

❑ Which other communication departments are key to consistent, broad-based organizational communications? Which managers need to support your communication strategy? Who are the key communicators in the organization (public relations, investor relations, industry relations, field communications, marketing communications, internal audience, specific communicators, respected leaders in the company, executives)? How often should the managers of these groups meet? How should they communicate when it is urgent? What is the process to communicate to all groups when one manager has a message to communicate to a constituency?

❑ How can you partner with organizational leaders and communicators across the company to build a successful communications and corporate journalism model? How can you track the pulse of various management teams, incorporating their communications objectives while sharing the broad organizational model? How can you integrate communication strategies specific to business units and help them align with the overarching organizational communications strategy?

❑ How can you help create a culture of information sharing and interaction?

VII. Resources

How well resourced are your communications teams?

If you are responsible for an organizational communications department, you must ask:

❑ What are the current financial and people resources available to support your communications department? How much is the organization spending vis-à-vis external communications departments? Can you benchmark against other organizations within your industry?

❑ Is the company growing or trying to cut costs?

VIII. Communications Infrastructure

How advanced is your communications infrastructure?

❑ What is the technical infrastructure of the organization? What is the voice mail infrastructure? Is teleconferencing widely used and easily accessible? Is the entire company on one e-mail system? Do all employees have the same operating system?

❑ Does your company have an intranet? Is there a corporate portal site? Is it global? What are the bandwidth limitations?

❑ Does your company have satellite broadcast capability? videoconferencing abilities?

❑ Is the rumor mill primarily verbally, or electronically propelled?

❑ How does the facilities infrastructure influence communication? Is the company a closed office or a cubicle environment? Are there venues for team meetings, departmental meetings, business unit meetings, and companywide meetings? How much communication happens over cubicle walls or in hallways? Are there company cafeterias, break rooms, or other open spaces for communications?

IX. Analysis of Current Communications Model

How effective is your current communications model?

❑ Is organizational alignment being achieved successfully? Could there be more effective alignment?

❑ What are the barriers to open, accurate, timely, weighted, and unbiased communication? Will there be executive resistance to corporate candor?

❑ Is it difficult to get a message through to the entire organization? Is it easy to target a specific audience?

❑ Do employees complain about "poor communications"? Do employees complain about (and subsequently filter or ignore) communications spam?

❑ Are corporate communications ignored or deemed corporatespeak, or propaganda? Is openness selective for the right reasons? Are corporate communications overly biased? Are they overly positive? manipulative? Are they myopic and focused on the function or geography in which the team is headquartered?

❏ Is the central communications team purely reactive to executive requests (or whims), or are they treated as consultants or advisors? Does the team have credibility with the executive team?

❏ Are communications too fragmented? Should a primary communications channel be created? How difficult would it be to create, manage, and acculturate central communications?

❏ Do organizational leaders understand their role in broad organizational alignment (as opposed to alignment within their specific function or geography)?

PART TWO: REQUIREMENTS FOR CORPORATE JOURNALISM

Introducing or building upon corporate journalism inside a corporation looks similar to the process for starting up a newspaper or magazine. Objectives are identified. The business model is crafted. The audience demographics (employee statistics) are analyzed. Strategic editorial calendars should be created, with input from readers (employees), owners (executives), and editors (communication managers). Editorial processes are created based on real-world journalistic principles and practices. Writers guidelines, article outlines and approvals prior to beginning, factual reporting, permission to snoop out angles and hidden facts, use of leads, writing that shows a well-crafted and intriguing style, research, encouragement to question behaviors perceived to be contrary to the organization's values, editorial review cycles, well-designed production . . . these all contribute to solidly produced journalistic features and publications.

Journalistic Elements

A publication needs relative *independence*. In the corporate world, the news organization is not usually designed (nor allowed) to earn money in the traditional way—selling advertising space or subscriptions—though this could become a future model. An internal news agency or intranet communications group, for example, could adopt a subscription model whereby the news organ sells space on its site or sells ads for outside products and services.

Currently in most companies, the news organization is fully funded by the corporation itself and is based on the model that the information it distributes is important news to be pushed (traditional corporate top-down communications). In adopting a strategic news and information model, the corporation more closely approximates a news organization (albeit with a different mission on which to report). To lay the groundwork for a corporate journalism model, you must consider both building reporting talent on the communications team and outsourcing the reporting and writing of the news. At the helm of the publication, you must also install a strategically oriented publisher and editorial team.

Access is everything in Washington, D.C. (or any political environment), and it is no less true in a corporation. To rise above the level of newsletter and bulletin board or local reporting, the corporate journalist and editorial team must use a combination of high-level access and solid research to get, and balance, the content of news stories. Networking, snooping, and working contacts for important nuggets of information are among the reporter's responsibilities. This means, of course, commitment on the part of leadership to allow the reporting to take place and to understand that doing so does not jeopardize either strategic or tactical activity, but rather opens up the process to some scrutiny and accountability, with potential for feedback and disagreement. This means having a leadership that is willing to face more accountability for how it leads. But the threat of giving so much access is not likely to intimidate strong, confident leaders who understand the dynamics and motivation of a knowledge workforce.

Attribution and by-lines build and keep credibility, and they keep people honest and accountable. Most newspaper columns are attributed to an author. Who owns the message, and who reports it?

Putting out propaganda without an individual declaring responsibility for it takes a toll instantly on the entire news organization.

Interactivity (such as letters to the editor) is critical so that redress can be sought and questions asked. A news hotline for both good news and the raising of issues is also powerful. Again, centralized journalistic interactivity is limited at best; broader, more local interactivity should augment strategic corporate journalism as part of an overarching organizational communication model.

Unlike the American media, which sees most of its revenues and readership in native terms, for global organizations strategic corporate journalism must by necessity have a *global focus*. In the corporate world, an American-focused media product cannot be distributed internationally unless it addresses the means by which it can function on a global scale. Consider the parallels in social journalism.

During the Gulf War, the only instantaneous and internationally accessible mass news source was CNN. Eyes around the world were glued to the network's green-tinted display and night-vision shots of antiaircraft fire dotting the Baghdad skyline as cruise missiles and other smart bombs laser-tracked their way to targets. Because the news was legally (and understandably) controlled by the U.S. military, the entire world received news reports angled and directed by the American military. This reality did not sit well with some European nations and broadcasters, despite the fact that their governments were part of the allied coalition.

A monopoly news source with a highly defined agenda rarely takes into account the needs and desires of a global audience. Reporters would talk about American soldiers as "our troops" and often lapsed into the language of accord, referring to the U.S. government as "we." Aside from the obvious concession of editorial independence through identification with the news source, it was also a blatant failure to recognize that the audience was not entirely American. The American foreign policy establishment may have been happy with this unconscious expressiveness, but few others whom it served were so sanguine. Of the three U.S. network news anchors, Peter Jennings (a native Canadian who was married to a native Hungarian) never identified the newsperson with the subject. Peter Arnett, a New Zealander by birth, always conscientiously referred to the warring parties in the third person while some of his American colleagues in Baghdad went so far as to relate the bombs bursting in air to a "Fourth of July" fireworks display, an analogy that was lost upon, or at least not appreciated by, some of the British audience.

Norms of consistency, language, design, distribution, feedback channel, anonymity, media, publishing frequency, and so on build credibility. All organizational communication norms must support the strategic corporate journalistic model. One norm out of line (for instance, publishing anonymous articles) can destroy the credibility of the model just as a bad column can have an impact on the credibility of a newspaper.

The concept of covering organizational *news* may seem obvious, but many organizations that use journalistic language and possibly even journalistic tactics overlook the concept of reporting organizational news. Writers need to become reporters, covering events, beats, and whatever appears to be news in the making.

With all of today's information technology, nothing beats *live coverage*. Many organizational communication teams understand the need to foster organizational interaction, but they often spend their time purely on event orchestration rather than ensuring that the event has live coverage that is broadcast to those belonging to the organization who are unable to attend the event. This concept of live coverage should extend beyond the events coordinated at the corporate level. Reporters should cover functionally and geographically specific events hosted throughout the company. One journalistic goal is to represent an integrated view of the organization. Live coverage helps achieve this objective.

For most audiences, *multimedia* has a much stronger impact than pure text does. Integrating multimedia into a journalistic model may involve adding imagery, audio clips, and video clips to journalistic reporting, or creating audio- or video-specific broadcast channels, or orchestrating events where attention-grabbing multimedia presentations take center stage.

In most companies, there are communications channels for different types of communication. *Target channels* are effective for providing specific context to a particular audience and are most useful when the distinctions among channels are quite clear and employees know which channel to use for which type of communication. Yet separate channels make the effectiveness of a journalistic model difficult to achieve. Employees usually only have time to focus on what is critical. If the critical broadcast channel is separated from the reporting channel or the feature channel, or if it is ancillary to the critical path, journalism does not have an impact. This channel distinction is one reason company newsletters have, in many cases, been deemed superfluous to the business objectives. If, on the other hand, there is a primary broadcast channel that *integrates* urgent announcements, strategic messages, journalistic reporting, and features and if the news diet is worked into the critical path, knowledge workers will consume the journalistic material. The equal footing given to urgent messages and journalistic reporting is critical for a solid journalistic stance.

Having a primary integrated broadcast communications channel does not mean that it should be used for all corporate broadcast communications. There are huge benefits to creating distinct channels for audience-specific or message-specific communications. For example, a sales organization may need a focused sales communication channel, and urgent "immediate reply to" messages should probably use whatever push medium of corporate dialogue is well acculturated (say, voice mail or e-mail). But when creating channel distinctions, it is important to work toward differentiation that does not dilute the effectiveness of the primary channel.

Strategic news coverage does not happen by accident. It takes both planning and building a process that allows for incoming news as well as future planning. The team's editorial calendars and forward-looking, strategic examination of what should be covered can be merged with reactive coverage of urgent, immediate news. Both the proactive and reactive reporting are critical and affect the other.

Assigning writers to target audiences or topic areas (beats) can create critical depth in a subject area. *Beat reporting* aids credibility as well as operational efficiency. In most organizations, there are usually many potential beats and a limited number of writers. How, then, do you choose the most important beats on which to focus? Choose the most critical focus areas for the company. Some suggestions common to most companies are to cover the executive beat, external press beat (perhaps public relations), industry beat (industry relations), investor relations beat (if the company is public), the customer beat (customer testimonials, success stories), a specific product or service beat (whatever the company's core production is), internal audience beats (engineering, sales, customer service), rumor mill beat, and specific technology beats (in a high-technology company, such beats could be operating systems, network structure, interfaces, graphics, etc.).

Journalistic Skills

The editorial team and reporters need to:

❑ Be trained in the skills of news gathering and the craft of writing.

❑ Be trained in the process, pace, and dynamics of publishing.

❑ Intimately understand the values and purpose of the organization.

❑ Support and promote the organizational purpose and values as long as they do not conflict with the laws, purpose, and values of the society in which they reside. In the same way that public journalists work to enforce and defend the laws of the land and reinforce cultural and social values, the same is true for the strategic corporate journalist.

❏ Strive for an unbiased approach. This is often easier to achieve by using external contract writers. Yet they should also understand the big picture well enough to craft integrated, in-context stories (this, by contrast, is sometimes easier to achieve with internal writers). These external writers must research well, ask tough questions, elicit interesting content, and write with ethical integrity.

❏ Understand the role of the ombudsman and the role of a news organization in an orientation of common business alignment. Much like a community paper, where the journalists and the people on whom they report are neighbors, the corporate news agency reports on those with whom they cooperate to meet a common business objective. The broad-scale U.S. news media have a tradition of printing allegations and rumors if substantiated by a credible enough source. This is not as common in small-community news, where the press plays a negotiating role since the people they report on are also the ones who advertise in the paper, whose kids play little league with the reporters' kids, and who share many of the same concerns and interests. The problem in small-community (or corporate) accountability, of course, is that it is possible to overlook misdeeds and problems because of cozy relationships between the management of the news organization and those who wield power in other realms of the community. Journalists in the real world more often identify with the underdog than with the power elite, and they are likely to be conflict-driven because doing so allows for narrative and drama. This inclination must be constantly checked and rechecked with those writing corporate news.

There are also some important advanced skills required to make strategic corporate journalism successful inside the corporation:

❑ *Business savvy.* To represent the organization, the organizational journalist must understand business strategy at a very intimate level. An organizational leader will not give the time of day to a corporate reporter who asks basic questions about strategic positioning.

❑ *Skill in influencing and confronting executives.* As a strategic corporate journalist or editor, you must be willing to influence executives to air their dirty laundry. This can be a challenging task. It's one thing for an executive to agree to the corporate journalistic model during good times but another entirely for an executive to agree to openly communicate about a difficult issue.

❑ *Broad-thinking, executive editorial skills.* An organizational communication executive editor must treat organizational communication just as a newspaper executive editor treats the planning, content, and operations of a newspaper. This includes both content and marketing analysis skills, such as attending to audience analysis, readership statistics, beat assignments, content sectioning, above-the-fold stories, serial columns, letters to the editor, etc.

❑ *Systems-thinking and pattern-recognition skills.* Both editors and writers must be acutely aware of the organizational communication system and how it is an aggregate of communications both internal and external, formal and informal, actual and inferred. This understanding should lead to highly integrated and synchronized communications.

❑ *Professional publishing skills.* The publishing operations should be professional, with an appropriate balance between multiple layers of editing, approval, and publishing execution.

Sample Staffing Template

This illustration posits a worldwide corporate journalism team in a company of five thousand to twenty-five thousand employees.

Executive Editor

❑ Sets the strategy for how primary communication vehicles play a role in achieving organizational alignment

❑ Determines overarching design and layout issues

❑ Analyzes target audiences and determines general focus of article categories (later analyzed by entire communications team and turned into a set of target stories to fill the story bank)

❑ Determines publishing guidelines, processes, and required journalistic standards

❑ Manages the editorial team, including the managing editor, assignment editor, writers (internal and external, although the assignment editor is directly responsible for managing writers' tasks and deadlines)

❑ Understands current organizational strategy and sensitivities of how articles should be treated

Managing Editor or Community Editor

❑ Manages day-to-day operations of primary communication vehicle

❑ Oversees feedback channels and replies directly to employee responses and letters to the editor; forwards feedback to appropriate figures in the organization for response

❑ Directs requests for coverage

❑ Understands the organizational pulse and psyche and how they affect all elements of organizational communication

❑ Coordinates messages with other key communicators

Assignment Editor

❑ Manages all writers and ensures that articles meet required deadlines and standards

❑ Snoops out stories and assigns them to appropriate writers

Executive-Beat Writer

❑ Focuses on executive strategy and changes

❑ Influences executive behavior and communication approaches through information about the employee pulse

❑ Writes executive communication and strategic features

Staff Writer or Full-Time Beat Writer

❑ Writes stories that require intimate knowledge of the organization

❑ Focuses on specific areas (such as those with a technology focus, or success stories)

❑ Acts as liaison with other communicators across the company

Production Artist

❑ Designs and produces feature stories

❑ Ensures that production elements meet the overarching goals of the primary communication vehicle as well as the specific goals of an individual article

Editorial Process Tools

Organizational journalism is more than reactive messaging. For a strategic corporate journalism model to succeed, alignment toward the overall vision and goals needs to be achieved. This is very difficult to do purely through reactive reporting. A marriage of reactive reporting and forward-looking editorial planning rounds out organizational alignment. Creating a story bank of potential articles that match the organization's mission is the first step. For example, if employee business literacy is an organizational goal, then the story bank should include articles that educate employees. The editorial team must then weave the strategic, forward-looking articles with organizational communications and "incoming" (urgent news announcements).

❏ *Story bank.* A strategic storytelling "map" of possible story topics sufficient for at least six months into the future. Possible topics include representative business units, all products (or at least product divisions), markets covered, competitive landscapes, customer profiles, success stories, executive and employee profiles, team or job summaries, major events for the company, external trends that affect the company, etc.

❏ *Editorial mix.* Balancing the types of stories identified as important to cover. For example, newspapers manage a mix of a certain percentage of news leads with entertainment or sports leads. A business editor might monitor the mix of news covered in market stories and technology stories. The important thing is that the editorial goals be set prior to the news coming in and agreed upon by executives and the "owners" of the press. Then the communications team takes on the management of fulfilling this mix.

❏ *Editorial calendar.* The editorial plan of stories to be covered in a given time period. Most editorial calendars in the external world are planned a year in advance so advertisers can target specific issues. This concern does not apply so directly to the halls of corporate journalism, but it is still valuable to plan coverage at least two quarters ahead. This allows you to share and leverage content with other communicators in the company and to manage a mix of planned stories with the inevitable incoming news.

❏ *Editorial guidelines.* The articulated purpose of each type of news published. For example, if you have features, short articles, and shorter news bites, you should have guidelines differentiating them all. What makes a feature? What are the requirements and suggestions for publishing content in a specific area or fashion?

❏ *Article templates.* Samples of common articles to help new writers easily understand what style and tone you are seeking for certain features.

❏ *Article proposal form.* An outline and guide to be completed prior to beginning the writing of an article. It should include purpose of the article, outline, sources, point of view, and cautions. A completed article proposal form should be signed by the article's sponsor. This keeps the tone and content of a feature on track. It also keeps objectives clear and covert agendas out of the copy.

PART THREE: RETURN ON INVESTMENT (ROI)

Analyzing communication investment paybacks requires understanding of the total cost of the current and new media, what alternatives these media may eliminate, human resource reduction as a consequence of the media, and how much value they add in communicating to the target audience. Unfortunately, as with some forms of advertising, measuring such a value is difficult. To further complicate the metric, an analysis must be performed with each communication.

ROI is easiest to calculate when you are presenting a communication option for an existing function that already has a hard cost. For example, training and eliminating print are two areas in which you can show discrete costs for both the existing communication and a media alternative. A well-orchestrated, virtual, multimedia broadcast training can not only be far more effective than in-person meetings using no media at all; it can also save the organization thousands of dollars in travel and opportunity costs, and it might even accomplish the communication goal better. Sometimes there are extra benefits with new delivery methods, such as automatic digital archiving from a Web-delivered communication.

Technology costs usually drop, and sometimes quickly, over time. Different media can become more useful depending on how they are used or as the technology advances. For example, to many audiences broadcast video technologies added little value until the quality reached a minimum threshold. Determining when the quality level is sufficient to create enough added value to justify the cost involves ongoing evaluations.

This ROI calculation grows more complex if you consider that some media can have a negative impact on communication. How can you calculate the missed opportunity or lost revenue of a flat product launch that went sour because of teleconferencing or audio-visual glitches? Any true cost analysis must consider this risk. Using technology that you know works, a production crew with whom you are familiar, or testing thoroughly may cost more up front, but the cost of things going wrong is often irrevocable. This risk should be factored into the calculation.

There are no hard rules when trying to determine whether or not to introduce new and expensive communications technologies. True, those who master virtual communication in an internal organization can leverage the communication value directly by using it for the customer base. Early intranet and Internet adopters were the first to parade out onto the e-business playing field. These companies, though unable early on to justify the expense of internal technologies, are now ahead of their competitors in translating direct value to customers.

PART FOUR: TRANSITION PLAN

Making the decision to transition to a corporate journalism model involves breaking through barriers. This transition should not be made lightly. If a communications organization cannot realistically achieve a strategic journalism mode, it is best not to attempt it. Pretending or promising to be open, accurate, timely, and balanced but ending up propagandizing leads to complete loss of credibility.

Gap Analysis

Regarding strategy:

❏ What are the differences between the current communication model and a strategic corporate journalism model?

❏ Is strategic corporate journalism necessary given the business objectives of your organization? Is it appropriate given the current internal climate? What would it take to move from the current model to one having strategic corporate journalism at its core?

❏ How long will it take for the organization to shift its expectations and information consumption? Will some employers react negatively to open communication?

Regarding commitments and skills:

❏ What level of commitment is required from executives? from key communicators? from the core communications team?

❑ To what level of journalistic standards should the team commit? Journalism is not simply about using certain language; it is an approach that requires discipline and ability to deal with controversy and conflict. Is the team prepared, trained, and supportive of this?

❑ Can your editors and writers push back on a leader who wants to overhype her organization? Will your team challenge or present a point of view in opposition to that of the executive team?

❑ Can you train them to become intimate with—but simultaneously removed from—the organizational rumor mill? Can they understand the essence of the organizational psyche without getting sucked into or manipulated by it?

❑ What new skills are required? What additional resources are needed?

❑ How do you achieve executive buy-in to a new approach? How do you make the executive team feel less vulnerable with comparatively open organizational communications?

Regarding resources and ROI:

❑ How do you justify the resource make-up (both people and finances) of the organizational communication team, and how must it shift to achieve a new communications model?

❑ Will you show decreased print costs? Will you show financial benefit from employee alignment? Will you calculate redundancies saved?

❑ Will you require additional finances or new team skills? Will you simply consolidate or eliminate certain activities in lieu of others?

❑ Will you work with outside vendors to fill gaps in the skills mix of current employees? (For example, when SGI shifted toward a corporate journalism model, the company's intranet portal became not just the primary communication channel but the *only* one as the print monthly newsletter and quarterly culture magazine were discontinued. The resources from print publications were diverted to hire two internal writers—both with journalistic backgrounds—and to contract with a suite of external freelance writers.)

The transition plan should detail exactly what a journalistic communications model looks like in the organization. What channels are to be used? How often? What level of business understanding is required? What publication processes are required? (To truly follow a journalistic model, it is necessary to study journalistic processes and roles.) Are you modeling your publication staff after that of a traditional newspaper (executive editor, managing editor, assignment editor, community editor, beat writers, etc.)? Are you modeling your publication vehicles after traditional newspaper departments (features, serials, headlines, classified, etc.)? Are you modeling your team functionality and processes after the traditional newspaper staff (daily front-cover planning; story critiques; fast-paced, over-the-transom reactions; setting up an office versus bullpen cubes; cooperation between editorial departments, etc.)?

PART FIVE: GETTING SUPPORT FOR THE NEW MODEL

Armed with analysis of the current landscape, the current communication climate, the benefits of corporate journalism, and the transition plan, your next step is to gain support from executives, other organizational communicators, and the organization—and not necessarily in that order. You must decide which group to target first. Once you have support from one person or group, you must build upon it. If you first communicate your plan to the executive team and get their support, then shop that fact to other key communicators in the company in soliciting their support. Likewise, visible cross-functional support from other organizational communicators strengthens your position with the executive team.

The organization leaders and executives must buy in to the idea of a journalistic communications approach, but the central organizational communications team should also work with other communications teams to ensure that they understand the new communications direction. The complexity of this relationship depends on how the various internal and external communications groups align within the organization and how political they are. If all internal communications responsibilities report to the same organization (for instance, corporate communications, sales communications, employee communications, etc.), then buy-in at the level of internal communications is easier.

More often than not, however, audience-specific communications teams try to bypass corporate communications to achieve their own goal. This hinders adoption of a strategic corporate journalism model. This dynamic is often seen in societal journalism, where community-specific newspapers view themselves as the primary communications source for a community and ignore alignment with the broader community newspaper (that is, neighborhood newsletters vis-à-vis city newspapers).

It is not uncommon for the central internal communications organization to report to a different organization than the external communications group. It is also not uncommon for these two organizations not to see eye to eye. Most communications organizations tend to view their constituencies as the primary target audience for all corporate communications. Our view is that the communications flow should be sequenced according to Figure Appendix 1.1.

This hierarchy does not imply that all communications are sequenced in this fashion; it indicates the hierarchy of alignment required for organizational success.

FIGURE APPENDIX 1.1. Corporate Communications Audience Sequencing

External communicators tend to rank external communications ahead of organizational communications. They want to ensure that organizational communication presents a positive image to the external world. Strategic corporate journalism, because of its tell-it-like-it-is nature, may threaten, or feel off-target to, external communications organizations.

In addition to achieving buy-in from executives and key communicators, the central communications team should also share its strategy with the organization at large. This is especially important if the organization is eliminating current publications or switching from a bulletin-board approach wherein any individual in the organization can influence corporate communications. Individual communicators understandably want to use the most credible broadcast communications vehicle available for their specific communication regardless of organizational relevance. Eliminating this ability may frustrate many individual communicators and derail organizational acceptance and buy-in.

PART SIX: THE TRANSITION

Don't underestimate the difficulty of the transition. Achieving initial organization buy-in does not mean that your team or the organization is then prepared for the transition. The pace of timely communications is grueling. You must beware of burning out your communications team. If you are retiring communications vehicles, there is apt to be some organizational mourning. Don't be surprised at the discontent when you begin to strategically weight communications and some communicators can no longer get their stories published. Prepare for struggles with external communicators as you begin to challenge timing and start to open communications more broadly. When you begin to challenge strategies, expose controversial issues, insist on accountability, publish external bad press, and surface the rumor mill, expect resistance and slow, incremental gains. Achieving credibility and trust is a slow, arduous process.

PART SEVEN: METRICS

Communications effectiveness is elusive and difficult to measure. There are, however, some measurement tools to aid you in determining what is and is not working. Feedback mechanisms need to match the culture. Some metrics can measure the effectiveness of and reaction to single messages, while others monitor overall communications effectiveness. You may also want to consider whether or not you need to measure each communicated piece (for example, using online automatic e-mail forms). Suggestions for gathering metrics include letters to the editor, online suggestion forms, statistics software that tracks usage patterns, surveys and pulsing mechanisms, focus groups, and e-mail contact submissions linked from each article.

APPENDIX 2

Glossary

Phrases of more than a word or two that are in quotation marks are dictionary definitions.

Alignment

"The proper positioning or state of adjustment of parts . . . in relation to each other"

Mechanistic alignment Alignment resulting in a centrally designed and controlled infrastructure made up of various interconnecting elements arranged to achieve a central purpose. For mechanistic alignment, each element in the system need only share information with the specific elements to which is immediately connected (as in an assembly line).

Organic alignment Alignment resulting from a completely decentralized system of self-selected elements collected around a central purpose. For organic alignment, the system must be "fully aware," with every element sharing information with every other element (as in the human body).

Representational alignment Alignment resulting from a hierarchical system of self-selected or elected elements collected around a central purpose. For representational alignment, the representatives must act as communication hubs passing information both up and down the hierarchy (for example, the U.S. political system).

Communication

"A process by which information is exchanged between individuals through a common system of symbols, signs, or behavior"

Broadcast communication channel A communication channel where information is "made widely known." The traditional definition of broadcast channels was limited to radio and video channels, but in recent years it has expanded to include any channel that reaches a broad audience in a short period of time (examples: the Internet, widely read newspapers, etc.).

Communication channel "A means of communication or expression." The spectrum of communication channels spans an enormous gamut, from face-to-face conversation to old-fashioned letter writing, and from e-mail to video walls.

Communication content The "substance, gist" transmitted over a communication channel; the words that are spoken; the text that is written; the video that is taped. Chapter Two of this book deconstructs communication content and defines each of the elements: completeness, accuracy, compellingness, consistency, contextualization, integration, and personalization:

❏ *Completeness* "Having all necessary parts, elements, or steps." Complete communications can stand alone and be understood without additional information or explanation.

❏ *Accuracy* Being "free from error." Accuracy is the most critical element in achieving credibility.

❏ *Compellingness* That which drives or urges forcibly or irresistibly. Compellingness may be inherent in the content (exciting news), or the communicator may create it in how the communication is distributed (eye-candy headlines or graphics).

❏ *Consistency* Being "free from variation or contradiction." Consistent communications result in a common understanding of the message across the organization.

❏ *Context* "The parts of a discourse that surround a word or passage and can throw light on its meaning." Context, which can be historical, referential, metaphorical, or localized, helps the communicator provide the audience with perspective.

❏ *Integration* Ability "to form, coordinate, or blend into a functioning or unified whole." Integrated messages need to combine multiple components to be complete (for example, organizational changes integrated with the strategy behind the change).

❏ *Personalization* Making a communication personal or individual. Personalized communications include content that resonates with audience members in a more intimate way.

Communication distribution "To . . . deliver" communications content "to the members of a group." Chapter Two discusses the three major components of distribution (channels, media, and production) and specific distribution elements necessary to achieving alignment: repetition, frequency, synchronization, sequencing, and interactivity.

❏ *Repetition* "To say or state again." Repetition is critical to branding a message into the organizational psyche.

❏ *Frequency* "Happening at short intervals." To many organizations in this age of Internet time, communication frequency means *constant*.

❏ *Synchronization* "Happening at the same time." Synchronization of communication is more difficult the more communicators there are. Synchronization is more important for some organizational communications than for others (it is critical that internal and external communication of a restructuring involving layoffs be synchronized).

❏ *Sequencing* "To arrange in a continuous or connected series."

❏ *Interactivity* Being "mutually or reciprocally active." For many organizational communications, interaction is a crucial requirement to achieve internalization and trust. It is usually through interactive communications that the communicator and audience truly internalize a message and make it their own.

Communication strategy "The careful plan or method" for developing and delivering communications. In *Beyond Spin*, the term is used in two ways: broadly as in an organizational communication strategy that refers to the overarching, organizationwide model and methodology to ensure organizationwide alignment and action; and narrowly when referring to the communication plan for a specific communication instance.

Crisis communications A communication strategy during "an unstable or crucial time or state of affairs in which decisive change is impending." A crisis communication strategy usually entails increased use of push communication channels and more frequent communication (as in wartime news coverage).

Landscape "A particular area of activity." In this book, *external landscape* means the aggregate of all external variables affecting the organization (such as competitive environment). The *internal landscape* refers to the aggregate of all internal variables affecting the internal organization (such as organization size).

Orchestrated communications Communications that are "arranged or combined to achieve a maximum effect." Orchestrated communications are carefully planned, crafted, sequenced, and often highly produced (an elected official's state of the union speech).

Organizational communications The aggregate of all communication within an organization; more specifically, the collective communication between two or more individuals within an organization.

Central organizational communications refers to communications coordinated by a central organizational communicator or communications team. *Broadcast organizational communications* refers to organizational communications delivered via a broadcast channel (as with executive messages delivered on the global Web).

Organizational communicator Any person who communicates broadly across the organization.

Organizational communications strategist A person who tries to influence the organizational communication norms. An organizational communication strategist is usually part of a central communications team responsible for determining the goals, standards, models, channels, media, frequency, and style used for organizationwide communication. Organizational communication strategists may also play a broad educational role in advancing communications skills within the organization.

Communication style "A particular manner or technique by which communication is done, created, or performed." Chapter Two discusses the primary determinants of communication style (culture, target communicator, content, and audience) as well as the central characteristics of authorship style (credibility, charisma, power, authenticity, and honesty).

❏ *Credibility* "The quality or power of inspiring belief."
A communicator's credibility lies in the perception of the audience. Many elements from the communicator's reputation as to the believability of content play into this perception. Since perception is individualized, any communicator's level of credibility may differ for each audience member.

❏ *Charisma* "A personal magic of leadership arousing special popular loyalty or enthusiasm. . . ."

❏ *Power* "Possession of control, authority, or influence over others." The effectiveness of different types of power depends on the organization (power derived from control is not as effective in a knowledge workforce as it is within a labor workforce).

❏ *Authenticity* "Being worthy of acceptance or belief as conforming to fact or reality; trustworthy." The level of required communications authenticity is largely dependent on the organizational communication norms (in some organizations, a polished style of communications is deemed "more professional" than an authentic, natural tone).

❏ *Honesty* "Being free from fraud or deception." Honesty means different things within different organizations. In some organizations, a lie of omission is understood as "communicating on a need-to-know basis," whereas in others, a lie of omission is deemed insidious.

Portal A portal is a Website that is a door or index into other Websites. Internet portals such as Yahoo help locate sites on the Internet. Intranet portals organize and provide search capability into intraorganizational (and sometimes extraorganizational) Websites. A corporate portal is the primary intranet portal for a company.

Push, pull, and push-pull *Push* communications are those delivered in such a way that the audience is forced to see and hear them (a Post-it note in the center of one's computer screen). *Push channels* refer to communication channels used to push information to an intended audience (billboards). Consequently, broadcast push channels are communications channels used to push information to a broad audience (community crisis alert sirens).

Pull communications are those delivered in such a way that the audience needs to consciously go retrieve the information (reference documents). *Pull channels* refer to communications channels used to publish information that is self-selected, or pulled, by readers, viewers, or listeners (bulletin boards).

Push-pull communication channels are pull channels that have become so acculturated that, for a large percentage of the target audience, the channel becomes a push channel (Internet portals like Yahoo that encourage audiences to point their browser's default home page to them are trying to turn a pull channel into a push).

Spam Spam is broadcast e-mail or voice mail that is deemed unnecessary to a portion of the audience receiving it. Spam is the electronic equivalent of junk mail.

Taxonomy "Orderly classification according to presumed natural relationships." Taxonomy refers to indexing, collating, or classifying information or Web links.

Journalism

"Writing characterized by a direct presentation of facts or description of events without attempt at interpretation."

Advocacy journalism "Journalism that advocates a cause or expresses a viewpoint."

Corporate journalism Journalistic principles and practices applied within an organization.

Eyebrow The headline or headline imagery used for visual relativity of interrelated articles. For example, in a crisis communication strategy where similarly themed news will be presented over a period of days or weeks (O. J. Simpson trial), a newspaper may create an eyebrow to be included over each thematic article. The eyebrow acts as a visual trigger so that readers can quickly identify the article with the theme.

Journalistic principles and practices The dissemination of open, accurate, timely, and strategically weighted information.

Pravda The communist official daily newspaper of the former Soviet Union (the name is translated as *truth* in English) which, because of the manipulative nature of its content, has widely become synonymous with *propaganda*.

Strategic corporate journalism Applying corporate journalism strategically to achieve alignment and action behind the organization's purpose, vision, values, strategies, operating principles, and priorities. Like societal advocacy journalism, strategic corporate journalism walks the narrow line between uninterpreted journalism and manipulation.

Management, Political, and Social Concepts or Theories

Chaord The combination of chaos and order, or any self-organizing, adaptive, nonlinear, complex community or system, whether physical, biological, or social, the behavior of which exhibits characteristics of both order and chaos. According to Dee Hock, founder of Visa International, a chaord is any chaotically ordered complex.

Chaordic organization A purely distributed, socialistic organization (chaos) with a few tenets tightly held (order).

Chaos and complexity theory A holistic systems theory where complex systems naturally achieve innate natural order (the universe, the flight patterns of migratory birds).

Darwinism A theory of evolution that predicts that the paths of evolution are defined by the survival of the fittest or the favoring of those traits that allow species to survive.

Dictatorial "Of, relating to, or befitting a dictator" (someone granted absolute power).

Egalitarian "A belief in human equality especially with respect to social, political, and economic rights and privileges."

Maslow's hierarchy One of the best known theories explaining people's actions. Conception by psychologist Abraham Maslow (see principally his *Motivation and Personality*, 1954) that people are motivated by a hierarchy of needs. Once low-level needs are satisfied, individuals are no longer motivated by them. As each level of needs is met, individuals progress to higher-level motivators. Here is Maslow's hierarchy, from lowest to highest:

1. Physiological: the need for food, clothing, and shelter.
2. Security and safety: the need to be free from physical danger and secure in the feeling that physiological needs can be met.
3. Social: the need to be loved, to be accepted, and to belong.
4. Ego: the need to be heard, appreciated, and wanted.
5. Self-actualizing: the need to achieve one's fullest potential.

PLUism The natural instinct to be more comfortable with people who share a similar culture, value system, language, background, etc. (PLU = people like us.)

Representative "Of, based on, or constituting a government in which the many are represented by persons chosen from among them."

Socialism Advocating collective ownership and administration of means or goods (for instance, shared ownership).

Systems theory The argument that however complex or diverse the world we experience, we will always find different types of organization in it, and such organization can be described by principles that are independent of the specific domain at which we are looking.

Taylorism An industrial-age, classically mechanistic management practice attributed to Frederick Winslow Taylor. Taylorism was an approach to organizing factories and offices that placed workers within a rigid system designed for maximum productivity.

Trends

Democratized workforce The trend away from hierarchical organizations toward flatter organizations with fewer layers of middle management.

Diversification "Increased variety." A diverse workforce is one that moves toward increased variety of backgrounds, cultures, languages, approaches, etc. The global economy is the trend toward a customer base consisting of an increased variety of backgrounds, cultures, languages, approaches, etc.

E-business The use of the Internet, extranets, and a corporate intranet to conduct business.

E-commerce The execution of monetary transactions with the assistance of Internet technologies.

Globality The linkage of events in one part of the world to places far distant.

Information age The era in which increased information quantity, information distribution immediacy, information technologies, and information overload preponderate.

Information overload The experience of being overwhelmed by too much information.

Increased pace of change The belief that almost everything is currently changing faster than has been the case historically.

Intellectual capital Intangible organizational assets related to organizational knowledge. The four primary categories of intellectual capital are:

1. Human-centered assets: the collective expertise of the organizational members

2. Intellectual-property assets: copyrights, patents, trademarks, etc.

3. Infrastructure assets: methodologies, processes, etc.

4. Market assets: branding, market dominance, etc.

Internet time Time sensed as instantaneous.

Knowledge equation Definition used in this book to declare that strategic corporate journalism, or SCJ (that is, fluidity of open, accurate, timely, and weighted information), added to organizational interaction leads to aligned innovation. In equation form:

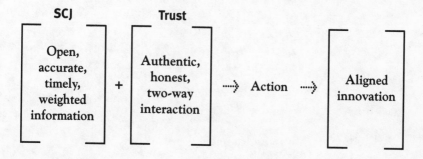

Knowledge management There are many definitions for knowledge management (KM) being bandied around in the business world today. Some definitions detail the need for KM infrastructural technologies and methodologies for organizing corporate information. Some definitions explore the subtle difference between capturing explicit and tacit knowledge. One simple definition that gets at the essence of knowledge management is: being able to quickly access what you need to know when you need to know it.

Knowledge workforce The trend away from the industrial-age dominance of a skill-based, labor or production workforce and toward an information-based workforce requiring higher and higher levels of knowledge to accomplish their jobs.

Moore's Law The observation that the logic density of silicon integrated circuits has closely followed the curve

$$\textbf{(bits per square inch)} = 2^{(t-1962)}$$

where t is time in years. That is, the amount of information storable on a given amount of silicon has roughly doubled every year since the technology was invented.

REFERENCES

The authors conducted numerous case study interviews in person, on the phone, and by e-mail with communication consultants, strategists, and leaders. Information and quotes from these personal case-study interviews are designated as such at the text citations.

Adams, J. *The Next World War.* New York: Simon & Schuster, 1998.

Armstrong, C. M. *Economist* ("The World in 1999" edition), [n.d.], p. 116.

Bohm, D. *On Dialogue.* London: Routledge, 1996, p. x.

Bohm, D. *Wholeness and the Implicate Order.* New York: Routledge, 1980, p. 1.

Branch, S. "The Hundred Best Companies to Work for in America." *Fortune,* Jan. 11, 1999, pp. 118–144.

Burrows, P., with Reinhardt, A. "What Makes Rick Belluzzo Run?" *BusinessWeek* [online], Feb. 1, 1999 (online version).

Collins, J. C., and Porras, J. I. *Built to Last.* New York: HarperCollins, 1994, p. xx.

Dahle, C. *Fast Company,* Dec. 1998, pp. 180–184.

D'Aprix, R. *Communicating for Change.* San Francisco: Jossey-Bass, 1996, p. 98.

Darlin, D. "The Core Problem." *Forbes,* Feb. 26, 1996, p. 48.

Davis, S., and Meyer, C. *Blur.* New York: Perseus, 1998, pp. 1, 5–9.

De Pree, M. *Leadership Jazz.* New York: Bantam Books, 1992, p. 8.

Dell, M. "The Virtual Firm." *Economist* ("The World in 1999" edition), [n.d.], p. 124.

Farney, D., and Seib, G. F. "The Statute Debate: Monicagate Left Few Reputations Enhanced." *Wall Street Journal,* Feb. 16, 1999, p. 1.

Foust, D. "Alan Greenspan: An Unlikely Guru." *BusinessWeek,* Aug. 24–31, 1998, p. 7.

Friendly, F. *Due to Circumstances Beyond Our Control.* New York: Vintage Books, 1967, p. 200.

Gates, B. "Bill Gates' New Rules." *Time*, March 22, 1999, p. 72. *From Business @ the Speed of Thought: Using a Digital Nervous System*. Warner Books, 1999.

Goleman, D. *Working with Emotional Intelligence*. New York: Bantam Books, 1998, p. 285.

Haberkorn, J. "I'm Losing My Job." *Measure Magazine*. [Employee magazine.]. Hewlett-Packard, Sept.–Oct. 1994.

Halberstam, D. *The Powers That Be*. New York: Dell, 1979, p. 625.

Heuerman, T., with Olson, D. "Authenticity." [Electronic pamphlet, self-published, distributed by e-mail.]. 1999.

Heuerman, T., with Olson, D. "Eyes That Do Not See." [Electronic pamphlet, self-published, distributed by e-mail.]. 1999.

Hill, G. C. "Silicon Graphics Loses Some of Its Luster." *Wall Street Journal*, Jan. 3, 1996, p. B4.

Hof, R. D. "The Gee-Whiz Company." *BusinessWeek*, July 18, 1994, pp. 56–64.

Hof, R., with Sager, I., and Himelstein, L. "The Sad Saga of Silicon Graphics." *BusinessWeek*, Aug. 4, 1997, pp. 66–72.

Horn, P. M. "The Future of Technology." *San Jose Mercury News*, Jan. 11, 1999, pp. 1E–5E.

Johansen, B. "Beyond Knowledge Management." [Pamphlet.]. Institute for the Future, 1997a, p. 6.

Johansen, B. "Digital Storytelling." [Pamphlet.]. Institute for the Future, 1997b.

Johansen, B. "Leadership in 21st-Century Organizations. 1999 Ten-Year Forecast." Institute for the Future, 1998, p. 180.

Kim, W. C., and Mauborgne, R. "Fair Process: Managing in the Knowledge Economy." *Harvard Business Review*, July–Aug. 1997, pp. 65–75.

"Knowledge Map, Part 3: The Culture of Knowledge Management." *Knowledge Management*, Dec. 1998, pp. 68–71.

Kuhn, S. E., Neumeier, S., and Sheeline, W. E. "Happy New Year: Your Best Investment Strategy for 1993." *Fortune*, Jan. 11, 1993, pp. 25–30.

Kutnick, D. "The Externalization Imperative." *CIO*, Dec. 15, 1998–Jan. 1, 1999, pp. 120–124.

Labovitz, G., and Rosansky, V. *The Power of Alignment.* New York: Wiley, 1997.

Malone, T. W., and Laubacher, R. L. "The Dawn of the E-Lance Economy." *Harvard Business Review,* Sept.–Oct. 1998, pp. 145–152.

Mandel, M. J. "The 21st Century Economy." *BusinessWeek,* Aug. 24–31, 1998, pp. 58–63.

Maslow, A. *Motivation and Personality.* New York: HarperCollins, 1954.

Naisbitt, J. *Megatrends: Ten New Directions Transforming Our Lives.* New York: Warner, 1982.

Naisbitt, J., and Aburdene, P. *Megatrends 2000.* New York: Avon, 1990.

Nauth, K. K. "Knowledge into Action." *Knowledge Management,* Oct. 1998, pp. 34–42.

Newell, C. "Fast Pack 1999." *Fast Company,* Feb.–Mar. 1999, pp. 135–150.

"Outlook Project Conversations and Summaries. Year 1998–1999." Outlook Project, 1998.

Parry, N. "The New Establishment: 50 Leaders of the Information Age." *Vanity Fair,* Oct. 1995.

Patrick, J. "Fast Pack 1999." *Fast Company.* Feb.–Mar. 1999, pp. 135–150.

Peetz, J. [Presentation]. Using Intranets for Effective Knowledge Management conference (Ernst and Young), San Francisco, Nov. 1998.

Petch, G. "The Cost of Lost Knowledge." *Knowledge Management,* Oct. 1998a, pp. 45–48.

Petch, G. "Leadership Challenge in KM's Deep Water." *Knowledge Management,* Oct. 1998b, p. 15.

Prokesch, S. E. "Mastering Chaos at the High-Tech Frontier: An Interview with Silicon Graphics' Ed McCracken." *Harvard Business Review.* Nov.–Dec. 1993, pp. 134–144.

Ries, A., and Ries, L. *The 22 Immutable Laws of Branding.* New York: Harper-Collins, 1998.

Robertson, E. "*Communication*: Applying Its Ancient Definitions to Today's Practical Problems." *Journal of Employee Communication Management.* [Internal Federal Express document.]. Jan.–Feb. 1994, pp. 6–7.

Robertson, E. "Five Common Myths About Communication." Manager's Pak. [Internal Federal Express document.]. Jan.–Feb. 1994.

Saffo, P. [Presentation]. Institute For the Future Outlook Project, 1999.

Senge, P. *The Fifth Discipline: The Art and Practice of the Learning Organization.* New York: Doubleday, 1990.

Senge, P. "Introduction." In J. Jaworski, *Synchronicity.* San Francisco: Berrett-Koehler, 1996.

"SGI Hitches Comeback to Win/NT Bandwagon." *Computer World,* Dec. 21, 1998.

"SGI Jockeys for a Comeback with Storage Agenda." *Computer Reseller News,* Dec. 14, 1998.

"SGI Plans Comeback on NT, Channels." *VAR Business,* Jan. 19, 1999.

Shaffer, R. A. "The Third Dimension." *Forbes,* Nov. 26, 1990, p. 266.

Shiltz, R. *And the Band Played On.* New York: St. Martin's Press, 1987.

"Silicon Graphics: Looking at the Future." *Economist,* Sept. 28–Oct. 4, 1991, pp. 72–74.

Smith, A. L. *Innovative Employee Communication.*

Smith, D. *Economist* ("The World in 1999," special report), [n.d.], p. 131.

Stephenson, K. "Fast Pack 1999." *Fast Company,* Feb.–Mar. 1999, pp. 135–150.

Stewart, T. *Intellectual Capital.* New York: Bantam Books, 1997.

Toulmin, S. *Cosmopolis: The Hidden Agenda of Modernity.* New York: Free Press, 1990.

Ward, J. "I Won't Dance. Don't Ask Me." *FinancialWorld,* Mar. 11, 1996, pp. 42–45.

Waugh, B. "Who's Fast '99? Unsung Heroes, Rising Stars: Radical Change." *Fast Company,* Dec. 1998.

Webber, A. [notes.]. Seminar, "The Changing Nature of Competitiveness," Dec. 28, 1998, Santa Clara, CA.

Weill, S. *Economist* ("The World in 1999," special report), [n.d.], p. 131.

Wheatley, M. J. *Leadership and the New Science.* San Francisco: Barrett-Koehler, 1992.

Wheatley, M. J., and Kellner-Rogers, M. *A Simpler Way*. San Francisco: Barrett-Koehler, 1996.

White, J. B. "The Line Starts Here." *Wall Street Journal* (Wall Street Journal Reports: The Millennium), Jan. 11, 1999, pp. R25–R28.

"The Wired Diaries." *Wired*, Jan. 1999, pp. 97–135.

Wolfensohn, J. "A Battle for Corporate Honesty." *Economist* ("The World in 1999" edition), [n.d.], p. 78.

Wycoff, J. "Who's Fast '99? Unsung Heroes, Rising Stars: Innovation Instigator." *Fast Company*, Dec. 1998.

Zander, B. "Who's Fast '99? Unsung Heroes, Rising Stars: Orchestrating Greatness." *Fast Company*, Dec. 1998, p. 112.

Personal Interveiws

Binney, J., Director of Internal Communications, Citibank.

Brennan, E., Corporate Journalist, Qualcomm.

Burks, S., Art Consultant, AT&T. Burks Consulting Group.

Coleman, J., Communications Manager, Hewlett-Packard.

Dillon, L., Managing Director of Corporate Communications, J.P. Morgan.

Duren, F., Manager of Employee Information, Caterpillar.

Froggatt, K., Former Vice President of Human Resources, SGI. Consultant.

Gayeski, D., Professor of Organizational Communication and Learning, Ithaca College. OmniCom Associates.

Georges, M., Managing Editor, *Junction*, SGI's Intranet Portal.

Gerstner, J., Communications Manager, Deere & Company.

Hill, N., Human Resources Manager, Tandem (formerly) and SGI.

Holtz, S., Former Communications Representative for Arco. Holtz Communication + Technology.

Jaco, C., Former NBC Reporter, CNN Broadcast Reporter.

Juarez, M., Communications Manager, Microsoft.

Jones, M., Communications Director, MIPS Technologies, Inc.

Maita, S., Former Director of Employee Communications for Pacific Bell. Maita/Saviano Public Relations.

Robertson, E., Employee Communications Director, Federal Express Corporation.

Solomon, J., Senior Editor for Time, Inc.'s Business Magazines.

Whitworth, B., Y2K Communications Manager, Hewlett-Packard.

Wolpe, M., Internal Communications Manager, Barclays Global Investors.

Woodall, K., Former Internal Communications Director for Levi Strauss & Co. Towers Perrin Consulting.

THE AUTHORS

Markos Kounalakis is a print and broadcast journalist who covers wars and revolutions, both civil and technological. He was the NBC-Mutual News Moscow correspondent in the early 1990s and covered the fall of the Soviet Union and Afghanistan. He reported the overthrow of communism for *Newsweek* in East Germany, Czechoslovakia, Romania, and Bulgaria; the rise of democratic institutions in Hungary; and ethnic strife in Yugoslavia. He was based in Rome and Vienna and later ran the magazine's Prague satellite bureau for more than a year. Kounalakis has written for the *Wall Street Journal*, the *Los Angeles Times Magazine*, the *International Herald-Tribune*, the *San Francisco Chronicle*, the *Dallas Morning News*, and many other regional and international newspapers and magazines. He holds a MSc in Journalism from Columbia University and a graduate certificate in International Journalism from the University of Southern California. He wrote the book *Defying Gravity: The Making of Newton*, a case study of Apple Computer's development of new technology, and is currently an executive communication strategist at Silicon Graphics.

e-mail: NewsScribe@aol.com

Drew Banks has a triangular background in technology, the arts, and business. He earned two B.S. degrees from North Carolina State University in electrical engineering and computer science, worked as a modern and jazz dancer in New York City, and received an MBA from MIT Sloan's School of Management.

Since 1989, he has worked at SGI in various information systems and human resource roles. In 1993, Banks co-led the team that created *Junction*, SGI's corporate intranet portal. His ability to synthesize different schools of thought have led him to roles where technology intersects with people to advance business strategies. He frequently speaks at professional forums such as the Fortune business conference series and Internet World conferences on topics such as knowledge management, the evolution of an intranet, and blurring boundaries of information. He is currently director of worldwide employee communications and integrated performance support. He lives in San Francisco.

e-mail: dbanks@alum.mit.edu

Kim Daus published printed business magazines and newspapers for ten years before digital and online technology attracted her attention. After years of writing, editing, and publishing regional and national news, she applied her communication, business, and journalistic skills to the digital publishing world. In 1993, at a San Francisco Internet start-up company, she worked on a team crafting virtual online communities.

From 1995 to late 1999, she worked at SGI in strategic communications marketing and business development roles. She was most recently an employee communications manager responsible for broad communication strategy and *Junction*, the corporate worldwide intranet gateway. Daus managed worldwide intranet operations, including strategic messaging and knowledge management architecture. In her roles, she blended classic elements of print newspaper editorial operations with intranet technology and communications principles. She currently consults and speaks internationally on communications strategies, intranet development, knowledge management architecture, and intranet design.

She received an undergraduate degree in English and philosophy and is currently pursuing a master's degree in theology and social ethics.

e-mail: kim@daus.com

ACKNOWLEDGMENTS

The authors collectively wish to thank the rest of the SGI World-wide Employee Communications team: Michelle Morgan, Mickey Georges, Tami Cowart, Trisha Ginsburg, Dee Street, and Diane Tedesco.

This book would not have been possible without the support of Ed McCracken, Rick Belluzzo, Kirk Froggatt, Bill Kelly, Bob Johansen, James Adams, Estee Solomon Grey, Noreen Lovoi, Kevin Burr, Tamar Elkeles, Peter Laufer, Cedric Crocker, and the entire fantastic staff at Jossey-Bass.

Markos Kounalakis
Journalists and editors: Judith Crist, Rod Nordland, Peter Laufer, Mark Bauman, Terry Philips, Susanne Biedenkopf, Jim Maceda, Heidi Bradner, Tom Ginsberg, Nick Gage, Pietro del Re, Josef Klima, Susan Koe, Nina Sederholm, Donald Shanor, Rachel Myers, Peter Sartorius, Marco Nicoletti, Maggie Cooper, Dave Bohrman, Murray Fromson, Hannah Bloch, Ed Rheingold, Ann Simmons, George Hatch, Claudia Fernandez, George Wood, Dana Adams, Tom Nagorski, Liz Shogren, Jay Carney, Doug Menuez, Margueritte Holloway, Andy Reinhardt, Pia Hinckle, David Streitfeld, Viva Hardigg, Christian Catomeris, and Joan McCraw.

For kindness and support: Susan Burks, the entire extensive Kounalakis clan, Karen Nazor, Mrs. Harley C. Stevens, Philip Krohn, Heidi Craig, Jodi Baron, Jim McKee, Lise Waring, Beau Vrolyk, Cindy Black, Richard Cohn, Julie Livingston, Sherry Whitely Roach, Nina Katz, Karen Schein, Barney Jones, and Lydia Weaver.

Drew Banks
First and foremost, thanks to my partner, Tom Perrault, who didn't forget about me while I was away. Kirk Froggatt ranks number two

for being a great boss, friend, mentor, and sounding board. To another good friend, Pedro Sanchez, thanks for trudging through the unbearable first draft and offering valuable guidance. Diane Perro let me delay our book to work on this one. My other friends and family members for allowing me to ignore them even more than I usually do.

In addition to the Worldwide Employee Communications team we have already mentioned, I would also like to thank the SGI Integrated Performance Support team—David Alcocer, Chris Bargeron, Ken Cushman, Anupam Garg, Hamid Ghods-Gooya, Lori Gibson, Scott Goodwin, Angela Janicki, Georgine Lindseth, Darryl Toney, Marhsall Uy, and Shawn Wilson—for supporting us and cheering us on.

My coauthors mentioned names that bear repeating: James Adams, Rick Belluzzo, Susan Burks, Kevin Burr, Heidi Craig, John Cristofano, Cedric Crocker, Estee Solomon Grey, Bob Johansen, Nina Katz, Bill Kelly, Ed and Rebecca McCracken, and Sherry Whiteley Roach.

Finally, I would like to thank everyone we interviewed for their wonderful stories, conversation, and insight: Ann Archer, Judith Binney, Eileen Brennan, Susan Burks, Jay Coleman, Laura Dillon, Lauren Dunbar, Francis Duren, Dr. Tamar Elkeles, Deborah Feinstien, Kirk Froggatt, Mickey Georges, John Gerstner, Nicolle Henneuse, Nancy Hill, Shel Holtz, Melissa Jones, Mario Juarez, Stephen Maita, Ed Robertson, Jolie Solomon, Brad Whitworth, Michele Wolpe, and Katherine Woodall.

Kim Daus

I am fortunate enough to work with an amazing team of people—both our employee communications team and the broader SGI employees. Thank you.

I am also grateful to my family and friends who supported this project with prayers, conversations, and patience when I didn't return phone calls: Margaret, Charlie, Jeff and Amy, Eric and George, Cathy, and David. Lisa Harvey, Jan, Lou, and Taylor Bock,

Beth Fraker, Karen Wilson, Gail Doering, Janet, Bo, and Andy Hawkes, Marian Andrin, Ernesto Mayans, Peter Hawes, Eric Seidel, Jane Ware, Justin Sherman, and Gena and Mary Stripling.

Special thanks go to my coauthors for the endless laughs and fascinating debates, and for making this such a fun project. More than all, I am humbly grateful to God, without whom none of this is possible for me.

INDEX

tion of, 71; internal, 70–78, 80
Laubacher, R. L., 183–184
Layoffs: accountability for, 49–50; organizational psyche and, 73; personalized communication about, 45–46; timeliness of information about, 106, 107, 148
Lead communicator, 43. *See also* Target communicators
Leadership: commitment of, 204, 216; democratized workforce and, 19–21; getting support from, 218–219; improvisational, 16–17; instantaneous information flow and, 26; knowledge workforce and, 16–18; scapegoating, 73; of subject-matter experts, 50. *See also* Executive headings
Leadership and the New Science (Wheatley and Kellner-Rogers), 25, 35
Leadership Jazz (De Pree), 16–17
Leaks, 58, 107
Learning, communication and, 187–188
Learning organization, 13, 188
Legal industry, 29
Legal trends, 190
Letters to the editor, 145, 205, 221
Levi Strauss, 7, 141
Lewinsky, M., 42, 92, 94, 100, 107
Life compression, 29
Linux community, 183–184
Live coverage, 206
Local communication: consistency in, 43; contextualization of, 44
Logical exactitude, 11
Lotus Corporation, 184–185
Lotus Institute, 184–185
Lotus Notes, 158
Lucent, 4

M
Macintosh computer, 157
"MacNeil-Lehrer News Hour," 93–94
Macro external climate, 69, 78
Macro socioeconomic factors, 16–34,

174–181, 232–233; of democratized workforce, 19–21; of diversification, 21–24, 177; evaluation of, 67–70; in future world, 174–181; of increased pace of change, 28–32, 181, 233; of information age, 24–28, 33–34, 177–179; of knowledge workforce, 16–18, 174–177; the new corporation and, 117–121; in new world, 16–34. *See also* Environmental trends
Macromedia, 5
Madonna, 114
Magazines, corporate: evolution of, 134–135; history of, 132; on push-pull continuum, 66
Maita, S., 143–144
Malone, T. W., 183–184
Managed journalism, 139–140
"Management by walking around," 61
Management theories, 147, 230–232
Manager-employee interaction, 58–59
Managers, in knowledge enterprise, 175
Managing editor, roles and responsibilities of, 211–212
Mandel, M. J., 179
Marketing, separation of organizational communications from, 102–103, 108
Marketingspeak, 126, 142, 160
Maslow, A., 175, 231
Mass media, 120
Mastheads, 146
Mauborgne, R., 52, 139
McCracken, E., 2–4, 136, 151–152, 154, 155, 156, 157–158, 162, 163
Measure, 140
Mechanistic model, 11–15, 223; controlled approach to communication and, 10–15; Ford's assembly line and, 12–13; in government, 15; persistence of, 30, 140–141; power style in, 50; shift from, to organic model, 13–15; shift from, to organic model, macro sociotechnological factors in, 16–34;